Since the first slave ships arrived in the U.S., efforts to dehumanize Afro-Americans have historically included outright bondage, discriminatory legislation, and the creation of demeaning stereotypes. Jane Campbell examines black literature as it seeks to reverse and supplant the various dehumanizing myths promulgated by white American culture.

Campbell analyzes fourteen literary works written over more than a century, from William Wells Brown's *Clotel* (1853) to David Bradley's *The Chaneysville Incident* (1981). She shows that this fiction celebrates blacks' efforts to preserve their humanity and also permits black authors to act as revisionist historians, offering a transcendent view of the future through an exploration of the past.

In searching for rhetorical devices, according to Campbell, black writers often draw on elements of myth, which by definition articulate a culture's most profound perceptions and can be used in fiction to awaken readers' deepest urges. For these writers, Campbell argues, the choice of historical romance facilitates the blending of myth and history because the genre characteristically imbues an ideal world with the trappings of verisimilitude.

The Author: Jane Campbell is assistant professor of English at Purdue University, Calumet.

Mythic Black Fiction

The Transformation of History

Mythic Black Fiction

The Transformation of History

Jane Campbell

The University of Tennessee Press

KNOXVILLE

Publication of this book has been aided by a grant from the American
Council of Learned Societies from funds provided by the Andrew W.
Mellon Foundation.

The paper used in this book meets the minimum requirements of the
American National Standard for Permanence of Paper for Printed
Library Materials, z39.48-1984. Binding materials have been chosen
for durability.

∞

Library of Congress Cataloging-in-Publication Data

Campbell, Jane, 1946–
    Mythic Black fiction.

    Revision of thesis (doctoral), 1977.
    Bibliography: p.
    Includes index.
    1. American fiction – Afro-American authors –
History and criticism. 2. Historical fiction,
American. 3. Afro-Americans in literature. 4. Myth
in literature. 5. Romanticism – United States.
6. Slavery and slaves in literature. I. Title.
PS153.N5C35 1986   813'.009'896   86-6909
ISBN 0-87049-508-9 (alk. paper)

For Beverly,
who taught me the meaning
of transcendence

Contents

Introduction

For Afro-American writers, whose ancestors were wrenched from their native country, enslaved, and forced to subscribe to damaging notions about themselves and their heritage, the creation of a distinct mythology has been almost essential to the artistic process. Afro-American historical fiction, from William Wells Brown's *Clotel* (1853) to David Bradley's *The Chaneysville Incident* (1981), has fused history and myth into a new reality that enshrines blacks' efforts to maintain their humanity despite the forces acting on them. Idealism pervades black historical fiction. Writers insist on heroism, even when such heroism seems inaccessible in everyday life. That mythic transcendence has continually preoccupied black men and women wishing to convey historical truths should not be surprising, given black literature's serious purposes, among them the countering of dehumanizing images imposed for generations. For, as Darwin T. Turner remarks, "a confident people must . . . have a transcendent vision of what might be, a vison drawn not only from their triumph but even from their despair."[1]

Because the black artist invariably writes from an intensely political perspective, he or she searches for rhetorical devices that will move the audience on the deepest possible level. Myths, by definition, voice a culture's most profound perceptions, and, when given fictional form, can awaken the audience's strongest impulses. Thus black artists who rely on myth have the potential to provoke whatever response they wish: to move the audience to consciousness, to attitude, even perhaps to action. "Pure myth" – in the sense of a literary mode revolving around a world peopled entirely by gods, demons, and other supernatural forces, a world, as Northrop Frye notes, which is abstract and not necessarily "attained or attainable by human beings" – has of course given way to other modes.[2] These modes (the romance, the confession, the picaresque, for example) present beings and actions closer to human experience at the same time as they may contain, in varying measure, myths or mythic elements.

Often black writers call upon earlier myths, those ancient expressions of power, of hope, of delivery. The myth of the messiah and that of the edenic garden, both of which cut across continents and cultures, are pivotal to black fiction. Mythmaking, the process whereby writers throw into relief the values, perceptions, and behaviors they want the audience to acknowledge within a particular culture, inheres in all of this fiction. As mythmakers, Afro-American writers imbue messianic figures and pastoral settings with new significance, overturning racist stereotypes. Even when a white audience is primary, as with early writers such as Charles Chesnutt and Pauline Hopkins, the author tries to appeal on some level to a secondary audience of black readers. As the nineteenth century gave way to the twentieth, heroes and heroines began to reject the delimiting values white culture attempted to impose. Instead, messianic figures began to point to and act out the real values at work, at times embracing the beauty of black speech, of violent revolt; at the same time, heroines and heroes began to discredit the promise of urban opportunity, rekindling faith in the abandoned South or the "primitive" agrarian homeland. Often protagonists appear superhuman, performing deeds that surpass those of ordinary mortals. But never are these messiahs literal gods; rather they are god-like, turning the seemingly unnoticed actions of everyday life into miraculous statements about the limitless power and possibility of Afro-America. At the same time as writers have reinvented old myths, they have inaugurated mythic elements in their fiction. This mythmaking, a process evident throughout Afro-American historical fiction, constitutes a radical act, inviting the audience to subvert the racist mythology that thwarts and defeats Afro-America and to replace it with a new mythology rooted in the black perspective. This tendency has manifested itself in fiction from Brown's era to contemporary times.

By its very nature, myth eludes definition, but for purposes of clarity it is crucial that its scope be somewhat limited here. Myth, then, is taken to mean a dramatic embodiment of cultural values, of ideal states of being found in Afro-American history and experience. Romance, the predominant device for presenting myth in black historical fiction, refers to the literary mode itself, in which heroes and heroines depict values that run counter to those of an oppressive culture. Despite the charges of sentimentality and escapism leveled at romance, it is potentially a radical literary mode, for it dares to posit a world of infinite possibility, a world in which cultural heroes and heroines come to grips with those negative forces, or villains, that interfere with the attainment of an ideal world. Romance can be used, in short, to reinvent reality. For these writers, romance transforms history and culture as whites have presented them into history and culture as blacks envision them. At the core of romance is "improbability," a notion undercut by the romance's seeming verisimilitude. It is in part this near verisimilitude that has encouraged scholars to describe most long black historical fictional narratives as novels and to deplore their failures to match novelistic demands of plausible plotting and complex characterization. For the most part, in fact, critics of black historical fiction have differentiated only between novels and short stories. Little attention has been accorded to fictional modes employed, scholarship about Ralph Ellison's *Invisible Man* and Robert B. Stepto's book *From Behind the Veil: A Study of Afro-American Narrative* providing the primary exceptions.[3]

Given the inattention to genre, this book explores the ways romance has served as the predominant mode of black historical fiction writers. As early as 1853, William Wells Brown seized upon the romance, one of the oldest literary forms in existence and a mode not limited to the Western world, as an ideal device for his purposes. During the fifties, to be sure, Ralph Ellison and James Baldwin deviated from the romance, and recent black historical fiction has continued this formal diversification, as evidenced by such writers as Leon Forrest and Alice Walker. Forrest (*There Is a Tree More Ancient Than Eden*, 1973; *The Bloodworth Orphans*, 1976; and *Two Wings to Veil My Face*, 1983) transmutes musical and oral modes into fictional form. Walker (*The Third Life of Grange Copeland*, 1970; *Meridian*, 1976; and *The Color Purple*, 1983) rejuvenates the realistic novel, going so far as to play with an old-fashioned epistolary form in the last of the three works.

Notwithstanding these and other formal experimentations, the romance flourishes, the mode having qualities particularly appropriate for depicting the black experience and for enhancing the mythmaking process. Black history is rife with suffering, alienation, and terror. For many

Afro-Americans, life has been earmarked by the extreme. With the romance, black writers can represent these heightened experiences. As distinguished from the novel, the romance allows for improbable events: characters extricate themselves from seemingly hopeless situations, perform incredible deeds, triumph over corrupt forces. Black historical fiction characters, who embody the strongest aspects of black culture, often effect miraculous escapes, and they rapidly acquire adulation and fame. Many become extraordinarily significant political figures with implausible rapidity. Typically, the romance emphasizes the characters' external rather than internal lives. Characters seldom develop; if they do, change is abrupt, even contrary to reasonable expectations. Ultimately, the characters function ideologically. Authors of black historical fiction, then, have not written myth, in the pure sense, nor have they written history in the official sense. Instead they have created mythic history. With the romance, the literary mode closest to myth in its idealized presentation of reality, Afro-American writers have found a way to anchor myth to accessible experience, to bridge the gaps between supernatural and "real," myth and history.

The fourteen works discussed here have been selected to provide a slightly abridged literary history from 1853 to 1981. In the first chapter Brown's *Clotel* (1853), the first known piece of historical fiction by a black writer, is paired with Arna Bontemps's *Black Thunder* (1936), thus beginning with slavery and moving from that period to the present. In succeeding chapters the works are handled chronologically according to the years when they were written. Up until the sixties, when historical fiction begins to proliferate, representative historical works have been selected. Excluded are relatively little-known and hard-to-obtain works such as John Paynter's *Fugitives of the Pearl* (1930); works about the black experience outside the United States such as Arna Bontemps's *Drums at Dusk* (1939) and Paule Marshall's *The Chosen Place, The Timeless People* (1969): and one work too long and cumbersome for this study — the W.E.B. Du Bois trilogy *The Black Flame* (1957-1961). Since the publication of Ellison's *Invisible Man* (1952), numerous writers have probed Afro-American history; among those authors not examined here are Margaret Walker, John Wideman, Ernest J. Gaines, John A. Williams, Leon Forrest, Octavia Butler, and Alice Walker. Several of these writers have penned more than one work of historical fiction. Alice Walker, in fact, asserts, "my whole program as a writer is to deal with history just so I know where I am."[4]

Critics might well question the inclusion of only three black women writers in a work that analyzes more than one hundred years of fiction. The fact is that until recently the historical romance has been predominantly a male canon. Before the sixties, black women no doubt wrote historical romances—in the sense of "historical" as defined below—however, when they did so their works were frequently ignored or suppressed, relegating the books to obscurity. With scholars' increasingly vigorous efforts to reclaim women's fiction, additional historical works will undoubtedly emerge. But what of those writers excluded from this study, authors such as Zora Neale Hurston and Gayl Jones? "Historical romance," as the term is used here, by necessity eliminated certain works, at the same time uncovering notable differences between male and female authors. As Claudia Tate observes in her introduction to *Black Women Writers at Work*, "black women writers, of course, are confronted with the same racial climate as their male counterparts, but by virtue of their gender their depictions of it often reflect differences . . . in tone, character selection, setting, and plot." Customarily, Tate points out, the black woman writer concerns herself with a heroine who is restricted by responsibilities to her children to "conduct her quest within close boundaries, often within a room."[5] In many cases, the woman writer is less concerned with external historical events than with how those events are filtered through the psychological process. It is interesting to note that although Morrison's *Song of Solomon* (1977) depicts both a male and a female questing figure, her primary protagonist is a man rather than a woman. In any case, black women writers' generic deviations from, and experimentations with, the historical canon as it is described here go beyond the scope of this book and warrant extensive study.

The term "historical" has been used to describe the works examined here, despite many of the romances' differences from the traditional definition of historical fiction. Although the early twentieth-century scholar Brander Matthews claimed that the best historical novels "are those which were a-writing while the history was a-making"—for example, *The Pickwick Papers*—more recent critics define an historical novel as one that returns to an era previous to the time of composition.[6] Turner agrees with the traditional position, defining the historical novel as "any long fictional story set in a time-frame at least one generation preceding the author's birth." Until the sixties, Turner points out, almost no Afro-American writers produced fiction of this traditional type, thus robbing themselves of opportunities "to improve Afro-American images by reinterpreting the past."[7] At the same time as one acknowledges that myth-making is inherent in Afro-American fiction, he or she must also understand that early black writers were virtually incapable of creating positive images of blacks at the same time as they fictionalized the past. Until recently, slavery was best forgotten; African culture was regarded with ambivalence or outright rejection. To be sure, Marcus Garvey did a great deal to dispel negative attitudes toward Africa, but even as late as the fifties many Afro-Americans had not gained the respect for Africa evident today. Closely related to the misconception that Africa was "savage" was the fact that very little accurate information was available to historical romancers. Thus, with the exception of Bontemps, who returns to Gabriel Prosser's rebellion of 1800, and Frances Harper and Pauline Hopkins, who dwell briefly on slavery, writers previous to Ellison eschewed the remote past entirely. Even Ellison and Baldwin, whose works provide a panorama of Afro-American history from slavery to the fifties, handle slavery symbolically, with little attempt at verisimilitude. Given the traditional definition, Turner's argument that Afro-American writers produced no historical fiction before the sixties is irrefutable. If one amplifies this definition, however, to consider another aspect of the historical novel, namely the degree to which history subsumes other concerns, a good deal of early black fiction is historical; that is, history is of primary significance. In every case, the impact of history on the characters, the characters' place in history, and author's concept of history are central to the work. Harriet E. Wilson's *Our Nig: or, Sketches from the Life of a Free Black* (1859), now known to precede Brown's *Clotel* as the first black romance published in this country, is not written from such an historical perspective and has not been explicated here, as such explication would move this book in a very different direction.

Fortunately for black fiction, the years since the fifties have wrought important changes. A large number of white Americans have finally begun to acquire an awareness of and sensitivity to the black experience. Blacks have gained stature in mainstream American culture, making equality felt by entry into the political and economic arena. At the same time, Afro-American historians and artists have launched a full-fledged exploration—and celebration—of the past, thus regenerating American fiction.

Acknowledgments

I formulated the central theory of this book — that beginning with William Wells Brown, romance has served as the predominant literary mode for transforming black history into mythic fiction — in 1977 while working on my doctoral dissertation. Since that time, my exploration of that notion through analysis of literature has undergone a great deal of revision and expansion. My original theory, however, has remained essentially unchanged. Thus this book has been nine years in the making. During that time, I have become indebted to so many people that I feel an exhaustive list is impossible. I do wish, however, to single out two people from the outset: James R. Giles, who furnished the original impetus for this study and who served as a critical source of information and perspective, and James M. Mellard, who guided me through the crucial early stages and whose amazing energy unleashed a great deal of my own.

My heartfelt thanks go also to those who offered advice and direction during the various stages of writing: James Andreas, Cynthia Davis, and Walter R. Davis; in this same context, I want to express particular appreciation to Trudier Harris and R. Baxter Miller, both of whom took special trouble to empathize with, and to help me realize, my vision.

I am grateful, too, to all those friends and colleagues whose genuine interest in my work contributed to my feeling that I was engaged in a vital project, among them Ann Blair, Brooke Battles, Jan Czarnik, Fran Fitch, Diane and Juan Guerra, Harvey and Tricia Kail, Mary Lerman, Saul Lerner, Zenobia Mistri, Donald Murray, Steve Pauley, John and Pat Rogalin, Robert Selig, Clement Stacy, Shirley Staton, Charles Tinkham, Wally Wold, and Ginny and Paul Wray.

Moreover, I would like to thank Carol Orr, director of the University of Tennessee Press, for her unflagging encouragement, and Purdue University Calumet, whose Summer Faculty Award offered vital financial aid. I commend Judy Bretz and, again, Ginny Wray for their excellent typing and Wanda Giles and Katherine Holloway for their invaluable editing.

I have reserved special accolades for Ellen Starkman, who coupled exceptional bibliographic knowledge with extraordinary emotional support, and Miguel Palacio, who read and critiqued the manuscript with a brilliance surpassed only by his faith in me. Without these sources of power, my book would have been a thousand times more difficult to complete.

Mythic Black Fiction

The Transformation of History

1   Celebrations of Escape and Revolt

William Wells Brown's *Clotel* and
Arna Bontemps's *Black Thunder*

William Wells Brown and Arna Bontemps have generally been designated as novelists; yet they might more properly be called romancers. Both *Clotel* and *Black Thunder* exhibit action freed from the confines of objective reality, allowing miraculous events to occur. Accordingly, these events often attain symbolic or ideological significance, contributing to a mythic aura. Although the characters may appear flat or poorly developed, they are in fact appropriate within the confines of the genre because the proper scope of romance characters is ordinarily not psychological. Rather, romance characters serve to depict ideal states of consciousness, states the artist may wish the audience to reflect upon. No doubt some readers will object to the implication that black writers have relied on white literary models. Given the educational background, however, to which black writers, particularly early ones, were exposed, it is impossible to ignore white cultural influences. Rather than "relying" on the romance as a model, black writers revitalized the genre, enriched it with history, with black folklore and the oral narrative, including the slave narrative. Taking for their own a mode that existed long before the United States, black writers have co-opted it, so to speak, for their purposes.

In order to explore the development of the romance, *Clotel; or, the President's Daughter* and *Black Thunder* will be examined together.[1] Each takes slavery for its subject; each proposes heroic modes of action involving rejection of the "peculiar institution," *Clotel* through flight, *Black Thunder* through revolt.

Brown lays the groundwork for the first stage of this mythmaking process, for he insists on blacks' innate humanity, responding directly to the "peculiar institution's" deliberate efforts to dehumanize its victims. He reifies blacks' humanity by emphasizing black potential to fulfill the fixed notions of human perfection prescribed by white American culture. Thus Brown lionizes the ideals of the ruling class: the Anglo-Saxon concept of beauty, mastery of white English and the Western rational heritage as proof of intellectual ability, identification with the American "aristocracy," and industriousness so as to acquire wealth. These, he believes, will allow blacks to erase the stigma of African "primitive" origins and the attendant stereotypes. His references to revolt, it must be made clear, posit a temporary solution: to allow blacks to enter the white world. Brown's work suggests that he, like some members of the immigrant population, endorses the melting pot analogy whereby the recently-arrived foreign born divest themselves of their ethnic heritage to realize the American Dream.

The fictional strategies of the romance clearly lend themselves to communicating this mythology and to making sure that his audience recognizes blacks' power to attain these deeply-felt ideals. Because the romance conveys an idealized reality, where superhuman characters exhibit their talents in order to make the improbable seem probable, Brown can employ god-like characters, inflated language, and incredible plotting. His three messianic figures, Clotel, Mary, and George, typify the heroines and heroes of abolitionist romance in their incomparable gentility and pulchritude, remarkable courage and virtue, and innate brilliance and ingenuity. Their language, which today seems stylized, serves Brown as an index to blacks' inherent "culture"; *Clotel*'s plot, which propels Mary and George out of slavery and into the mainstream of white society in an incredibly short time, testifies to their industry. Like other romancers of his day, Brown need not be criticized for depicting characters with ideological rather than psychological dimension, or chastised for his contrivances of plot. Granted, *Clotel*, like other abolitionist romances, does not successfully synthesize the didactic intent of oratory with fictional rhetoric. Moreover, Brown, being primarily an historian, gratuitously includes historical events, giving the narrative a disjointed quality. Otherwise, however, *Clotel* is as effective as most abolitionist romances in offering a sense of the enormous human waste slavery enacted, insisting that the institution be eliminated so that Afro-American potential could be fully realized.

Janheinz Jahn has shown that abolitionists learned to eschew all that might be interpreted as "primitive."[2] The first task for Brown, then, involved creating characters whom the audience would view as "civilized." One device Brown uses is that of making all major characters house servants by virtue of their fair skin. Such contact with whites as these characters' positions afford them endows them with traits both historically verifiable and ideologically prudent for the abolitionist audience. Further, these characters, rather than speaking black English, employ a stylized diction exemplified by Clotel's refusal to meet again with Horatio Green, the man who has taken a white wife despite his marriage to Clotel: "To meet thus is henceforth crime" (108). In addition to diction, Brown emphasizes the characters' clothing and politeness. With his female characters, these traits are shored up by the sentimental literary legacy of Charles Brockden Brown, a tradition that insists on depicting women as consummately gentle, forgiving, and supportive. Even when Horatio Green abandons Clotel and their daughter, for a white woman, Clotel, rather than feeling anger or a sense of betrayal, pities his white bride and refuses to disrupt Gertrude's household or cause her sorrow. Clotel's "earnest prayer was, that [Gertrude] might not know of her existence" (111). For Brown, gentility serves to reinforce the notion that abolition is necessary; for not only are some "blacks" actually "white", many are socially acceptable by white middle-class standards.

Examining *Clotel*'s detail, one is struck by the primary characteristic that earmarks Brown as a nineteenth-century romancer: his unabashed allegiance to Angle-Saxon lineage. Most of Clotel's characters are mulatto; in fact, Clotel herself is Thomas Jefferson's daughter. Jefferson's parentage of white children has been difficult to verify, leading Brown to change Clotel's father to an unnamed senator in his second edition, which he published in the United States rather than Great Britain, where *Clotel* was first published. Sexual relationships between master and slave constitute historical fact, of course, but more than history influenced Brown to create a heroine of mixed lineage. In fact, Brown continually stresses the Anglo features of his characters. Early in Brown's romance,

Clotel appears on the auction block; the narrator laments: "there she stood, with a complexion as white as most of those who were . . . to become her purchasers; her features as finely defined as any of her sex of pure Anglo-Saxon . . ." (62). And Mary, Clotel's daughter by a white man, exhibits a complexion "still lighter than her mother. Indeed she was not darker than *other* white children" (80, italics mine). Not only did Brown's own white ancestry influence his depiction of nearly white heroines; the tragic mulatto theme appears in numerous abolitionist romances and in Dion Boucicault's play, *The Octoroon*, as well as in post-Reconstruction works. Catherine Starke has gone so far as to insist that the mulatto represents the tragic archetype in American literature.[3] Brown's hero, George, is "as white as most white persons. No one would suppose any African blood coursed through his veins. His hair was straight, soft, fine and light; his eyes blue, nose prominent, lips thin, . . . and he was often taken for a free white person . . ." (222). Clearly, Brown's emphasis on a Caucasian standard of beauty raises profound questions about his views of white supremacy. But the reader must also take into account Brown's abolitionist audience, many of whom were white. For this audience, the mulatto's plight furnished a two-fold message. On the one hand, the mixture of the races suggests the exploitation of female slaves by their masters; on the other, it intimates an affinity between blacks and whites, an affinity that might, to Brown's way of thinking, lead to equality and integration. The modern reader may react with anger and dismay at Brown's dependence on the tragic mulatto motif, and rightly so. But for Brown, mythmaking was impossible without this motif.

To further his mythmaking, Brown turns to the romance, a form particularly common to the historical fiction writer and destined to attract a wide audience. George's heroism comes into play when he participates in Nat Turner's rebellion. He is captured with the rest of the rebels, but he inexplicably happens to be standing by the courthouse when a fire erupts, threatening to destroy some invaluable deeds. Predictably, George rushes into the raging fire to rescue the deeds. Whether his act stems from civic loyalty or calculated risk is unclear; however, the result is the same: his trial is delayed a year because the city recognizes his meritorious service. Further reward comes when the judge allows

him a fairly lengthy speech in his defense, a speech so eloquent it melts
the hearts of all the jurors. His eloquence notwithstanding, George is
convicted of high treason. Yet his oration serves the purpose of eluci-
dating the hypocrisy of a country which hangs rebels while it glorifies
the American Revolution. At the same time, George himself invites the
audience to revere those Afro-Americans who dare to be militant.

With the freedom of action the romance allows, Brown can fabricate
a world where the reader readily accepts numerous escapes. Whereas the
realistic novel might delineate one escape, Brown details at least five.
One is that of Clotel, sold to a slave speculator when Horatio Green's
evil wife decides to punish Clotel and Horatio. In this episode, Brown
fictionalizes the account of William and Ellen Craft. Clotel's hair having been shorn by her new family in an effort to destroy her beauty, she
and a fellow slave, William, conceive a plan to escape whereby she will
disguise herself as a gentleman with William as her slave. Although the
escape proves successful, Clotel is recaptured directly after Nat Turner's
rebellion and escapes again, ending her life by jumping into the Poto-
mac when she discovers she can no longer elude her pursuers. Clotel's
death would seem to relegate Brown's fiction to sentimental nineteenth-
century romance, in which the heroine often dies, but Brown in fact regards Clotel's suicide as the quintessential heroic act. Entitling his chapter "Death is Freedom," Brown mythologizes the courage of those Afro-
Americans who preferred death to enslavement. Plunging to her death
in full view of the White House, Clotel, the President's daughter, symbolizes rebellion against the rape of an entire people.

Another escape, that of George, reworks the Ellen Craft episode.
Mary, whom Horatio's wife has taken as her slave, persuades the imprisoned George to don her clothes, leaving her in his cell. In this disguise, he manages to travel toward Canada undetected until he begins
to suspect that two slavecatchers are following him. In an episode based
on Brown's own escape, a family of Quakers hides George in their barn,
knowing that the law will soon arrive. During an amusing chain of
events, the Quakers manage to stall those seeking to enforce the Fugitive Slave Act so that George can evade them.

Like many romances, *Clotel* abounds with coincidences. After George
escapes from slavery and travels to Canada, he persuades a missionary

to return to Virginia to find Mary. She has, however, been sold. That Mary would have been sold for helping George escape could be easily accepted. But the events that follow strain the modern reader's credulity almost to the breaking point. After years in England, where his industry and intelligence put him "on the road to wealth," George decides to travel (232). In France he encounters a mysterious veiled lady weeping over a grave. Seeing him, she faints. Later invited to her house (she learns his address from a book he has accidentally left by the grave), George discovers her to be Mary, now conveniently widowed by the Frenchman who bought her for his wife in New Orleans. The two marry immediately. Astonishing as these events may seem, they serve to assure the audience that no obstacle is insurmountable, that visions should exceed common sense.

Often historical romances move characters from one geographical area to another with astonishing rapidity. In *Clotel*, the action begins in Richmond, moves to New Orleans and Natchez, and then back and forth among these three cities. In the concluding chapters, the reader accompanies George to Canada, England, and France. For the nineteenth-century readers who had no doubt spent most of their lives in one or two towns, the characters' peregrinations provided exhilarating fantasy. But George's journeys are otherwise significant. In the first sections of Clotel, characters move through the South as a result of the vagaries of fortune; the masters decide where the slaves will locate. In the concluding chapters, George's horizontal mobility signifies vertical mobility as well. George and Mary are not only free instead of enslaved and reunited as lovers, but both are apparently well-to-do rather than impoverished. This rags-to-riches formula was exhibited by numerous nineteenth-century romancers; even today it represents a stock device in popular historical romance.

Taking into account Brown's remarkable life, one might expect a sanguine attitude. But the social climate itself strengthened such hope, for the Enlightenment had left a legacy in the doctrine of progress. Early and mid-nineteenth-century Americans saw humanity as perfectible, particularly in a democratic nation. Further, Americans believed, perfectibility must lead in time to an even more ideal society. At the same time Dostoevsky was denouncing as simplistic such a concept, ignoring as it did the complexity and waywardness of human nature, for most people – not only in Europe and Great Britain but in the United States as well – the belief in humanity's innate goodness prevailed. What caused this notion to carry even more weight in the United States than abroad was America's idealism, shored up by the expanding population and burgeoning agriculture and industry between the War of 1812 and the Civil War. These social and economic realities suggested that with proper application, anyone could achieve affluence. For Brown, the black man or woman is destined to progress toward a perfect being, if he or she is freed from enslavement. The irony produced by the use of Thomas Jefferson's relationship to Clotel derives from the fact that Jefferson himself espoused the principles of humanity's innate goodness, of the ultimate creation of a perfect society. Yet the same person seen as the spokesman for the "common man," who decried slavery because it robbed blacks of their right to the "pursuit of happiness," himself owned slaves, may even hypothetically have produced mulattoes like Brown or Clotel. What Brown perceives as Jefferson's hypocrisy does not, however, prevent Brown from embracing the tenets of Jeffersonian democracy, and does not inhibit him from presenting contemporary events with a view toward concretizing these same tenets.

The eighty years that elapsed between the publication of *Clotel* and that of Arna Bontemps's *Black Thunder* brought with them some marked changes in attitude toward history. Whereas Brown perceives history as an upward spiral that, with the proper degree of enlightenment engendered by writers such as himself, will produce a progressively better society, Bontemps has likened history to a pendulum. Examining the characteristics of the period from which *Black Thunder* derives may provide understanding of the genesis of his theory.

From the Golden Age preceding the Civil War, the country moved into the Gilded Age: industrialization led to despair and poverty in the masses. Even Jefferson's much valued agrarianism showed signs of defeat when droughts destroyed crops year after year. For blacks, continuing oppression underlined these grim agricultural conditions; though slavery had been abolished, the plantation economy was resurrected in the form of sharecropping and tenant farming. After the turn of the century, the First World War's pyrrhic victory generated a wave of cynicism and despair nearly opposite to the pre-Civil War optimism Brown embodied. Growing out of this despair, the Lost Generation and the Harlem Renaissance alike produced some of the twentieth century's most brilliant art. The allegiance that Bontemps felt toward the Renaissance resulted in much of *Black Thunder's* flavor, but before discussing the Renaissance influence, it would be helpful to look to the thirties and its influence on Bontemps's view of history.

If the aforementioned burdens of exploitative industry, floundering agriculture, systematic disenfranchisement, and cosmic despair were not enough to crush U.S. optimism, such problems were compounded by the Depression. Yet, although economic failure at first impoverished the spirit, nihilism rather quickly gave way to a new wave of hope, less abandoned than that of the nineteenth century, more realistic, but nevertheless much different from the dreariness that might have been expected, given the decade's conditions. Both black and white writers responded to a national urge to redesign values. This mood manifested itself in the social protest of William Attaway's *Blood on the Forge* (1941), of John Steinbeck's *Of Mice and Men* (1937) and *The Grapes of Wrath* (1939), of James T. Farrell's *Studs Lonigan* (1932-35), and of John Dos Passos's *U.S.A.* (1930-36). But in all these works the nineteenth-century concept that the individual can shape the future is dampened by cynicism and despair. Revolt, if engaged in, is viewed as absolutely necessary – but somewhat futile.

Bontemps shares this sense of revolt's minimal impact at the same time as he remains convinced of revolt's necessity. Just as vehemently as Brown denies folk cultural realities in favor of white middle-class mores, so does Bontemps reverse this stance. *Black Thunder* hinges on the notion that the unschooled common folk are more likely to initiate and sustain revolt against oppression than are the "favored" blacks, especially the house slaves. Bontemps believes that those who have retained their own tribal literacy, as Robert B. Stepto uses the term, rather than assimilating to the manners and values of the white majority, are those least conflicted about their politics.[4] Revolt, Bontemps maintains, will generate from those in touch with black folklore and the supernatural, those who have not lost their affinity for nature or their impulse for freedom. His idealized folk world focuses his audience on Afro-America's heroic power, dramatized by Gabriel, a messianic figure contrasting sharply with those in *Clotel*.

Bontemps's romance fictionalizes Gabriel Prosser's revolt of 1800, in which 1,100 blacks organized against whites in Henrico County, Virginia. Structurally, *Black Thunder* is divided into two parts. The first part involves what Bontemps views as the naive preparation for a plan that is logistically doomed. The second part not only emphasizes the monstrous measures whites will take to punish blacks, but also analyzes the social influences determining the revolt's failure. Bontemps employs a number of successful fictional strategies. Avoiding conventional narrative plotting, he offers instead a series of brief, dramatic scenes providing sketches of characters pivotal to the revolt. As these scenes progress, very little action, as such, occurs. To depict his mythic vision of a universe where good and evil struggle to displace each other, Bontemps juxtaposes scenes of the anguished black slave community with the corrupt white political one. Moving his fiction away from verisimilitude, Bontemps exerts poetic license, endowing actual hisorical figures with mythic characteristics. *Black Thunder*'s heroine Juba, for example, serves as the embodiment of the powers of nature and the supernatural. To emphasize and exalt black speech, Bontemps employs oral narrative devices. A work that has not received its fair share of critical recognition, *Black Thunder* demonstrates remarkable mastery of historical documentation, romance tradition, and oral narration. Despite tendencies to sentimentalize and to present a heroine reinforcing the stereotypic "lusty wench," Bontemps largely achieves his aims, marrying history and myth by way of the romance and making an outstanding contribution to the black historical literary canon.

During the first part of *Black Thunder*, one gets both a sense of the growing power and solidarity among the blacks and the growing curiosity and bewilderment among the whites, who sense a political undercurrent. The revolt is already planned when one of the slaves, Bundy, is murdered by his master, but this death spurs the rebels on to implement their scheme. However, a huge storm prevents the plan's execution. Although Gabriel hopes to begin again the next day, after the storm dies out, two slaves, Ben and Pharoah, betray the plot, resulting in the hangings of innumerable blacks. Most studies put the figure at about thirty-five; *Black Thunder* gives one the sense that hundreds are executed. Bontemps declines to offer a specific number, instead allowing Pharoah to admit, chillingly, "some's catching the rope what ain't done nothing."[5] Although Gabriel manages to elude the whites who search for him, he refuses to run away, remaining in the county in hopes of re-organizing. When he realizes the futility of this plan, he secretes himself on a ship, where he is eventually captured. *Black Thunder* concludes with Gabriel's heroic death by hanging, followed by a scene of Ben, who has revealed numerous rebels' names, fearful that those who have not suffered hanging will avenge his betrayal. Although Bontemps holds Ben responsible for his treachery, he makes clear that Ben represents only one cause of the slaughter that follows the revolt.

Throughout *Black Thunder* Bontemps emphasizes the larger world by a montage of newspaper accounts, prowling militiamen, and reward posters issued by Governor Monroe, a world that determines the rebels' fate. Reinforcing this sense of the world beyond Henrico County, Bontemps includes a portrait of Thomas Callender distributing anti-slavery letters to the editor of the Norfolk *Epitome of the Times*, while at the same time imprisoned as a result of the Sedition Act; emphasized too is the harassment of alleged "Jacobins." With these details Bontemps suggests that the powers beyond Gabriel and the rebels are exceedingly vast and complex. Even beyond political forces lie natural forces that seem to conspire absurdly to determine the outcome. Alexander Biddenhurst, a white liberal, voices this sentiment: "It was everywhere conceded that barring the storm, the blacks could hardly have failed to duplicate the recent successes (within certain bounds) of their brothers in San Domingo. But life was like that: beauty beats a frail wing and the scales of fate are shaken by a bubble. Now the hope of freeing the slaves was more remote than ever in the United States . . ." (152).

To Bontemps, "history is a pendulum that does recur. But in each recurrence there is a difference . . . ."[6] And as he suggests in his 1968 introduction to *Black Thunder,* though Martin Luther King's death seems to parallel Gabriel's failure, this is not to say that either should not have acted as he did; each must certainly be regarded as a hero. Like other fiction of the thirties, then, *Black Thunder* reflects the belief that though one may do little to ameliorate injustice, he or she must, with a kind of existential courage, lash out against oppression; and because of this dictum, Gabriel's revolt deserves glorification. The nineteenth-century belief in the individual that allowed Brown to pin all his hopes on one or two characters had by the thirties been superseded by the notion that most social action demands collective effort; still, that notion does not negate the necessity for a hero with whom the audience can identify. This hero differs greatly, however, from *Clotel*'s George. In 1800 Gabriel had represented heroism primarily to a counter-culture; by 1936 he appealed to a much larger audience. Bontemps asserts that in the thirties "even conservative people could understand why certain writers could be taking positions that were quite radical."[7] In addition to his militancy, *Black Thunder*'s protagonist possesses other traits that endear him to his audience, making him a mythic hero.

Bontemps began the work while still involved in the Harlem school, before it dissolved. It is important to remember that this literary movement fictionalized modes of being appealing not only to the school's members, or even to the larger black audience, but to those whites caught up in the twenties mystique. Despite the fact that most of the Harlem school artists were highly educated, their work repeatedly yields two outstanding tenets: the reliance on instinct over reason and the belief in fold wisdom over academic knowledge. With these features in mind, it is possible to appreciate Bontemps' Gabriel. Although some historians claim Gabriel was literate, Bontemps chooses to depict him as illiterate; furthermore, were he able to read the volume of Roscoe's Leo X that George peruses, he would not choose to do so. Neither intellectual nor philosophical, Gabriel, when asked for his last words, replies, "Let the rope talk, suh" (223). While historians claim Gabriel possessed knowledge of military science, Bontemps never touches upon this fact, preferring to de-emphasize the plan so that it appears the essence of simplicity. It is clear that Bontemps wishes to create a cultural hero for black audiences, one who deifies those very qualities Brown tried to avoid. Interestingly, whereas Jean Toomer sought to appeal primarily to a white audience with *Cane*, Bontemps goes beyond Toomer's scope, capturing both black and white readers.

Moving beyond this depiction of Gabriel as a cultural hero, Bontemps also creates an entire world of mythic proportions, a world inhabited by characters serving as legendary black figures. Most significant of these are three slaves, Bundy, Juba, and Ben. When Bundy's master whips him to death, aside from informing the readers that slaves suffered such fates, Bundy's death carries larger significance. As Robert Bone suggests, it "does duty for all injustice of master to slave, making it unnecessary to belabor the point. . . ."[8] Further, Bundy's funeral sets the ominous tone appropriate to *Black Thunder*'s outcome, foreshadowing the approaching deaths and capturing the tenor of slave experience, dominated by loss and sorrow. Bundy's characterization, like Gabriel's, is possible largely because the Harlem Renaissance encouraged Bontemps to confront his own past, to portray honestly characters like Bundy who were not intellectual, complex, nor particularly noble but who achieved greatness through suffering. Although it triggers the revolt, Bundy's death effects little historical change, given the revolt's outcome; however, it possesses legendary significance, and it is this significance Bontemps emphasizes.

Another character who attains mythic stature with assistance from Harlem Renaissance tenets is Juba. Herbert Aptheker points out that Gabriel's wife was in fact named "Nanny."[9] Probably Bontemps's change derived from a desire to present Juba as larger than life, Juba having traditionally served slaves both as a nickname for Jupiter and as the name of a joyful dance originating in Africa. Emphasis on Juba's sensuality enhances her mythic proportions. Bontemps takes pains to describe her posture upon the black colt Araby, her thighs glistening with sweat, her thin waist, and the scarcity of her garments. Regrettably, Bontemps carries this sensuality to extremes, repeatedly underscoring her one-dimensional role: Juba is described as "the tempestuous brown wench" who twitches "her wet skirt lasciviously," "haughty and aloof as a harlot" (29, 108, 166). It is not, however, Bontemps's aim to deprecate his heroine. Rather than a mere sex-object, Juba typifies the Renaissance fusion of instinct and wisdom, a majestic, courageous young woman whose loyalty to Gabriel and determination to save him with a conjure bespeak the agonizing yet hopeful quality of the folk tradition Bontemps celebrates. Richard Wright's review of *Black Thunder* insists that Gabriel reveals "a quality of folk courage unparalleled. . . ."[10] Juba too reveals such courage, she and her unbroken colt signalling the revolt's beginning. Later, when Juba suffers a vicious whipping, she stands up to this torture with superhuman strength and dignity, refusing to flinch or cry.

Ben's characterization is unrelated to Bontemps's Harlem school involvement, yet he too emerges as a legendary figure. Rather than offering, however, as do Gabriel, Bundy, and Juba, an ideal mode of action, Ben plays an undesirable but realistic historical role: that of the house servant who betrays the hero. Ben receives fuller treatment than Gabriel, causing the reader to wonder whether Bontemps's sympathies lie more closely with Ben than with Gabriel. Admittedly, Bontemps treats Ben sympathetically in *Black Thunder*'s first three books, but he modifies this sympathy greatly after Ben betrays the plot and its leaders. At this point, the narrator recedes from a sympathetic stance, and Bontemps juxtaposes Ben's comparative opulence with the situations of Mingo and Gabriel, doomed to imprisonment and death: militiamen patrol the streets "periodically dragging anonymous Negroes before the justices." The daughter of the man killed by Criddle, another rebel, waits "hungrily for each new kill"; most of the victims are innocent (168). Nearby, Mingo lies bound, face down to the jailhouse floor, listening for the gallows' trap to fall, kicking wildly, "imagining that he [cannot] bear the gruesome horror another time." Ben is close by, "clean and well-favored, wearing new driving gloves and a hat in neat trim . . . and satin breeches" (169). Gabriel, meanwhile, sits "on a heap of filthy straw . . . his hat . . . battered beyond recognition" (170).

Clearly, Bontemps considers Ben a reprehensible character, but his strategies for communicating that fact are subtle. Continually juxtaposing the rebels' condition with Ben's well-being, Bontemps emphasizes that Ben has traded his integrity for the comfort to which he has grown accustomed. Moreover, as *Black Thunder* concludes, Ben is obsessed with a vision of "Gabriel's shining, naked body" and "the arc inscribed by the executioner's ax," an arc that has lingered in the air moments after Gabriel's death (224). Bontemps juxtaposes this final image of Gabriel, reinforcing his mythic proportions, with Ben's escape into his sensuous fantasy life, where the mare of the coach he drives plays "a soothing tune on the cobblestones" with her feet (224). Therefore, it seems clear that Ben should be viewed as both a foil for Gabriel's militance and a believable portrait of those oppressed people who cannot divorce themselves from their allegiance to the ruling class. Ben typifies those who, while sympathetic to the idea of revolt, are incapable of acting out that sympathy. He makes clear the fact that not all people, black or white, have the courage to translate their words into action. Bontemps does not eulogize Ben, or men like him; rather, by portraying rather than avoiding such a character, he enhances the complexity of the mythology he presents.

Clearly, the thirties influenced Bontemps's concept of history, and the Harlem Renaissance affected his mythologizing of that history, allowing him to create a fictional world filled with characters who both embody and contradict ideal modes of being. It is apparent also that Bontemps's selection of literary mode shapes his fictionalization of history. As has been demonstrated, Bontemps was the first black romancer to confront rather than repudiate the past, choosing to endow his characters with traits eschewed by Brown and other early writers. To enhance his depiction of the past, it was necessary to find a literary form that would convey the resonance of the era he portrayed.

Black Thunder is a romance augmented by the oral narrative tradition. Bontemps has stated: "Blacks were the foremost proponents of the tale told for entertainment or instruction. And it was always oral."[11] Northrop Frye, Milman Parry, Scholes and Kellogg, and others have explored the oral narrative, a mode dating from the days when the first storytellers entertained their audiences. This mode, although written, seeks to duplicate the features of an oral tale. Although certain conventions typify the oral mode, these conventions need not all be present for a piece to be defined as oral narative. One may expect some of the following: a frame narrator, stock characters (such as the old story teller or the trickster figure), formula plots (such as rescue of the heroine or tricking the trickster), formula episodes (such as a chase or the surmounting of three obstacles), and parody or burlesque. The oral mode strives for authenticity by employing a demotic "folk style," characterized by simple diction, similes (the figure of speech commonly employed in everyday conversation and storytelling), and formulaic expressions or epithets. Although most readers regard the oral narrative as a mode limited to the epic poem, the tall tale, the ballad, and the folk tale, one adopted primarily by

Henry Wadsworth Longfellow and Mark Twain, scholars have shown that many modern writers, among them J.D. Salinger, William Faulkner, and Flannery O'Connor, make use of the oral tradition. Oral narrative is frequently pivotal to black American literature, especially in those writers concerned with preserving the folk tradition. One modal element previously discussed in reference to *Black Thunder* is a hero with whom the audience can experience immediate identification. James Mellard has described these types of heroes in the following manner: "Protagonists are not anonymous actors but identifiable models who project the values of their culture. . . . The hero absorbs the value of his culture and his deeds transform those values into actions."[12] Obviously, Gabriel can be viewed as this sort of hero.

Another distinguishing feature of the oral narrative evident in *Black Thunder* is its use of demotic rather than formal language; language is "of the people." Whereas *Clotel*'s principal characters avoid black English, those in *Black Thunder* use black English freely. Their language is demotic in another sense. In *Clotel,* as in other romances of its day, characters often lapse not only into poetic diction but into poetry itself. *Black Thunder*'s language, rather than relying on literary allusion, makes use of the simile. Similes vary from the ordinary "it's something what'll burn yo' ears like fire to hear . . ." to the original "the stars shook like lamps swinging in a storm" (118 and 17). When a startling semi-literary figure of speech appears, the narrator is responsible. Often the narrator combines simile and metaphor: "Little splinters of moonlight showered the dark hut. They fell in gusts as fair and fine as the spray of imaginary sparklers on an imaginary holiday" (116). The narrator inevitably calls up the elemental, primarily death, animals, or both: "A swarm of sparrows covered a green coppice like flies on a carcass" (19).

In conjunction with the tendency toward simile, or toward language suggestive of the folk, Bontemps uses formulaic expressions, analogous to the Homeric epithets appearing in ballads. As one of the primary devices for describing characters in *Black Thunder,* these epithets are particular, since they are not interchanged between characters; rather, each is used in connection with one character. Juba is described as "that brown gal" (34), Melody as "the apricot-colored mullatress" (39), Pharoah as "that pun'kin colored nigger" (44). Not only are these epithets repeated, but they are varied within the boundaries that their formulaic nature allows. Thus, Juba is also called the "brown girl," "the girl," and "the tempestuous brown wench." Melody, "the beautiful temptress," is always described in connection with garments suggesting the lure of the material and the romantic aspects of nature at the same time: she wears, in different scenes, "a leaf-green petticoat," "a rose-colored headcloth," and a "leaf-green dress." Criddle, too, is surrounded by formulaic language: "his little stupid head was a bullet; his eyes were no more than white spots on a domino" (16). Later, he is called "the short black stable boy with eyes like spots on a domino" (31) and still later: "the two little domino spots [show] plain on his bullet head" (32). With such epithets Bontemps underscores those personality traits on which he wants his audience to reflect. Melody, for example, reveals the conflict between material comfort and political commitment.

In addition to the formulaic description of characters, *Black Thunder* presents a recurrent motif: "Anything wants to be free" (68). Many characters repeat this refrain, one that emphasizes the theme of rebellion and undergoes innumerable variations, among them: "A wild bird what's in a cage will die anyhow, sooner or later" (69), "Everything what's equal to a ground hog wants to be free . . ." (77). With not only the epithets that surround characters but with this formulaic motif, it should be remembered, Bontemps *strives* for recurrence. In the actual oral tale or song, the narrator relies on repetition, on refrain, both to speed the tale's movement and to give the audience a comforting sense of familiarity and identification with the material. With *Black Thunder* Bontemps imitates oral presentation to evoke in his audience the same responses they would have were they listening rather than reading, both to tap the readers' urges for simplicity and to remind them of their folk origins. In this attempt Bontemps is far ahead of his time, for he is the first black historical romancer to return to these origins fearlessly, without sham or pretense. Bontemps remarks: "I don't know whether I was consciously yearning for the past. I don't think that I ever believed that I could recapture the past. I had a yearning for something in my own life. Unlike most black writers I yearned for something in my past . . . . A great many writers whom I have known have wanted to forget their pasts."[13] In an effort to recreate the past, Bontemps chooses a form that corresponds to the character's actual speech, a form that reveals the poetry and beauty of that speech. His oral narrative embodies his conviction that black history demands celebration. Within black history lie the seeds of mythology, seeds Bontemps wishes to nurture. Brown, on the other hand, believing that black mythology must look toward the future, creates dialogue that seems to assure white social acceptability, his characters' speech reflecting their degree of assimilation rather than identification with black culture.

Thus, though Brown and Bontemps transform the slave experience into fiction, they approach it from very different perspectives. Brown's method is essentially one of avoidance. Like many writers who followed him, he is concerned with humanity's place in history, with the effects of socio-historic events on humanity; but unlike James Fenimore Cooper and other historical romancers of his day, he cannot blithely return to the past in order to examine these matters. For Brown's second concern is with mythmaking, and past history yields no myths to deny the stereotypes he wishes to refute. Consequently, he not only places his characters in the present but impels them beyond the present. Accordingly, his characters, like him, serve as luminaries of the concept of assimilation, itself a symbol of perfectibility for him. Bontemps, in contrast, enjoying the good fortune of living in an era that embraced those qualities previously anathema to blacks desiring social acceptance, can confront blacks' place in history through actually looking at that history and can create viable myths out of that history. The ideological tendencies of the time affect all writers. Not until the twenties and thirties, however, did the climate allow black writers to create fictional worlds inhabited by genuine black characters rather than figures embodying the whites' expectations of them.

2   Female Paradigms

in Frances Harper's *Iola Leroy*
and Pauline Hopkins's *Contending Forces*

The period between the first publication of *Clotel* (1853) and that of Frances Ellen Watkins Harper's *Iola Leroy; or Shadows Uplifted* (1892) was a dormant one for black romancers. One major work emerged: Harriet E. Wilson's *Our Nig; or Sketches from the Life of a Free Black* (1859), the first black romance published in this country, explores the plight of a woman whose life as an indentured servant duplicates that of her enslaved sisters. That blacks produced little fiction during this period should not be surprising; social conditions did not lend themselves to literary productivity. Freed by the Emancipation Proclamation, blacks found that in some ways life proved even more difficult than it had before the Civil War. Many freed men and women, released from bondage with few skills except those of field labor, went to work on plantations leased by former Southern planters. August Meier and Elliot Rudwick have shown that though "a significant number of ex-slaves bought farms after the war," many more black laborers worked for very poor wages on these leased plantations.

> In some arrangements, blacks were paid partly in food, clothing, and medical care, but lessees had endless opportunities to fleece the Negroes of what little they had, and medical care was practically never provided. Government agents interested in the Black's welfare attemped to draw up regulations to mitigate the problems, but at best these were compromises with the demands of the plantation owners and the lessees. At worst they were flagrantly ignored.[1]

Such conditions are fictionalized by W.E.B. Du Bois in *The Quest of the Silver Fleece* (1911), but more than forty years of such suffering preceded the transformation into fiction.

Other conditions following the war evolved from the despair, rage, and frustration of white Southerners propelled into a way of life entirely foreign to them. Raised under a strict caste system, they were suddenly forced to overturn their perceptions of themselves and of blacks, to reverse behavior to which they were conditioned. Such demand asked for more than the old racist code could handle; thus, Southerners set about reinstituting the old South under the facade of Northern mercantilism and industrialization. The sharecropping system provided one strategy for this reinstitution, and the Black Codes provided another. Under these statutes, enacted in 1865 and 1866, unemployed blacks were declared vagrants. Contracts between laborers and employers often emphasized their relationship through use of the terms "master" and "servant"; blacks could not own firearms. Other efforts toward reinstating the old order involved violence in the form of race riots (more properly, pogroms) and harassment by the Klan. These efforts, in conjunction with Northern disenchantment at the lack of immediate "progress" by blacks, culminated in the Compromise of 1877, legislation that withdrew Federal troops from the South, more or less abandoned the ideal of total equality, and ushered in the post-Reconstruction period about which Pauline Hopkins, Sutton Griggs, Charles Chesnutt, and W.E.B. Du Bois write.

A series of court cases followed the compromise, reflecting what C. Vann Woodward calls "The cumulative weakening of resistance to racism."[2] In the *Civil Rights Cases of 1883* the Supreme Court decided that the Fourteenth Amendment allowed Congress to prohibit states, but not individuals, from racial discrimination. This and other court decisions attest to the climate of the late 1890s, one in which aggression toward blacks reached a new high. Various signs from American culture served to legitimize such aggression: conciliatory Northerners, an imperialist national temper, and the submissive philosophy of Booker T. Washington.[3] Although Washington intended to better the situation for blacks, it is probable that the concepts expressed in his Atlanta Compromise Address of 1895, in which he warned against forcing political or professional goals, suggested that he himself felt blacks were inferior. With a major spokesman for black people implying black inferiority, one gets a sense of racism's pervasiveness at the time. Not only politicians, but historians, anthropologists, and sociologists enunciated racist views. To underscore notions of Afro-America's inadequacy, authors of popular literature mapped out the plantation tradition, whipping up the emotions of any reader entertaining doubts about the mood's legitimacy. Joel Chandler Harris and Thomas Nelson Page, popularizers of the stereotypes of benevolent masters, comic darkies, tainted mulattoes, and loyal mammies, surfaced partly as a result of the South's desire to return to a mythically ideal past and partly because the Genteel Tradition demanded denial of ugly reality in favor of mawkish fantasy. The loyal mammy, in particular, deserves mention here, for this stereotypically adamantine, kind, unattractive, and sexless woman was beloved by white Southerners immersed in nostalgia for the antebellum South. The mammy, as Barbara Christian has pointed out, served as a correlate for the mythically dainty, "refined" plantation mistress, a being supposedly far above the vulgar duties of nursing babies or performing the menial tasks associated with childcare.[4]

The mammy stereotype, one which typified stoic endurance, was, of course, both limited and harmful, justifying abusive treatment of black women on the grounds that they were impervious to pain. The stereotype of the promiscuous black woman, closely akin to the mammy stereotype, likewise justified the historical sexual exploitation of black women, a practice as old as slavery. After the Civil War, when black men by the score experienced lynching for allegedly violating white women, black women writers and lecturers continued to testify to the reality of the situation: black, not white, women were more often the victims of interracial coercive sex, brutality, and rape. Whereas white women did indeed suffer sexual exploitation, such exploitation occurred more often within their own race than it did between the races. It would be naive to assume that sex never happened between black males and white females. But crucial to the racist attitude is whites' flat refusal to acknowledge that sex between black men and white women could be mutually voluntary, that white women were seldom victims. "Not all of those innocents existed in reality," Trudier Harris writes. "But all acquired innocence in the white male imagination."[5] Ultimately, most sex between white and black victimized blacks, not whites. The white female suffered few legal consequences from voluntary liaisons, whereas the black male could be put to death at the whisper of a rumor. At the same time, numerous black women, assertive enough to speak for the legions who suffered similar fates, report repeated sexual harassment by slave owners and employers, as well as more direct attack in the form of rape, an ultimate violation used as a weapon of terror for centuries. Whether wielded as an expression of dominance by an individual or launched as a tool for mass subjugation by a gang, rape of black women by white men swells the annals of black history. Not only did white men systematically assault black women during slavery, but rapes accompanied riots of the 1890s and the blood baths engendered by the Klan. Regardless of the degree of force and violence involved, such sexual exploitation posited its justification on the myth of the promiscuous black woman. Although Harris and Page cannot be held responsible for perpetuating the image of the oversexed black woman, an image that would have marred the facile surface of the genteel plantation living they depicted, Christian notes that not only was this image present in post-Civil War popular literature, but in Southern white women's diaries.[6] In any case, the image of the black "wench" persists today, sanctioning abuse on the grounds that the victim elicits it.

Both Frances Harper and Pauline Hopkins write in direct response to these historical conditions and cultural images, but in many ways their mythmaking hearkens back to *Clotel*. Thus they provide a bridge between Brown and the male post-Reconstruction writers Sutton Griggs and Charles Chesnutt. Like Brown, Harper and Hopkins set as their task the reification of Afro-American humanity, and they laud many of the same white American ideals with as much enthusiasm as their predecessor: a Caucasian standard of beauty, high regard for industry, uncritical admiration for Anglo-Saxon "culture" and "refinement," and firm belief that education will allow blacks to surmount prejudice and attain equality. Yet, they write their romances forty years after *Clotel*'s publication, and as a result, *Iola Leroy* and *Contending Forces* reveal post-Reconstruction's influence. Harper and Hopkins touch on the problems of lynching, of voting disenfranchisement, of the difficulties of educated blacks finding and retaining employment, and of expatriation to Africa. *Iola Leroy* and *Contending Forces* exhibit other striking similarities as well. Pivotal to Harper and Hopkins are their outrage at women's victimization and their notion that black women must resist such victimization whenever possible. Reverence for motherhood also informs their romances. In accordance with their sanctification of motherhood, both writers celebrate the reunion of families splintered by slavery and underscore the need for the black extended family to stabilize. A final similarity which deserves notice is the relative critical neglect which Harper and Hopkins have suffered; this obscurity must be attributed, at least in part, to the fact that they were women.

Contending Forces; a Romance Illustrative of Negro Life North and South, originally published in 1899, might appear at first glance to be a traditional historical romance, one that fictionalizes the past, for its action begins during slavery and jumps to post-Reconstruction, just as *Iola Leroy* begins during slavery and moves to the Reconstruction period immediately after the war. As with most black historical romancers of the nineteenth and early twentieth centuries, however, Harper and Hopkins find mythmaking incompatible with a detailed depiction of slavery, given its attendant humiliations. Thus, although they do fictionalize the antebellum South, and Harper applauds blacks' participation in the Civil War, their treatment of slavery is brief and symbolic, their romances moving rather quickly to the period after emancipation. Consequently, the central characters' enslavement receives short shrift. Harper never presents the lives of Iola and her mother as property, and Iola's bondage appears to last a few months, at most. Grace Montfort dies almost immediately after she is remanded to slavery in *Contending Forces,* and Hopkins glosses over the slave experience of Grace's two sons. Moreover, the enslaved characters are all so light-skinned as to pass for white, so that the romances focus more clearly on the tragic irony of mulattoes suffering along with dark-skinned Afro-Americans than they focus on the questions of slavery's horrors for multitudes of black people.

Harper infuses *Iola Leroy* with the central notion that black women possess the power to effect historical transformation. In order to change history, however, black women must insist on their dignity, shunning victimization and excoriating racist stereotypes. But it is not enough for black women to shape history through enhancing their own self-worth, Harper argues. Black women should embrace the role of motherhood, acting as culture bearers while simultaneously fostering pride in their children so that future generations can serve as race leaders. Finally, by playing an equal role with the black man in engineering social reform and racial equality, the black woman can come to view herself as the apotheosis of intelligence, courage, and self-sacrifice, instrumental in the historical process.

Harper's strategies for relaying these fictional messages parallel those of her literary contemporaries, black and white, male and female. Commingling woman's romance conventions with Afro-American historical concerns, she coaxes her audience into accepting the innate significance of black women. Proclaiming the need for women to acquire marketable job training, her heroine Iola serves as a black feminist prototype in fiction, despite Harper's tendency to assign her artificially feminine characteristics such as fragility. Iola, a talented and predictably tragic octoroon cast out of the white mainstream and into black culture, functions as a messianic figure (notwithstanding her sentimental treatment) by choosing to identify with blackness. Tapping the romance for its inherent faith in the remarkable, Harper avows that the black family, though estranged during slavery, can reunite, allowing women to assume their proper historical role. Harper's very real rhetorical talents, admirably displayed in her lectures, do not translate well into fiction, resulting in a work that resembles a series of political debates. Yet *Iola Leroy* is at least as good as *Clotel,* and Harper's romance deserves more critical attention than it has heretofore received.

Iola Leroy begins during the Civil War, when black men and women eagerly took up the opportunity to participate in a conflict they believed would eliminate slavery. Twenty years before the war, Iola's mother, Marie, has been freed and married by her master. Despite Marie's protests, her husband Eugene Leroy insists on "protecting" their three children from knowledge of their black heritage; thus all three children grow up believing themselves to be white. As soon as Eugene dies, his reprehensible cousin finds loopholes in Marie's marriage contract and manumission, takes possession of the Leroy plantation, and remands Marie and her children to slavery. When the reader first encounters Iola, she has been freed from enslavement to serve as a nurse in the war. Soon afterward, she rejects a white doctor's suggestion that she marry him and pass for white, her rejection based on two principles: first, she has decided to identify with her blackness, and, second, she has determined to embark on a quest for her mother after the war. Subsequently, Iola reunites her family and marries a mulatto doctor, both of them dedicating their lives to crusading for the race.

Harper's historical concerns are imbued with romantic elements. Her characters are extraordinary mulattoes created to transform whites' notions of blacks. According to Iola, Dr. Frank Latimer, her fiancé, exemplifies "high, heroic manhood." In fact, she declares, "he belongs to the days of chivalry."[7] Dr. Latimer's veins run with "the blood of a proud, aristocratic [white] ancestry," but it is his black mother who aids him in his highest achievement, for after being freed from slavery in the early 1800s, she works for thirty years so that he can become a doctor (239). Eventually, he attains the title of "The Good Doctor," signalling his mythic status. Not satisfied with confining his influence to medicine, Dr. Latimer is "a true patriot" and "a leader in every reform movement for the benefit of the community" (279). Evidently, Iola's beau serves as the model of race leadership.

Despite Dr. Latimer's heroic qualities, it is Iola in whom reside the central tenets of Harper's mythmaking. Harper, a dedicated abolitionist and feminist, herself boasted a long career of leadership. During her illustrious tenure as a lecturer, she toured for such organizations as the State Anti-Slavery Society of Maine and helped to found the National Association of Colored Women. From Harper's point of view, "it is the women of a country who help to mold its character and to influence if not determine its destiny."[8]

Iola epitomizes the qualities Harper envisions as fundamental for a messianic woman. Highly intelligent and well-educated, she is also self-sacrificing, devoting her life to a series of jobs that prove her bravery and selflessness: nursing wounded soldiers, teaching poor children, instructing Sunday school students, and helping a young pastor. Independent and assertive, she speaks out against oppression without regard for censure. And although educated in private schools, she makes clear that she has attained her education at the expense of black people, whose unpaid labor has made possible her privileges. Her decision to refuse a white man's marriage proposal and decline to pass for white further reinforces her heroism, as do her indignant rejections of white men who assume her sexual availability during her enslavement. Enraged by the historical sexual exploitation of black women, Harper repeatedly underlines Iola's virtue, at the same time clarifying, for her white readers in particular, the coercion involved in sex between master and slave. Furthermore, Harper insists that such sex, proceeding from woman's powerlessness, degrades white men more than it does black women. As Iola puts it: "I have heard men talk glibly of the degradation of the negro, but there is a vast difference between abasement of condition and degradation of character. I was abased, but the men who trampled on me were the degraded ones" (115). Black women, Harper believes, must view themselves as actors in, rather than victims of, history. Thus, although Harper does not directly depict slavery, she does anticipate later reflections on it by writers of the mid-to-late twentieth century, her ruminations on slavery offering the beginnings of revisionist history from a feminist perspective.

Hampered by racism, Harper's mythmaking has of necessity to fuse the refutation of deplorably stereotypic views of black women with the romance conventions of her day, thus leading her into the same traps that ensnared Brown and, later, Hopkins and Chesnutt. In order to telegraph Iola's singularity to an audience surrounded with images of black females as either unattractive superwomen or comely "wenches," Harper fuses the motif of the tragic mulatto with that of the Sentimental Heroine. Despite Iola's initial description as a "spitfire," she is at the same time "a trembling dove [snatched] from the gory vulture's nest" when a young black soldier named Tom Anderson rescues her from her lascivious slavemaster. Until she reunites with her family, Iola remains heartbroken, "homeless and alone," by her own admission, animated by a terrible secret sorrow (60). In the tradition of the tragic mulatta, Iola has blue eyes and is indecipherable from a white woman. Her beauty, which Harper repeatedly emphasizes, earmarks her as extraordinary, but it also reinforces the concept that one must be white to be beautiful, a distressing idea for a writer dedicated to racial equality. *Iola Leroy*'s heroine decides to turn down the white doctor's suggestion to pass for white early in Harper's romance; yet Iola harbors a disconcertingly ambivalent attitude toward her lineage throughout most of the book. Although declaring the best blood in her veins to be African, when she decides to pass in order to get a job, she believes it unnecessary to announce that her great-grandmother was an Afro-American, evidently forgetting for the moment that she has dedicated herself to insisting her grandmother, her mother, and she herself are Afro-Americans as well and that they should identify with that heritage. Recounting her slave experience to her future husband, Iola maintains, "you cannot conceive what it must have been to be hurled from a home of love and light into the dark abyss of slavery; to be compelled to take your place among a people you have learned to look upon as inferiors and social outcasts" (271). One gets the sense that it is Iola's reversal of fortune that marks her as more noble than she might have been were she born among her "inferiors," as she expresses it. In the same vein, one apprehends that Harper milks Iola's transformation (Iola changes from a girl who defends her father's slave ownership into a young woman who speaks out against slavery) in order to appeal primarily to white women who had mixed feelings about the "peculiar institution" before emancipation.

Another influence signalling the mythmaking qualities of *Iola Leroy* and at the same time marring it is that of the Genteel Tradition, a flaw typifying black historical romance from Brown to Du Bois. Aside from repeated references to Iola's "refinement" and Dr. Latimer's "aristocratic" lineage, Harper points to her central characters' gentility by way of their regal bearing and courtly manners. Their associates are often intellectual, well-turned-out, and well bred, obvious especially at the *conversazione*, as Harper calls a gathering in which they hash out Reconstruction issues. Here, race leaders convene to present papers on expatriation, the black mother's moral responsibilities, the meaning of patriotism in a racist country, and the prejudice of the courts. Stilted, painfully learned dialogue predominates, characters occasionally slipping into allusion, as when Marie remarks, "the true strength of a race means purity in women and uprightness in men; who can say, with Sir Galahad: 'My strength is the strength of ten / Because my heart is pure'" (254). Elsewhere Harper's presentation of history exhibits the marks of excessive decorum;

lynching is "perfectly alarming," while housing discrimination against Iola's brother is attributed to the discovery that he is not white but a member of "an unfashionable and unpopular race" (217, 190). But the passages which display most tellingly Harper's struggles to present history in a genteel manner are those involving Iola's experiences as a slave, which she declines to describe to her own mother because this "fearful siege of suffering . . . would only harrow up [Marie's] soul to hear" (196). Considering that Marie, too, suffered enslavement, Iola's discretion seems unnecessary. But for Harper, mythic history demanded characters epitomizing gentility and erudition, characters who could furnish a counterstatement to the demeaning visions of Afro-America that permeated white culture. During an era when literacy among blacks in general, and black women in particular, was exceptional, Harper's intellectual female characters transmit important messages.

Another device Harper employs in her mythologizing of history is that of coincidence, a romance strategy well suited to communicating to her audience that blacks can surmount hardship and forge meaningful lives. The disruption of black families is emblematic of the mendaciousness of the "peculiar institution," a system which reduced human beings to property bought and sold according to economic considerations, reinforcing a sense of powerlessness and subjugation. Yet, *Iola Leroy* abounds with improbable reunions between members of families that slavery has torn apart. While nursing soldier Robert Johnson, Iola sings him a tune she learned from her family, thus setting in motion a chain of events leading to the discovery that Robert is Iola's uncle, whom she has never before met. After the war, when the two embark on a quest for their mothers, they easily discover Robert's forbear at a meeting held in a black settlement. That this meeting, called primarily for the purpose of fellowship, appears to be the only one Iola and Robert attend testifies to the unlikelihood of Robert's reunion with his mother. That she is the first speaker at the meeting to recount the story of watching her small children wrenched from her arms and sold points up the romantic quality of Harper's book. An equally remarkable twist of fate enables Iola's mother to find her son Harry, wounded in a hospital where she just happens to visit. Their moment of mutual recognition occurs when Marie, equipped with fruit and flowers, bends over Harry's bed to comfort the anonymous young man she has inexplicably selected to receive her gifts. Coincidence follows coincidence when Harry encounters Iola at a conference where she reveals her identity by narrating her personal history to the assembled company. Harper chooses to fictionalize family reunions at such meetings in true romance fashion, ignoring the realistic necessity for Afro-Americans to attend dozens, perhaps hundreds, of such meetings, attendance which produced infrequent reunions. Yet Harper, writing in the tradition of black historical romancers, fictionalizes the historical truth that some families did reunite by this method; thus, she reformulates history, simultaneously encouraging readers to continue seeking lost family members.

Harper also can be credited with a prodigious feat: refuting dehumanizing images of black women by presenting a heroine strong enough to change the course of history yet at the same time genteel and fragile. In order to succeed at this herculean effort, she merges historical concerns with the conventions of nineteenth-century women's fiction. Nina Baym, in her study of women's novels and romances written between 1820 and 1870, has noted patterns that one may observe even in later fiction of the century.[9] Although Baym suggests that the pure genre of women's fiction, as she defines it, disappears after the Civil War, many of the individual characteristics she identifies persist in popular romances today. Such fiction usually centers on a heroine who is either an orphan or has experienced separation from her family. As has been shown, Harper fictionalizes the historical reality of families fragmented during slavery by presenting a lonely, alienated young woman whose mother has been sold away from her. Like most nineteenth-century heroines, Iola suffers abuse, in her case from cruel slavemasters who seek to sexually exploit her. For the most part, this abuse is reported rather than shown, Harper recoiling from fictionalizing such demeaning experiences in connection with her rarefied heroine. Ultimately, Iola claims that her suffering has enhanced her character, a given for much nineteenth-century fiction. Typical of most heroines of her day, Iola escapes her potentially disastrous fate with the aid of a guardian figure, Tom Anderson. When Tom dies from battle wounds, Iola eventually re-encounters Tom's friend Robert Johnson, who acts as another guardian, supporting her efforts to find her mother and to locate employment, which Iola insists a woman must have, whether married or single. In women's fiction of the 1800s, Baym notes, the function of the guardian, or surrogate father or brother, supersedes that of the aspiring suitors, some of whom pursue the heroine for spurious reasons. Usually, the heroine sees through such unscrupulous suitors and refuses their advances. Not only does Iola reject sexual advances, she turns down a marriage proposal, well-meaning though it is, that threatens to repeat her mother's history, Dr. Gresham offering her the tenuous security of posing as a white woman. Women's fiction of Harper's era generally concludes with the heroine triumphantly successful, having transcended her misfortune by dint of her own talents, character, and efforts. Although Iola does receive aid in escaping slavery, Harper bases her heroine's subsequent good fortune on her mythic qualities. From her graduation speech, which reduces every member of her audience to tears, to her work at the hospital, where Dr. Gresham describes her as quintessentially tireless and devoted, to her visionary expression as she rhapsodizes about a race leader's responsibilities, Iola remains a mythic character.

Iola's mythic capabilities stand her in good stead even after her marriage; rather than offering her an identity, Iola's marriage provides her with a partner in her struggle to bring about racial equality, allowing her to devote herself to educating mothers and children for Afro-America's benefit. Throughout *Iola Leroy,* Harper synthesizes woman's historical role with these fictional conventions, clarifying the need for black females to set their sights beyond their personal happiness and contribute to a better world. That Iola, married to a successful doctor, has the luxury of working without pay rather than toiling at domestic service, field labor, or the narrow range of other occupations open to the majority of black women of her time who struggled to feed themselves and their children may suggest that her audience was comprised primarily of middle-class white females. Yet for those black women who read *Iola Leroy* in 1892, and for those who read it today, Harper's insistence that black women must change the course of history deserves commendation. For even those readers who see their lives as circumscribed by economic and familial concerns can take notice of the primary tenet of Harper's mythmaking: the value of motherhood.

Naturally, many contemporary feminists would deplore the relegation of women to the domestic life that Harper's romance appears to sanction. Yet, given the few avenues open to Afro-American females in Harper's day, one must regard her sanctification of motherhood as ingenious, a way of telegraphing to nineteenth-century black women that child rearing designated them as instrumental in historical process. Celebration of motherhood inheres in nineteenth-century fiction, but Harper infuses this convention with the respect for motherhood central to Afro-American culture, placing her firmly in the mythmaking tradition of black historical romance. Harper, writing from within Afro-American culture, had plenty of opportunity to base *Iola Leroy* on motherhood's significance to that culture, where, as Robert Staples has noted, "motherhood represents maturity and the fulfillment of one's function as a woman."[10] Although, as Christian points out, motherhood is a mixed blessing, serving as "a battleground for racist and sexist ideology," reverence for motherhood is so pivotal to both black and white nineteenth-century women readers as to represent a fortuitous choice for Harper's historical romance.[11]

The value of motherhood takes various forms in Harper's mythmaking. Several characters sanctify this role. During the war, one man decides not to join the fight for emancipation, though he fervently wants to do so, because becoming a soldier would force him to leave his mother behind. Robert never loses a chance to remind his companions that being sold away from his mother constitutes the greatest catastrophe of his life, equating loss of mother with loss of self. Since for Harper one of slavery's primary injustices was its destruction of families, Robert's repeated references to this experience simultaneously decry injustice and exalt motherhood. Iola and Robert's quest for their mothers comprises a large portion of the narrative, fleshing out the concept that Robert enunciates and transforming the romantic rescue of a damsel in distress to the rescue of the estranged mother. Marie elucidates one of Harper's views of black women's exploitation during slavery when she laments that black women who bear illegitimate children by their white masters are as victimized as their children because the mothers are denied all respect due them; instead, they are branded as temptresses. Obviously, Harper avers, slavery, by its very nature, mitigated against reverence for motherhood, thus depriving black women of self-respect and happiness.

Writing her romance after slavery's demise, however, Harper concerns herself with how her black sisters can redress these past injustices, turning around their victimization. Iola, who admires a young female's efforts to initiate a school to train future wives and mothers, herself delivers a paper on educating mothers. From her perspective, mothers can change history by passing on appropriate values to their children, thus enlightening future generations about racism and how to combat it. Harper interweaves this view of mothers' role with her adulation for education in general, which she envisions as blacks' primary hope. Deploring the ignorance and uncouthness of her own pupils during her brief stint as a public school teacher, Iola, like Harper, insists that educated blacks must "elevate" those without education.

Although beset by post-Reconstruction demons such as lynching, disenfranchisement, and stereotyping, Harper manages to formulate a positive concept of history. She realizes that emancipation has not inaugurated the joyous era envisioned by Brown but has installed slavery in new guises. Yet she feels blacks must resist the temptation to adopt corrupt white cultural values, supplanting greed, ruthlessness, and racism with selflessness, generosity, and love. Harper remains convinced, in fact, that blacks, given the power, would overshadow whites, and she contends that eventually the Afro-American civilization will surpass the Anglo-Saxon, black America led by partnerships of women and men such as Iola and her husband. For, Harper writes, "the world cannot move without woman's sharing in the movement, and to help give a right impetus to that movement is woman's highest privilege."[12] Harper's evolutionary concept of history, assuming that Afro-Americans will lead Anglo-Americans to a higher state of being, is not, however, based on militant or separatist principles. Instead, Harper espouses a union of "the best of both races," together forging a new culture deriving from equality rather than expediency. Investing her mythmaking with religious fervor, Harper maintains that whites can progress at the same rate as blacks if they emulate Christian virtues.

Pauline Hopkins's *Contending Forces*, like *Iola Leroy*, mythologizes black history of the 1890s; and Hopkins also reveals a preoccupation with the after-effects of slavery without devoting a great deal of space to depicting slavery. Hopkins introduces the reader to the Montforts, an extravagantly wealthy couple living in Bermuda in the year 1800. When Charles and Grace Montfort agree to relocate their plantation and their seven hundred slaves to North Carolina, friends enjoin them to reconsider, given the South's barbarity at the time. Unfortunately, Charles ignores this plea, moving to the States, where the family passes for white. Not long afterward, the white community, who suspects that the Montforts are mulattoes, gets wind of Charles' plan to emancipate his slaves gradually and conspires to subvert this plan. Murdering Charles, the whites seize the plantation along with its human cargo and remand to slavery Grace and her children, Charles, Jr., and Jesse. Driven to near insanity, Grace drowns herself, resulting in Charles, Jr., and Jesse being left alone with Anson Pollack, the malevolent character who has spearheaded the plot to destroy the Montfort family. Subsequently, an Englishman buys the young man Charles from Pollack, taking him to Great Britain and freeing him. Jesse, who has also reached adulthood, manages to escape, fleeing to Boston. *Contending Forces* then leaps from 1800 to 1896, where a new generation, Jesse Montfort's grandchildren, live comfortably with their mother, "Ma" Smith, in Boston. The vast majority of Hopkins's book centers on the post-Reconstruction lives of these grandchildren, Will and Dora Smith, and their friend Sappho Clark. Sappho, who resides at the Smith boarding house, falls in love with Will, but their engagement founders when John Langley, Dora's fiancé, a scoundrel determined to seduce Sappho at any cost, blackmails Sappho. When Langley convinces Sappho that Will would reject her if he knew she had an illegitimate son, she secretly leaves Boston for New Orleans, repairing to a convent with her child. Meanwhile, Dora and Will learn that Sappho's son has resulted from an abduction by a white man, and they agree on her innocence. Dora breaks her engagement to the scheming Langley, and Will pledges himself to marry no one but Sappho. Several years later, a British citizen named Charles Montfort Withington appears to announce his kinship with the Smiths: a direct descendant of Charles Montfort, Withington is the Smiths' cousin. Sometime after this joyous family reunion, Withington helps the Smiths recover their stolen inheritance of $150,000. When Will by chance finds Sappho in New Orleans and marries her, *Contending Forces* concludes happily.

To some degree, one might view Hopkins as a pioneer, for *Contend-*

ing Forces encourages interest in and repect for investigating personal history, anticipating contemporary writers such as Alex Haley, Toni Morrison, and David Bradley. Hopkins enlists her audience to consider the possibility that history can repeat itself by her daring to provide a glimpse of black women's humiliation during slavery at the same time as she cautions black women to prevent sexual exploitation from recurring in the present. Renouncing racist myths that erode self-respect, myths posited on the alleged wantonness of black Americans, Hopkins challenges her readers to contextualize those myths in order to understand the historical origins of them. She urges solidarity among women for the purpose of engendering self-esteem and historical transformation. At the same time as she excoriates white America for its mistreatment of blacks, however, she props up her mythmaking with inflated reverence for Anglo-American culture.

Hopkins's predominant mythmaking strategy is the romance typical of popular nineteenth-century white women writers. *Contending Forces* abounds with the trappings of domestic fiction: Hopkins juxtaposes imperiled heroines, concupiscent villains, and tragic misunderstandings with serene domestic scenes symbolizing cosmic harmony. At the same time, rhetorical devices with serious political implications permeate this apparent melodrama. The central heroine of *Contending Forces* may possess predictable beauty, but Hopkins uses Sappho's attractiveness to suggest the victimization that has accompanied beauty for black women in a racist society. Her villains perpetrate crimes against Afro-America, be it sexual coercion of women or ritualized murder of men. And Hopkins infuses the cult of domesticity with political messages, so that seemingly innocuous gatherings of women proclaim the significance of the black women's club movement, and joyous reunions among kin betoken the vibrancy of the black family. Sad to say, not only does she transmit assimilationist concepts through the devices of tragic mulatto and Genteel Tradition (motifs Brown, Harper, and Chesnutt employ with equal vigor), she allows her narrator to relay white supremist cant. Finally, *Contending Forces* reflects the deep confusion post-Reconstruction racism engendered in its writers, for Hopkins also affirms the need for mulattoes to take pride in their African lineage. Compared with the other writers of her day, Hopkins is quite a skillful author, managing an adroit fusion of women's romance and black historical concerns; and given her attempts at revisionist history, it is time she received recognition.

Hopkins transforms history into a cloak and dagger romance designed to keep a wide audience spellbound. Basing the early chapters involving the Montforts on an actual occurrence, she entwines fact with fancy to craft a mythic history. Through the romance, Hopkins's central concerns, the disruption of the black family during slavery and the sexual abuse of black women, emerge. Coincidences abound: the Englishman Charles Montfort Withington happens upon the Smiths when he meets Will purely by chance in Boston. Meretricious John Langley, whose unrequited lust for Sappho drives him to wreak havoc with her life, turns out to be the grandnephew of Anson Pollack, who two generations before punctured Grace Montfort's tranquility because she refused to encourage his sexual advances. And Sappho Clark's tragic story of being sold into prostitution by her white uncle surfaces when a stranger narrates the story to the American Colored League, unaware that Sappho sits in the audience.

Another device of romance, the supernatural, plays an important part in *Contending Forces*. Madame Frances, Sappho's aunt and a highly esteemed fortune teller, predicts several characters' futures when they consult her. Had Langley heeded her prognostications, he might have prevented a disastrous chain of occurrences: his loss of Sappho, his jilting by Dora, and his freezing to death in the Arctic, a fate he has seen suggested on the magic screen of Madame Frances. Buttressing the miraculous quality of romance, the supernatural also serves to remind Hopkins's audience of Afro-America's latent power, for as the narrator notes, "the occult arts . . . were once the glory of the freshly imported African."[13] Hopkins believes that Afro-American culture would benefit if blacks could resurrect this power.

Aiming "to raise the stigma of degradation from [the] race," as Hopkins points out in her preface, she lit upon the strategies evident in nineteenth-century women's fiction, novels and romances whose popularity surpassed all other fiction of their day (13). Using these strategies, Hopkins hoped, as did Harper, to garner the largest possible audience for her mythmaking. In the manner of Harper and other women writers, Hopkins fashions a romance about a lonely young orphan with a violent, subterranean past who must prove her virtue through additional suffering and is eventually rewarded with an ideal husband. Mabelle Beaubean, alias Sappho Clark, functions to acquaint her audience with the grim historical convergence of racism and sexism at the same time as she serves as a paradigm of black womanhood, a counterimage to the same stereotypes that plagued Frances Harper. Perhaps even more than Harper, Hopkins is appalled by the myth that black women invite sexual overtures. No one could imagine a less consciously seductive heroine than Sappho Clark, who views her beauty as a curse rather than an asset, and whose son has resulted from rape and enforced prostitution when Mabelle is only fourteen. Highly cultivated, Sappho is variously described as a saint and a Madonna. A vulnerable woman with a slight frame, tiny hands, and a frail constitution, the heroine of this romance is the an-tithesis of the earthy siren so beloved by racist ideology. Sappho, who with other rape victims shares guilt about her victimization, tries to make amends by her cool distance in the presence of men, whom she freezes out when they approach her with any behavior that one might construe as dishonorable. For example, when she discovers that Will Smith has repeatedly entered her room in her absence to make fires for her, she indignantly orders him to cease. Her responses to Langley's unscrupu-lous advances demonstrate her ethics as well, since he is engaged to Dora. Furthermore, her shrewd assessment of him transmits the notion that women can intuit truth and thereby control their fates. From the out-set, Sappho dislikes the necessity of hiding her past from Will, and when she departs for Boston, despite her love for him, she does so in order to preserve his family's respectability. In short, Sappho testifies to the innate morality of black women who have suffered sexual abuse.

Emblematic of her virtue is Sappho's beauty, which Hopkins has wrought by means of the tragic mulatto motif intertwined with the Sen-timental Heroine formula. Her hair has a golden cast; her skin boasts the attributes of a lily. This demure heroine can be recognized by her "aquiline nose, rosebud mouth, soft brown eyes veiled by long, dark lashes which swept her cheek, just now covered with a delicate rose flush" (107). True to form for such a heroine, Sappho not only blushes prettily but trembles, faints, or weeps under pressure.

At the same time Hopkins mines the Sentimental Heroine device,

however, she invests her romance with feminist leanings. Not only does
Sappho's personal history emphasize the interplay of sexism and racism;
Sappho herself stands as a counterimage for Dora, her foil. For while
Dora exults in her good fortune at not having to work outside the home,
Sappho recounts stories of her own problems keeping jobs, fictionalizing the difficulties blacks have faced in a white male dominated market-
place. Whereas Dora serves as a mouthpiece for the ideas espoused by
her friend and eventual husband Arthur, a Booker T. Washington figure, Sappho denounces Arthur's faith that "industrial education and the
exclusion of politics will cure all our race troubles" (124). Dora confesses
that the subject is "a little deep" for her and admits that she accepts
whatever values men subscribe to, a fortunate position since Arthur
"thinks women should be seen and not heard" with regard to political
discussion (123–24). Sappho is disgusted.

Further inklings of feminism mingle with the sentimental depiction
of Grace Montfort, who experiences a sadistic whipping only moments
after being remanded to slavery. It is interesting to compare Hopkins's
mythmaking with regard to Grace's beating with Bontemps's vision of
Juba in *Black Thunder,* Juba refusing to cry or flinch as she suffers the
same fate as Grace. The victim in *Contending Forces,* on the other hand,
shrieks for her husband, whom she knows to be dead, to save her, as
the lash descends on her "frail and shrinking form." Not satisfied with
allowing Grace to lapse into unconsciousness once, Hopkins subjects
her to a series of "fainting fit[s]" (69). The reader may wish that Hopkins had created a more stoic heroine, a woman more akin to Juba, in
order to fictionalize the suffering and humiliation of hundreds of thousands of black women during slavery. Yet, she navigates a nearly impossible course: the communication of the agony of black women during
a time when most writers chose to ignore slavery entirely because it in-
terfered with mythmaking. In an effort to provide a counterstatement
to the notion of the invulnerable black woman, she goes a bit too far.
One must remember, however, that Hopkins generates her romance out
of the conventions of her time, as do her male literary peers. Moreover,
as Baym notes in her analysis of fiction of Hopkins's day, female writers
committed themselves to illustrating woman's dilemma: "mistreatment,
unfairness, disadvantage, and powerlessness, recurrent injustices occa-

sioned by her status as female . . . ."[14] Hopkins's impulse to infuse the conventions of white women's fiction with the particulars of black women's history is noteworthy.

Hopkins's mythmaking, like Harper's, resorts to the Genteel Tradition. Although the modern reader may find the earmarks of this tradition comical, one must appreciate the degradation whites sought to visit upon blacks during the 1890s and the necessity for providing rebuttal to such degradation. In an era when popular literature, from Thomas Nelson Page to Mark Twain, insisted on Afro-Americans' "primitiveness," ignorance, and illiteracy, Hopkins may be forgiven for contriving characters who curtsy, lapse into verse, and otherwise proclaim their refinement and intellect. If today one chortles at Charles Montfort "cast-[ing] himself upon the velvet turf," or "myriad stars . . . bespangling the firmament," he or she must remember Hopkins's literary models (74, 334). As will become obvious in analysis of Sutton Griggs, Charles Chesnutt, and W.E.B. Du Bois, such devices prevailed as a result of a painfully constrictive socio-political climate, and mythmaking was impossible without such devices.

Another aspect of romance, the presence of villains lying in wait for unsuspecting victims, is evident in *Contending Forces*. In every case such villains are men seeking to exploit black women; inevitably, these men evince admiration for the victim's charms while harboring violent hatred. When Anson Pollack approaches Grace Montfort, her rejection spurs him to revenge, so that his victory involves her being whipped nearly to death. Sappho's white uncle, who appears "extremely fond" of her, sells his niece into prostitution (259). Whether he himself rapes her is unclear; however, his "fondness" clearly involves lust mixed with hatred. John Langley, Pollack's grandnephew, likewise appears wildly in love with Sappho, yet his real aim is to secure her sexual favors while he marries Dora for her fortune. Underneath Langley's desire, "he longed to crush her . . ." and he achieves his aim when Sappho cowers in terror before him as he threatens to expose her to Will Smith (317). To accuse Hopkins of melodrama circumvents her wish to admonish women that what passes for love often masks hate; in the case of white men, black women must exercise special caution. Hopkins's mythmaking goes even further than Harper's in cautioning readers to ruminate on black history, for she not only decries black woman's sexual exploitation, based as it is on the myth of her sexual availability, she illuminates its companion myth: the black rapist.

Several chapters of *Contending Forces* center on reaction to a lynching involving skinning and dismembering the victim for his purported rape of a white woman. White and black speakers urge Boston's American Colored League to excuse the white community for these atrocities. Two black speakers, Luke Sawyer and Will Smith, register their alarm, however, at this accommodationist stance. Narrating the story of Mabelle Beaubean, Luke offers an oral history about the violation of black, rather than white, womanhood, violation that he feels must be avenged. In response to Sawyer's story, Will Smith proclaims that the notion that black men pose a serious threat to white women represents a subterfuge justifying lynching. The truth is, Will continues, "lynching was instituted to crush the manhood of the enfranchised black. . . . Irony of ironies! *The men who created the mulatto race, who recruit its ranks year after year by the very means which they invoked lynch law to suppress,* bewailing the sorrows of violated womanhood!" (271). In order for Afro-Americans to understand the impetus for lynching, Hopkins insists, they must dissolve the cant surrounding lynching. Angela Y. Davis revoices Hopkins's analysis: "In the history of the United States, the fraudulent rape charge stands as one of the most formidable artifices invented by racism. The myth of the black rapist has been methodically conjured up whenever recurrent waves of violence and terror against the Black community have required convincing justifications."[15] The reality of black women's violation stands as bitter reminder that whites have rewritten history for their own benefit. Hopkins insists that black women must beware white men, for underneath burns "a living fire of hatred" (51). Such men, Hopkins implies, project their lust, their obsession with domination, onto black men, the latter of whom are allegedly consumed with desire for white women. At the same time, white men project their appetites onto black women, branding them as lascivious. Such binary thinking, conveniently equating blacks with "evil" sexuality and whites with "virtuous" chastity, inverts the historical reality of racism, suggesting that Afro-Americans are ruled by savage instincts. For Hopkins as well as for

Harper, black women must refuse to capitulate to this oppressive set of myths.

Contending Forces fictionalizes women's collective efforts to create a countermythology. In the chapter entitled "The Sewing Circle," a large group of women gather to make garments for a church fair. Mrs. Willis, who plays a significant role in this chapter, serves as the embodiment of the black women's club movement. Although women's organizations existed before the Civil War, during the 1890s these clubs, led by such esteemed members as Frances Harper, Mary Church Terrell, and Fannie Barrier Williams, achieved greater prominence than they had earlier, in part because of the formation of the National Association of Colored Women in 1896. Gerda Lerner notes that it is unclear whether this association spawned new clubs or whether existing clubs began to attain recognition; nevertheless, the club movement as a whole deserves credit for uniting black women in the crusades against lynching and Jim Crow and for integration.[16] When characters in the sewing circle discuss woman's role in racial upbuilding, they turn to Mrs. Willis for direction. Mrs. Willis echoes Harper's injunction that mothers, as culture bearers, constitute black America's future, and she applauds African women's native virtue, suggesting that black American women, by extension, are innately virtuous. She goes on to caution her listeners that black women must not assume responsibility for the sexual exploitation of their ancestors and themselves. With this chapter, Harper charts black woman's role in changing history through her solidarity with other women, who help her to forge a new vision that runs counter to the one white culture promulgates. At the same time, the cult of domesticity, a motif pervading *Contending Forces,* enshrines the possibilities inherent in the home, where a sewing circle can become a political forum.

Hopkins's concept of history, exhibited in the aforementioned chapter and elsewhere, presupposes an educated, "cultured" class of leaders who will foster the rest of Afro-America so that it may evolve into ideal humanity. Patronizing as her mythmaking seems, it mirrors the attitudes of other post-Reconstruction black writers in its evolutionary concept of history. Unlike Harper, however, Hopkins conveys no notion that blacks are inherently more moral than whites or that black leaders will enhance white evolution. If anything, Hopkins hazards the idea that racial intermixture with Anglo-Saxons, however much it exploits women, has improved Afro-Americans, infusing blacks with characteristics of "the higher race" (23). This blatant endorsement of racial supremacy has been responsible, in part, for the critical neglect of Hopkins' fiction; whether she was collapsing under the weight of the dominant cultural ideology or merely appealing to a white audience fails to excuse her. Yet paradoxically, Hopkins insists that, regardless of skin color, African descent people must identify with Afro-America. In addition, she avows in her epigraph from Emerson that whites have debased themselves by racial oppression. Finally, *Contending Forces* challenges "the best" of both races to consolidate in order to bring about historical change. Denouncing violence for agitation, Hopkins seeks to arouse moral urgency in black and white readers alike.

Struggling under the suffocating mantle of post-Reconstruction, Harper and Hopkins fashion romances that reveal their vital awareness of history, even while they employ the cult of domesticity, lauding the family as the circle within which moral harmony can reign. *Contending Forces* concludes with the two branches of the Montfort family—English and American—reunited after years of estrangement. As if to retrieve their European heritage, Dora and her husband, Dr. Lewis, "Ma" Smith, Will, Sappho, and her son Alphonse embark on a trip to England, underscoring the significance of the family unit. Hopkins sanctifies motherhood as vigorously as did Harper, for Sappho has reclaimed Alphonse, exulting in her renewed role; in fact, under her influence Alphonse blossoms despite his previous years of neglect. *Iola Leroy* and *Contending Forces* resemble each other in additional ways. Wrestling to abolish dehumanizing stereotypes, both writers create legendary heroines who surmount historical difficulties without jeopardizing their much vaunted gentility or femininity. As orphans victimized by racism, Iola and Sappho triumph over the vicissitudes of personal history through nearly superhuman virtue, offering radiant hope to women who have endured similar fates. Able to pass for white, these heroines decry the need to do so and ally themselves with Afro-America, to some extent at least. Both romances end with marriage to enterprising, peerless suitors, but *Iola Leroy* and *Contending Forces* should not be dismissed as "love stories" or "domestic fiction," for both authors speak out against racial oppression and mythologize history. Amidst attention to other issues, Harper reminds her readers that those Afro-Americans who fought and nursed during the Civil War deserve equality. That these books end optimistically, despite being composed during one of the most oppressive eras in black history, invites charges of escapism; however, writers respond differently to oppression. In an effort to reach a wide female audience, these two authors relied on the formula plots of nineteenth-century women's fiction, literature that inevitably ended with marriage. Heroic roles for women were limited in the 1890s; faced with mob rule, Jim Crow humiliation, and sexual exploitation, Harper and Hopkins took refuge in a mythic future, hoping to communicate the transformational possibilities of marriage and motherhood to readers—both black and white—at the same time as they infused their narratives with the realties of black history.

3   A Necessary Ambivalence

Sutton Griggs's *Imperium in Imperio* and
Charles Chesnutt's *The Marrow of Tradition*

The fiction of Sutton Griggs and Charles Chesnutt emerges from post-Reconstruction despair, both writers crafting romances that bespeak vast promise, that give voice to black heroism in the face of devastating odds. Both resort to the Genteel Tradition in order to supplant degrading stereotypes. At the same time, both launch indictments of education for the limited advantages it offered Afro-Americans. Finally both create two heroes, one militant and one accommodationist, heroes that reflect Griggs's and Chesnutt's ambivalence toward their mythmaking role.

Griggs especially strives to awaken his audience to blacks' innate power; his notion of black solidarity, autonomy, and separatism cemented by creative thinkers conjoins the myth of the messiah with his faith in Western rationality. His saviors must unite their intellectual and visionary capacities to deliver Afro-America from its sense of powerlessness, effect political change, and, ultimately, reorder the world. For Griggs, post-Reconstruction's overwhelming constraints on black America dictate identification with transcendent figures, for suffering and death constitute everyday realities. Although Griggs's ideal leadership rests on an educational foundation, he insists that black thinkers must not forget their folk roots or seek to assimilate. In keeping with such thinking, he jettisons Brown's reverence for light skin, encouraging pride in blackness. Given the dangers implicit in Griggs's endorsement of revolt, however, his dramatization of revolt divides in two, and one of his messiahs becomes an accommodationist.

Griggs employs a number of strategies in the mythmaking process. Romance, his primary device, serves him well for projecting his utopian vision of black political power embodied in a gigantic secret society designed to rectify social injustice. His heroes and heroines occupy the upper reaches of human possibility, hovering close to divinities in their abilities to survive attempts on their lives, and in their intellectual and artistic talents, qualities that occasion instant stardom. Just as the romance allows for characters of ideological rather than psychological magnitude, so too does romance plotting free the narrative from the burden of verisimilitude. His heroes' talents enable them to unify Afro-America, creating a national organization that exceeds the limits of plausibility in its size and power. To elucidate his allegiance to blackness, Griggs designs a subplot in which one of his heroines commits suicide rather than produce light-skinned children with her suitor. To dramatize the healing power of laughter, Griggs makes use of the oral narrative mode, reinforcing trickster figures' centrality in black life. Aside from his reliance on Sentimental Heroines, the Genteel Tradition and inflated diction, Griggs has trouble incorporating historical events into his narrative, and he repudiates African historical connections. Despite his limitations, however, Griggs remains the first black artist to dramatize an appreciation of dark skin and political separatism and as such anticipates later historical fiction.

Imperium in Imperio presents an account of the lives of Belton Piedmont and Bernard Belgrave, childhood companions who struggle to develop and receive recognition for their talents in a racist society. Whereas their white grade-school teacher victimizes Belton because of his poverty and dark skin, he appears to favor Bernard, a well-to-do mulatto. Despite their opposite treatment, the two protagonists achieve equal academic credentials in grammar school and enter college. Belton's political leanings become clear when he launches a successful student protest on campus, subsequently organizing a secret society to secure black rights. After Belton and Bernard graduate from college, both embark on careers, encountering all the stumbling blocks that typify post-Reconstruction. Eventually Belton builds his secret society, the Imperium in Imperio, to great proportions and recruits Bernard to serve as president. Ultimately, when Belton refuses to join a militant plan, he agrees to be executed by the Imperium, as policy dictates. Griggs's romance concludes with an epilogue written by the man who has betrayed that plan in order to subvert the race war that would result.

Griggs's protagonists are essentially one-dimensional, representing two heroic alternatives: pacifist and militant.[1] Both undergo numerous trials that demonstrate to the audience the value of "manly" behavior, offering a mythology of power and heroism. Repeatedly mistreated and thwarted by the grammar school teacher who considers him a "nigger brat," Belton still develops into a superior student who receives a full scholarship to a black college on the strength of his commencement address. When Bernard is being considered for president of the Imperium in Imperio, he undergoes initiation rites including a real firing squad and actual gallows. Both characters repeatedly receive accolades; Belton's graduation speech is "everywhere . . . hailed as a classic."[2] Bernard's achievements at Harvard are likewise "so remarkable that the Associated Press telegraphed the news over the country" (85). The demonstration Belton organizes at Stowe University is so successful that it triggers similar revolts in many schools throughout the United States. Both become involved in politics. Bernard, in fact, is elected to Congress but is denied the office because of typical post-Reconstruction fraud at the polls. Ultimately, when the two are involved in the Imperium, nearly every black in the country regards them as heroes.

Like other romances of its era, Imperium in Imperio reflects the Genteel Tradition, an unfortunate but inescapable influence. Not only Belton and Bernard but their lovers Antoinette and Viola reach the zenith of middle class respectability. It would never have occurred to Griggs to have created heroes and heroines who speak black English. Rather, he employs diction epitomized by the formula, "Take that, you knave" (185). Viola leaves a suicide note paralleling in style most of the sentimental romances of the time: "If in the shadowy beyond, whose mists I feel gathering about me, there is a place where kindred spirits meet, you and I shall surely meet again" (175). Another device with which Griggs underlines his characters' gentility is their attire. Belton, though making his initial appearance in a patched jacket and an elaborately described collection of hand-me-downs, later sports "a most beautiful and costly silk handkerchief" that he stows "in the tail pocket of his handsome Prince Al-bert suit of lovely black" (70). Inevitably, houses are furnished with "exquisite taste."

Female characters are both genteel and remarkable, befitting their suitors: "Miss Viola Martin was a universal favorite. She was highly educated and an elocutionist of no mean ability. She sang sweetly and was the most accomplished pianist in town. . . . She was most remarkably well-informed on all leading questions of the day, and men of brain always enjoyed a chat with her. . . . In all religious movements among the women she was the leading spirit" (100). Antoinette is no less extraordinary. She is "famed throughout the city for her beauty, intelligence and virtue. . . . She neither sang nor played, but her soul was intensely musical and she had the most refined and cultivated taste in the musical circle in which she moved" (113-14). According to the dicta of the popular sentimental romance, women must not only be described as virtuous, but they must prove their virtue through suffering. Just as Belton and Bernard undergo trials to prove their manhood, Viola and Antoinette demonstrate that they are appropriate models for their audience. Because Viola believes that a union between two mulattoes such as herself and Bernard will cause the race to grow pale and to deteriorate, she commits suicide, an act the reader is encouraged to view as a noble, if misguided, sacrifice. Antoinette, too, possesses heroic powers. When she gives birth to a white baby, Belton abandons her, assuming she has been unfaithful. Later, of course, her virtue is revealed, but her suffering continues when Belton is executed by the Imperium. Significantly, Griggs, unlike Brown, Harper, and Hopkins, refuses the tragic mulatto theme, maintaining that black skin is purer than white. And although Griggs's emphasis on gentility seems quaint, even amusing, to contemporary audiences, he wrote as do all writers from within a particular era, and his insistence on racial pride and heroism far outweighs his conventionality. Of primary significance is the characters' participation in the myth-making process that Griggs deems indispensable to fiction of historical nature.

For Griggs as for Brown the miraculous creates a sense that not only survival but transcendence of oppression are within reach. As do most romances, *Imperium in Imperio* abounds with coincidences, escapes from peril, and astounding, even improbable, events. Often such events inter-

twine with post-Reconstruction conditions to suggest that with suffi-
cient agility and ingenuity blacks can combat their situation. One of the
most spectacular of such incidents involves Belton's entrapment by the
Klan (called "Nigger Rulers") who shoot and hang him as punishment
for entering a white church and helping a white girl find the correct place
in her hymnal. By chance the bullet merely penetrates the skin at the
base of his skull, failing to enter the brain; luckier still is the whites'
impatience to get on with the dissection of "such a robust, well-formed,
handsome nigger," for they cut him down before he has time to die (156).
Once on the operating table, Belton has his valor tested when the doctor
cuts and pricks the victim's skin to assure himself that he is dead. Belton, of course, does not flinch. When the doctor conveniently places his
dissecting tool next to Belton, the protagonist seizes the opportunity to
stab the doctor, lay him out on the table, and leave a note to head off
his pursuers. Even carrying a bullet in his head, Belton makes his way
to Baton Rouge—not to escape, but to turn himself over to the governor.
When it seems that Belton is doomed, Bernard is employed as a *deus
ex machina*. With an eloquence comparable only to that of Daniel Web-
ster, the narrator informs the audience, Bernard pleads the case before
the Supreme Court and secures an acquittal.

Dramatizing these events without excessive narrative intrusion, Griggs
leads the reader to identify with his protagonists and thus succeeds in
indirectly commenting upon many aspects of contemporary history. That
blacks were segregated from white churches and subject to lynching for
infractions of the Jim Crow code is illustrated by the results of Belton's
"impudence" in suggesting that a white girl was too stupid to locate the
correct page in her hymnal. Since post-Reconstruction, blacks have been
caught in a double-bind: self-assertion assures chastisement for impudence; aloofness from whites guarantees castigation for surliness. *Imperium in Imperio* as well as *The Marrow of Tradition* and *The Quest of
the Silver Fleece* abound with scenes fictionalizing this historical truth.
Also illustrative of the mood of the time is the suggestion of the white
church's hypocrisy (a legacy from the slave narratives) and the utter corruption of supposedly moral members of white society. The postmaster,
a government employee, heads the Nigger Rulers, and the doctor, who
has dedicated himself to saving lives, finds joy in sacrificing this "fine

specimen" to an experiment that is clearly counterfeit. Because the nineteenth century regarded science with both awe and suspicion, the scene
becomes doubly significant. For murdering Belton, the postmaster receives from the doctor a keg of whiskey, symbolic of dissipation in much
black literature. Ultimately, these incidents conclude so as to satisfy the
tastes of a late-Victorian audience: the postmaster is punished, the hero
resurrected.

Thus these events describe the mood and morals of the time; furthermore they illustrate the oral narrative, a tradition rooted in folklore and
music, a tradition crucial to black literature. Because Griggs established
his own publishing company, promoting his fiction among the entire
black community, Gloster postulates that his novels were more widely
read than those of Chesnutt and Dunbar.[3] Whatever the case, Griggs,
like Harper and Hopkins, strove to approach his audience by way of the
popular mode, one that would appeal to a wide readership. The popular mode deriving from the oral narrative utilizes formulaic style (epithets) and protagonists with whom the audience can easily identify, and
it relies on formula episodes as well. Most familiar of these formulas
are those employed in the western or the detective story. In "Prolegomena to a Study of the Popular Mode in Narrative," James Mellard asserts: "If we are going to understand 'pulp' fiction or the 'slicks,' the
western, the detective or science fiction, the soap, the confession, or the
adventure, we must come to understand their structural conventions
and formulas as fully as the scholars of the oral tradition understand
Homer's themes and plots."[4] By the same token, to read *Imperium in
Imperio* properly, the reader must view it according to the conventions
Griggs employed, rather than denigrating it because it fails to satisy demands outside its scope.

The episode described above, that of Belton's capture, escape, and
acquittal, presents him with several obstacles he must overcome. By
considering for a moment the fictional forms mentioned earlier—the
western, for example—the reader may realize that the protagonist often
confronts several obstacles within an episode, each of which must be
dispensed with in order for the protagonist to triumph. Viewed within
this context, Belton's actions seem predictable to the extent that the
reader assumes he will ultimately outsmart his antagonists. Yet in much

the same way that the audience of a tragedy knows the outcome of events but is engaged by the working out of these events, the audience of the popular narrative stays with the story in order to discover the author's variation of the formula. Employing the conventions of the popular mode, Griggs suggests that, though seemingly entrapped by a kind of historical destiny, blacks can attain heroic or mythic stature and eventually change the course of that destiny by outwitting the opponents they confront.

Robert E. Fleming speaks of Griggs's use of comedy to "ridicule the exaggerated dignity of the white master race"[5] Particularly does he refer to those scenes involving the practical jokes played on Tiberius Leonard, Belton and Bernard's grammar school teacher. From placing a tack on Leonard's chair to contriving an elaborate device to drop him into a cistern at the culmination of graduation exercises, these scenes derive from a humorous tradition easily recognizable as oral. The gradual piling up of details which lead inevitably to a disastrous conclusion is a device which demands that the audience, consciously or unconsciously, predict that conclusion. As with the episode involving Belton's escape, the audience waits to see the way the teller will vary this formula. Griggs, of course, assumes that the audience has as little regard for Leonard as do he and the romance's characters. In transforming a figure who is historically real, who is indeed horrifyingly familiar, into a victim of clever jokes, Griggs reiterates much the same notion as with the use of formula episodes. Blacks may respond to oppression in various ways; by laughter they may revolt against and transcend it. Thus black oral tradition contributes to the mythology Griggs creates.

Many of the jokes achieve success because they are directed at a teacher. For an audience whose primary identification does not lie with the academic world, the teacher functions as a time-worn target for humor. Contemporary American films, televison programs, and comic strips continue to exploit the audience's ambivalence toward and alienation from education, as well as their anger toward authority figures. For Griggs's audience, Leonard is drearily emblematic of teachers available to blacks. Griggs takes pains to describe the stigma attached to teaching in a black grammar school and makes clear that Leonard's criminal past has made him unfit for any other career. But Griggs's mythologizing of history reaches far beyond a condemnation of the poor quality of teachers. *Imperium in Imperio* fictionalizes historical reality and at the same time debunks the educational theories of Booker T. Washington and William Wells Brown.

The romance opens with Belton's mother sending him off to school because she is determined to expose him to all available education. Tiberius Leonard favors Bernard over Belton because of his own shady associations with Bernard's white father; however, because he pits the two boys against each other, they strive to outdo each other. Upon graduation Belton obtains a teaching position, yet when he starts a newspaper that decries fraud at the polls, he is fired. With this incident, Griggs exposes the relationship between education and politics, suggesting that the teacher must function as a puppet to survive, that the intention of education is not to encourage independent thinking or integrity but to reward students and teachers for docility. Thus Griggs implies that the educational philosophy of Booker T. Washington accommodates itself to political corruption. To undermine Brown's concept that black education will inevitably lead to joy and prosperity, the narrator informs us that though Belton's aid to the Republican party entitles him to a high position in the post office, his color consigns him to a post as stamping clerk. Shortly afterward, his refusal to support a racist candidate for Congress causes him to lose his job with the post office. Although educated, Belton is victimized by a corrupt environment because he lacks Bernard's influential white father and his light skin. Contrary to Brown's and Harper's doctrine of black "perfectability" leading to the creation of an ideal society, Griggs maintains that this "perfection" leaves Belton at the mercy of a society preferring expediency to integrity. Finally Belton takes a position as president of his alma mater. Significantly, the only hope for an educated black man during post-Reconstruction is to return to his own community; white culture refuses to acknowledge his talents. En route to his new life Belton encounters the ethic of Jim Crow: he is literally thrown off a train for refusing to leave a first-class coach; he is refused service in a restaurant; and he is harassed by the Klan. Promising prosperity and joy, education brings instead frustration, alienation, and a more acute sense of injustice.

But *Imperium in Imperio* does not totally indict education. Rather,

Griggs rejects the myth that education necessarily serves as a tool by which blacks can achieve material success in white society and replaces this notion with an emphasis on education as a process that should develop critical and creative thinking so that blacks can alter oppressive conditions. Such thinking is essential for the members of the Imperium, the secret society Belton creates. An organization intended to operate in the political arena, the Imperium suggests Du Bois's Niagara Movement (of which Griggs was a member) that later evolved into the NAACP. The Imperium, however, limits its membership to blacks. The legendary quality of the Imperium is clear, for its members number 7,250,000 and its treasury $850 million. Further, the Imperium represents a separatist government that will settle legal differences without needing to resort to the bigoted white system. The Imperium boasts an army, a congress, and a constitution.

The political philosophy of the Imperium crystallizes when a black postmaster's house is burned, he and his family shot. This event, one that actually occurred in 1898 in Lake City, South Carolina, precipitates a meeting to decide black-white relations in this country. There follows Bernard's discourse on injustices of the period: the relegation of blacks to a physical rather than a mental plane, the Jim Crow laws, the emasculating intentions of education, the prejudice of the courts, and the practice of mob rule. Imperium members propose three solutions: amalgamation, African emigration, and war. At the third suggestion Belton recoils, his rebuttal taking an accommodationist position. Attributing to the Ango-Saxon a culture superior to that of "primitive" Africa, he urges the Imperium to adopt the tenets of Christianity taught them by this "superior" culture. Rather than engage in race war, he resolves that the Imperium devote four years to impressing whites of the New Negro's talents. Should that fail, Belton proposes that the members of the Imperium emigrate to Texas, "working out our destiny as a separate and distinct race . . ." (245). Belton's proposal is defeated the next day by that of Bernard, who resolves to enter into secret negotiations with foreign enemies and seize Texas by force. Because Belton will not accede to this plan, Belton agrees to be punished by execution.

Belton and Bernard, then, occupy the two horns of the dilemma faced by blacks in turn-of-the-century America. With the suggestion to "work out destiny," Belton echoes Booker T. Washington's Atlanta Address of 1895. Possibly, Griggs had in mind the Washington-Du Bois controversy, with Belton representing Washington, Bernard, a more militant Du Bois. But both positions created doubts for the black audience. Belton's non-violent stance and his insistence on Christian humility gained a sympathetic ear; in fact, such tactics later proved effective for Martin Luther King. But his notion of the inferiority of African culture mirrors the very indictments that whites were using to perpetuate oppression. Tragically, Belton has come to accept a stereotyped, erroneous view of Afro-American history, a view that remains dominant until well into the twentieth century. Bernard's insistence on militance, though laudable for its loyalty to the black community, raised fears of race suicide, heroic but futile. To ascertain Griggs's position, the reader might be tempted to take Belton's death as an endorsement of militance. But Berl Trout, who foils the Imperium's plans, urges in the epilogue that humanity must unite to secure black rights "because love of liberty is such an inventive genius that if you destroy one device it at once constructs another more powerful" (165). *Imperium in Imperio*, then, should be read both as an incentive to black solidarity and as a warning that unless the black's place in history changes for the better, violence will inevitably erupt.

Griggs shies away from returning to his racial past, and in *Imperium in Imperio* he concentrates most of his energies on analyzing the historical moment, on creating a mythical society to rectify the horrors of that moment. The work begins about the time of the Compromise of 1877; unlike Harper and Hopkins, Griggs chooses not to approach the subject of slavery at all. Instead, *Imperium in Imperio* focuses on events contemporaneous with the time of its publication and reveals that late nineteenth-century blacks were largely controlled by prejudice. Even so, his mythology insists, blacks can reshape their environment, primarily through education and adoption of white middle-class speech and cultural mores. Griggs believes that Afro-Americans' political understanding must be sophisticated; however, the action taken on the strength of that understanding remains unclear. Unable to endorse either total accommodation or total militance, Griggs merely depicts these two positions through Belton and Bernard. And much of *Imperium in Imperio*'s strength and complexity derives from Griggs's failure to take a position, for his romance documents the ambivalence characteristic of the period's black intellectual.

Charles Chesnutt's *The Marrow of Tradition* (1901) also fictionalizes the bewilderment of a man full of righteous anger but incapable of abandoning hypnotic security. Far angrier in tone than any of Chesnutt's earlier works, this romance, like *Imperium in Imperio,* employs two black characters, one conciliatory, one militant. Unable to embrace militance, yet consumed with rage, Chesnutt remains ambivalent toward blacks' proper position in history; each character depicts a possible mode of being. As Griggs responded to post-Reconstruction's socio-historic pressures, so too did Chesnutt. Just as an actual event – the murder of Postmaster Cook and his family – spurred Griggs on to interpret contemporary history, so did the race riot in Wilmington, North Carolina, provide part of Chesnutt's impetus. Occurring in the same year – 1898 – the two events furnished Griggs and Chesnutt with dramatic material to transform into fiction and myth at once. As Chapter Two has shown, such events are not isolated ones, the climate of the 1890s being so vicious that it allowed for numerous such occurrences. The year 1898 spawned mobs in Greenwood County, South Carolina, where many blacks were shot and hanged. In 1900, mobs robbed and assaulted blacks for three days in New Orleans. During this time, in fact, the proportion of lynching was increasing in the South.[6]

Like his fellow post-Reconstruction writers, Chesnutt responds to the dehumanization of blacks, and his primary emphasis is self-definition. In the manner of many black writers, he uses messianic figures to point to traditionally Christian virtues without making direct reference to Christianity. Thus he mythologizes endurance and dignity in the face of adversity, demonstrating the transcendence of suffering he wants his audience to acknowledge in the black community. Moreover, Chesnutt depicts black visionary qualities, particularly intuitive wisdom, to arrive at a notion of the various ways Afro-Americans are empowered to change history. Literacy, a central fixture of Chesnutt's mythmaking, has the potential to demonstrate black intellectual agility, if not to provide social mobility.

The romance, with its emphasis on heroic characters who triumph over corrupt forces, is an ideal strategy for depicting Chesnutt's myth. His three central characters form a kind of trinity engaged in battle with the unholy "Big Three," Chesnutt's fictionalization of typical post-Reconstruction politicos. Romance also allows him to uproot prevailing stereotypes, particularly those promulgated by the Plantation Tradition, and redesign them from a black perspective. Generally speaking, Chesnutt's mythmaking in *The Marrow of Tradition* centers on educated blacks, fleshed out by the Genteel Tradition, the Sentimental Heroine, and the tragic mulatto, devices to further his insistence on assimilation. At the same time, however, he offers an uneducated working-class hero, Josh Green, whose messianic capabilities emerge when he avenges slavery's injustices. Two other paradigmatic characters, William and Janet Miller, both of whom are educated, dramatize dignity and refusal to misuse power. Both can see beyond the mammoth injustices inflicted on them to envision an ideal world, and they behave according to the dictates of that world without sacrificing their integrity. Perhaps because Chesnutt views his racial past as humiliating, or perhaps because he assumes his audience views it thus, he cannot incorporate that past into his mythology. While such omission may or may not constitute a fictional flaw, one cannot ignore more obvious flaws: *The Marrow of Tradition* suffers from the stock devices of the sentimental romance, including overplotting, and its language is as stilted as that of most romances of its day. Nevertheless, if examined within the mode Chesnutt chooses, *The Marrow of Tradition* cannot justly be criticized for melodrama or implausibility or for flat characterization or plot contrivances, for Chesnutt deliberately employs such strategies to convey his fictional mythology.

Both Griggs and Chesnutt sought to counteract stereotypes and create heroes for their audiences, but these audiences differed from one another. Earlier it was noted that a larger number of blacks read Griggs' fiction than read either Chesnutt's or Dunbar's. Chesnutt failed to reach a large black audience, in part, because in some instances he chose not to reach that audience. In a letter to Houghton Mifflin, December 14, 1899, Chesnutt wrote that he did not favor advertising or reviews from the majority of black newspapers. His reason involved this theory: "Most of them are grossly illiterate, and their readers, generally speaking, buy comparatively few books."[7] Thus while he, like Griggs, tried to merge

historical issues with popular fictional strategies to attract a large readership, his major audience was not the black working class but those whites
and middle class blacks suffering the influence of the plantation tradition of Joel Chandler Harris, Thomas Nelson Page, and, later, Thomas
Dixon.

Harris and Page's fictionalization of pre-war times, albeit ludicrously
simplistic or historically inaccurate, did provide impetus for Chesnutt.
In addition, Chesnutt reacted as vehemently as Hopkins to newspapers
of the time that vilified blacks as brutes lurking in the shadows, intent
on raping innocent white women. With *The Marrow of Tradition,* he
wished to confront the lack of reality of black characters presented to
American society. Moreover, Chesnutt envisioned himself as crusading against what he perceived as the "subtle, almost indefinable feeling
of repulsion toward the Negro, which is common to most Americans."[8]
As a result, *The Marrow of Tradition* strives to develop multi-faceted
characters.

Chesnutt accomplishes this characterization in part because he realized that black characters, though functioning as counter-stereotypes,
need not necessarily appear divine. White characters, he saw, needed to
occupy roles other than villainous ones—or at least needed motivation
for villainous acts. Proceeding from these assumptions, Chesnutt created Jerry, a black character whose class interests preclude moral action,
and Old Mr. Delamere, a truly benign member of the gentry. During
slavery Jerry would have experienced a certain degree of protection from
his master, but as a freedman he is on his own, shrewdly ascertaining
that his well-being depends on obsequiousness. Disloyal to whites and
blacks alike, he contributes to the near-lynching of an innocent black
man. Although a victim of racism, Jerry is at no time presented sympathetically. Rather, he reveals the dehumanization resulting from the
New South's mores. Whereas the Plantation Tradition made much of
the suffering freedman, Harris and Page chose not to depict the reality
of his condition as did Chesnutt. Many of Chesnutt's characters resemble Plantation Tradition types; however, each transforms the original to
explode and replace contemporary myths. Consequently, *The Marrow
of Tradition* both parallels and parodies the romances of its literary ad-
versaries, revising both history and historical fiction.

Primarily, Chesnutt addresses the Plantation Tradition through contrasting the old and the new. For Harris and Page, who wished to perpetrate the notion that the South had deteriorated since the Civil War, it was necessary to show the benevolent paternalism of the old masters. Old Mr. Delamere, whose faith in the innocence of his servant Sandy Campbell obliterates his faith in his own grandson, exemplifies this sort of ideal gentleman. In contrast, his grandson Tom, emblematic of the new order, is portrayed as a whiskey swilling, insensitive rake, who not only cheats at cards, defying the code of the Southern gentleman, but robs (and possibly murders) his own aunt to pay off his gambling debts. More hideous still, he frames the loyal servant who raised him, almost causing Sandy's lynching. Had Chesnutt depicted Old Delamere as a stereotypic Southern gentleman, the reader might feel bewildered by Chesnutt's apparent use of the Plantation Tradition. Actually, Chesnutt transmutes stereotypes into real historical figures, presenting Delamere's loyalty to Sandy in historically accurate fashion: Sandy is found innocent simply because Delamere's blacks had been carefully raised, in other words, socialized. White romancers would have lionized the beatific Southern gentlemen of the past; however, they would have avoided showing that men such as Delamere produced dissolute grandsons such as Tom. Chesnutt's mythmaking, then, recreates and undercuts the Plantation Tradition.

Servants, too, embody contrasts between antebellum and post-Civil War periods. Just as Chesnutt opposes Sandy, the ultimate innocent, to Jerry, the sycophant, he juxtaposes the faithful old Mammy Jane with a combative new nurse. Significantly, however, Mammy Jane, while genuinely kind, is appallingly self-righteous, as shown by her response to her employer's claim that Mammy Jane has no peer: "Deed dere ain't, honey; you is talkin' de gospel truf now! None er dese yer young folks ain't got de trainin' my ole mist'ess gave me. Dese yer new-fangle schools don' l'arn 'em nothin' ter compare wid it."[9] Through this speech, Chesnutt underscores the nature of the servant's compliment to her mistress, her firm resolve to identify with the power of the ruling class. In contrast, the nameless nurse is described as passing through racial adolescence: "she was in what might be called the chip-on-the-shoulder stage, through which races as well as individuals must pass" (42). With the phrase "as well as individuals," Chesnutt slyly suggests that all readers, white as well as black, have at one time manifested the "pugnaciousness" which post-Civil War blacks stood accused of originating. Through these and other devices, Chesnutt seeks to dispel Plantation Tradition myths.

To further mythologize black history, Chesnutt resorts to the Genteel Tradition, that delimiting but inevitable set of values in the turn-of-the-century romance. Amusingly, when Chesnutt wishes to symbolize Tom Delamere's utter depravity, he reveals a bureau drawer's contents. To his horror, Old Mr. Delamere discovers "bottles of wine and whiskey; soiled packs of cards; a dice-box with dice; a box of poker chips, several revolvers, and a number of photographs and paper-covered books at which the old gentleman merely glanced to ascertain their nature" (223). Chesnutt's handling of black characters further reinforces genteel values. William Miller, the young doctor, is rarely called by his first name; that the reader knows him as "Dr. Miller" seems pretentious and formal. In addition it has led several critics to call him "Adam," his father's name. Miller and Janet, his wife, speak white English at all times and struggle to influence "the best people" (190). In one episode a train conductor forces Miller to ride in the Jim Crow car, and he briefly shares his quarters with some farm laborers whose noise and dirty clothes he finds "offensive" (61). That he must ride with them galls his class sensibilities. Chesnutt's willingness to exploit the tragic mulatto theme constitutes a more serious limitation. Miller and Janet are both mulatto; in fact the primary emotional impact of *The Marrow of Tradition* hinges on Janet's relationship with Olivia Carteret, her half-sister, and Olivia's refusal to acknowledge Janet's existence, much less her right to their father's estate. Bearing a strong family resemblance to Olivia, Janet is nevertheless denied social acceptance by the white community. Chesnutt's purpose in emphasizing Janet's color is much the same as his predecessors; by stressing the physical similarity between Olivia and Janet he hopes to elicit white sympathy and identification. Whereas Harris and Page emphasize the mulatto's "tainted nature," Chesnutt deplores the racial mixture because it leads to isolation. Janet and her husband, though financially stable, are as Chesnutt described himself, "neither 'nigger,' white, nor 'buckrah.' Too 'stuck up' for the colored folks, and, of course, not recognized by the whites."[10]

As with Brown, Harper, and Hopkins, the appeal to whiteness suggests an underlying sense of racial supremacy disturbing in a writer seeking to counter white supremist's romances. Chesnutt himself, however,
would have found such criticism irrelevant because he unabashedly envisioned part of his "high, holy purpose" as promoting assimilation.[11]
Through assimilation, he felt, racial prejudice would vanish. That such
a notion is politically anathema to black nationalists is obvious. But even
in Chesnutt's time the tragic mulatto theme was considered sentimental. According to the 1860 census, only 12 percent of the black population was mulatto.[12] By 1900 the census did not solicit such information,
but there is little reason to believe the figures had altered significantly.
For most blacks the mulatto was not tragic but fortunate, enjoying special privileges denied darker Afro-Americans. Thus for some black readers Chesnutt dwelled on sentiment for its own sake. Significantly, neither
Griggs nor Du Bois exploits the tragic mulatto theme. Finally, the reader
must regret Chesnutt's use of the theme as indicative of his imprisonment in a cliché.

A more appealing device of Chesnutt's romance to counter stereotypes is his emphasis on characters' extraordinary qualities. Josh Green,
Dr. Miller, and Janet Miller possess heroic potential, each serving a distinct ideological function. Josh Green exhibits the most obvious heroism, and the modern reader can identify with him more easily than with
the Millers. The reader first glimpses Josh, "a huge Negro, covered
thickly with dust," through Miller's eyes. Poles apart from the well-
mannered doctor, Josh immerses his head in a water trough and shakes
himself "like a wet dog." In contrast to Miller, who has paid first-class
train fare, Green has hopped on a car without paying. To Miller, Josh
is "an ordinarily good-natured, somewhat reckless, pleasure-loving negro" (59). Therefore he is surprised to see Josh's expression change to
one of intense hatred when he glimpses Mc Bane, a fellow passenger.
During a Klan incident Mc Bane has shot Josh's father and traumatized
his mother so that she has never regained her sanity; Josh is determined
to avenge these deeds. Even while he regards Josh as a "dusty tramp,"
Miller admires his dedication to revenge (59). Most blacks, Miller admits to himself, want to forget their history, a "dark story." Josh, on the
other hand, remembers his and "shapes his life to a definite purpose"

(112). Josh remains unintrigued by middle-class manners and mores. His sympathy, language, and behavior lie entirely with the black working class, and his life purpose is to rectify the wrongs done to them, wrongs symbolized by his mother's disrupted sanity.

Chesnutt further stresses Josh's heroism through opposing his militant stance to Miller's accommodationist principles. Whereas Miller attempts, with no success, to convince the indifferent whites of Sandy Campbell's innocence, Josh proposes that blacks take up arms and surround the jail. Even when Miller refuses to join Josh's resistance group against Mc Bane and Carteret's raid on the black citizenry, the rebels proceed fearlessly without him, disregarding his warning that resistance is suicidal. The ensuing riot provides Josh with his long-awaited confrontation with Mc Bane. While more than one critic has lambasted this scene for its melodramatic qualities, the scene clearly ignores the demands of verisimilitude and moves into the realm of romance. Josh, a "black giant, famed on the wharves for his strength," amazes the crowd with his immunity to the endless rain of bullets. "Armed with a huge bowie-knife, a relic of the civil war," and a smile which "seemed to take him out of mortal ken," Josh plunges the weapon into Mc Bane's heart. Given the post-Reconstruction era, Chesnutt cannot endorse Josh's violence, finding it necessary to query, "One of the two died as the fool dieth. Which was it, or was it both?" (309). Nevertheless, Josh's larger-than-life status remains intact. He occupies a pivotal position in black historical fiction, a man who would "ruther be a dead nigger any day dan a live dog," thus contributing to the mythologizing process (284).

Dr. Miller's heroism is more elusive, but Chesnutt does mean him to serve as a paradigm, even though Miller laments his own advice to disband the resistance group as "not heroic but . . . wise" (283). Dr. Miller belongs to the segment of black culture Du Bois designated as the "talented tenth." Colleagues here and abroad regard him as the best in his field, and he has performed a remarkable operation that has gained him recognition in a medical journal. Moreover, his humanitarian instincts have led him to dedicate personal funds to establish and maintain a black hospital in the South rather than in the less oppressive North or in Europe because he regards his mission as remaining with his people, contributing "to their uplifting" (51). Despite repeated slights and insults, such

as being denied entrance to Carteret's home, where a Northern doctor
has invited him to assist at a delicate operation, he maintains impecca-
ble dignity. The romance's final scene pushes Miller's self-command beyond the point any ordinary man could endure. His hospital reduced
to rubble by a racial massacre perpetrated by Carteret, his own son shot
during the holocaust, Miller is approached by Olivia Carteret to save
her son's life by performing a tracheotomy. During several impassioned,
irrefutable speeches, Miller outlines the moral situation: Major Carteret
is a murderer, while he is a victim; Major Carteret represents injustice,
while he represents justice. In short, Miller, as the only doctor who can
save Carteret's son from death, occupies the messianic throne of power.
Satisfying as his power appears to the audience, Miller, like Chesnutt,
cannot reconcile himself to the militance his position suggests. Just as
Chesnutt edges away from Josh's violent attack on Mc Bane, he takes
the reins from Miller and hands them to Janet, allowing her to perform
her mythic function.

 Janet's heroic potential is almost as difficult to perceive as is Miller's,
but when viewed within its historical context, her heroism emerges
clearly. Serving, like her husband, to counter prevailing Plantation Tradition stereotypes, she is college-educated, well-read, and unlike the so-
called "impudent new negroes," unfailingly gracious and polite. In fact
Janet is the quintessential Sentimental Heroine: aside from her role as
tragic mulatta, she is "an exhaustless fountain of sympathy" who all her
life has "yearned for a kind word, a nod, a smile," from her sister Olivia
Carteret (65–66). Despite Janet's self-abnegation, Chesnutt wants his
audience to view her as an extraordinarily sensitive and introspective
woman. In reflecting on her all-forgiving nature, Janet muses that she
has often rebuked herself for her spineless behavior and poor self-concept.
She attributes these flaws to the "taint of slavery" (66). Janet's medita-
tions are not apt to arouse in the reader a sense of her heroism, in the
traditional sense. Unlike Josh, her remembrance of her history does not
lead her to "shape [her] life to a definite purpose" and avenge the wrongs
done to her ancestors. In contrast to Josh, she feels more shame than
anger in connection with the history that has "tainted" her; or, more to
the point, she has internalized her anger rather than directing it toward
an appropriate target. What is heroic is her willingness to confront her

own docility and to examine its supposed origins. Chesnutt obviously views Janet as a woman concerned with the nature of truth, a woman who has access to profound realities. His confidence that "when the heart speaks, reason falls into the background" explains why Janet's decision to allow Miller to perform the tracheotomy is not simply a retreat from militance, for Chesnutt believes she possesses a penetrating intuitive understanding of truth (66).

The Marrow of Tradition's final moments permit Janet to turn around a potentially humiliating confrontation with her sister and achieve tragic greatness. Chesnutt stresses her mythic qualities: "she towered erect, with menacing aspect, like an avenging goddess" (326). When Olivia, fearing that Janet will not send Miller to her baby's aid, exercises her last effort at manipulation by offering Janet the portion of their father's estate to which his will already entitles her, Janet retorts scornfully, "I throw you back your father's name, your father's wealth, your sisterly recognition. I want none of them—they are bought too dear!... But that you may know that a woman may be foully wronged, and yet may have a heart to feel, even for one who has injured her, you may have your child's life, if my husband can save it!" (329). Compared to the narrow, petty selfishness of her sister, she emerges as heroic, almost saintly. *The Marrow of Tradition* concludes with Miller entering the Carteret house. Still, the reader remembers not this seeming defeat but Janet's superb victory over the groveling, ignominious Olivia. Indeed, Janet's nearly superhuman dignity during her last speech ensures her mythic stature. Each of the romance's heroic characters has suffered tremendous loss: Josh Green lies dead, Dr. Miller's hospital stands in ruins, Janet is deprived of her child and her inheritance. But the three characters remain ennobled—not by suffering but by their ability to transcend that suffering. Putting aside personal, selfish motives, each acts with dignity even in the face of degrading circumstances. Each, larger-than-life, achieves legendary status, suggesting that blacks would be better equipped to lead than whites if given positions of power.

Did Chesnutt's characters not triumph in this fashion, his romance would be unbearably depressing, for he fictionalizes in meticulous detail post-Reconstruction politics. Carteret, Belmont, and Mc Bane convey through their values and actions Chesnutt's concept of history. With the leaders of the white supremacy movement, Chesnutt explains the forces behind disenfranchisement. Major Carteret, editor of the *Morning Chronicle,* the organ of the political party defeated in the last election, seeks to reinstate the old South for his son's sake. Carteret, who believes in "the divine right of white men and gentlemen," represents those for whom the Southern code's external manners easily symbolize true morality (34). As William L. Andrews has demonstrated, Chesnutt has modelled Carteret on an actual person, Josephus Daniels, "who, as editor of the *Raleigh News and Observer* . . . conducted an anti-fusion, anti-Negro press campaign during the election year of 1898." General Belmont, Andrews establishes, is likewise based on a real historical figure in Wilmington politics, Alfred Moore Waddell.[13] Belmont, a lawyer aspiring to be governor, is entirely unscrupulous. In Chesnutt's moral hierarchy, Belmont retains his gentlemanly position primarily as a result of birth, education, and shrewdness. In short, unlike Carteret, he is the sort of man who before the war would have turned his head when his slaves were mistreated. "Captain" Mc Bane, whose title is purely fictitious, epitomizes the old South's obliteration. Whereas before the war Mc Bane would have served as an overseer, slavery's abolition, coupled with his ambition, has allowed him to move from manual laborer to political aspirant. Benefiting from illegally-acquired wealth, Mc Bane seeks a political office to ensure the status formerly denied him. Thus he perches on the bottom rung of the ladder, below Carteret and Belmont.

Their campaign to repeal the Fifteenth Amendment through convincing North Carolina that blacks should never have received the vote is for each of these men only a tool to further his own ambitions. Finally, they possess a frightening amount of political power. What Carteret and Belmont lack in effrontery Mc Bane makes up for; what Mc Bane lacks in influence Carteret and Belmont counterbalance. As a result, "the Big Three" constitute an invincible force. With these characters and the massacre they bring about (for which Carteret disclaims responsibility when the wholesale murder repels his sensibilities) Chesnutt suggests that if history is cyclical, it is so because men like these desperately need the security previous eras afforded. To be sure, blacks are floundering in a post-Reconstruction morass, but the Big Three, as well, stumble through unknown territory, struggling to forge stable identities. Carteret and Belmont can best forge these identities by reinstating the old order. By identifying with this order, Mc Bane can blot out his past's humiliation. Through these characters, John Reilly writes, "Chesnutt exposes the fundamental similarity of white men who mistakenly believe themselves to be distinctly different because of social class and manners."[14] *The Marrow of Tradition* demonstrates that history is shaped by humanity's psychological needs, its insecurities and weaknesses. Analyzing the white supremacy campaign's success, the narrator reflects that selfishness, rather than patriotism, humanism, or spirituality, "is the most constant of human motives . . . burrowing unwearingly at the very roots of life" (239). Perhaps because Chesnutt spent much time with whites, he arrives at a vision of history that recognizes the degree to which blacks' and whites' fates intertwine. Selfishness motivates all of us, the only hope lying with those who can put aside selfishness and behave morally. Both black and white characters exhibit this ability: Old Delamere, who intervenes on Sandy Campbell's behalf, acts as morally as do Josh, Miller, and Janet. J. Noel Heermance makes a case for the optimism Chesnutt exhibited most of his life. Pointing to a statement to Walter Hines Page in 1899 that blacks were "moving steadily upward," Heermance argues that even in the period of Chesnutt's most profound despair, he never failed to believe in the future amelioration of blacks' condition.[15] For Chesnutt, as for Griggs, life is grim. Yet while *Imperium in Imperio* reveals bewilderment at the proper means to confront that life, *The Marrow of Tradition* conjectures that even when nothing can be gained except the assurance of dignity and heroism, by refusing to misuse power blacks can transcend oppression.

Griggs and Chesnutt both rely on their own era's historical events to furnish fictional material. Like Brown, they do little more than allude to a past whose "primitiveness" precludes the possibility of heroic figures for their audience. Both flirt with militance, yet neither can fully endorse that militance. Whereas each decries the paucity of reward gained through education, each takes pains to provide genteel, educated blacks to counteract stereotypes. Both romances embody the desire to provide legendary figures who dispel myths of inferiority and populate a realm of heroic possibility. For the post-Reconstruction romancer, the need to create a positive mythology was monumental. But the unabashed heroism of *Iola Leroy* and *Contending Forces* ultimately eludes Griggs and Chesnutt. To repudiate white cultural values as does Josh Green, or to embrace militance, as do both Josh and Bernard, suggests the very dehumanization these writers fight so hard to erase. Accordingly, to accept white mores while refusing to fight back, as do Belton and Dr. Miller, means betrayal of one's race, loss of integrity. Even Janet achieves her heroism at the expense of joy. Many blacks today believe their dilemma mirrors the one Griggs and Chesnutt depict. Yet *Imperium in Imperio* and *The Marrow of Tradition* disclose a far more constrictive culture, one that totally denies black humanity and achievement, forcing its writers to take refuge in a heroism tempered by bitterness and ambivalence.

4 Visions of Transcendence

in W.E.B. Du Bois's *The Quest of the Silver Fleece*
and William Attaway's *Blood on the Forge*

W.E.B. Du Bois represents a transition from Griggs and Chesnutt to the writers of the Harlem Renaissance and those of the thirties, particularly William Attaway. Written in 1911, Du Bois's *The Quest of the Silver Fleece* contains both a larger vision than those in *Imperium in Imperio* and *The Marrow of Tradition* and limitations similar to them. Concerned as he was with many of the same historical conditions as were his literary contemporaries, Du Bois brought to these conditions a more sophisticated historical and cultural understanding. That he chose to fictionalize the political arena by way of techniques similar to those of Frank Norris's *The Octopus* is fortunate. That he could romanticize the common people (*The Quest of the Silver Fleece*, unlike the two earlier romances, calls them "folk") may explain why Arthur P. Davis credits him with preparing the ground and planting the seeds of the Harlem Renaissance.[1] Both Du Bois and Attaway present the plights of sharecropper and millworker. Both reveal the disenchantment attendant upon urban migration. Both employ the supernatural in their romances. And in both, Marxism enters into the conception of history; though Herbert Aptheker denies that Du Bois is a Marxist "in any meaningful sense," his emphasis on the relationship between the white and black masses leans toward the thinking of the thirties.[2]

Transfiguration, the myth that informs *The Quest of the Silver Fleece*, moves black historical literature in a startlingly new direction and initiates the passage back to Africa that crystallizes in the sixties and seventies. Whereas earlier writers seek to deny the past, Du Bois proposes that blacks must confront and transform history. This transformation, according to Du Boisian mythologizing, occurs under the guidance of the "talented tenth," those blacks whose intelligence, ingenuity, and vision, buttressed by education and gentility, equip them to lead the masses. With Du Bois, the means to reclaiming black culture from poverty and oppression — and the locus of wisdom — are not within the white political structure but within the black rural community.

Du Bois employs the romance as the form best suited to conveying his notion that the pastoral is a repository of redemptive power. He does not fictionalize Afro-America's past, but he allows his characters' quest for union with the earth to symbolize their gradual immersion in their African history. Going one step further, he lets the Swamp, where his sharecroppers live, suggest economic exploitation and racial oppression. When the sharecroppers reclaim their swamp to plant cotton, their own golden fleece, they turn upside down the sharecropping system and the myth of powerlessness they have introjected, thus transfiguring history. In conjunction with the pastoral, with its suggestions of an edenic garden, Du Bois uses other familiar romance elements. Supernatural occurrences and characters point toward a world a few steps away from verisimilitude, as do his heroes Zora and Bles, who wrestle with a gallery of villains. The romance's plot, which can plant the seed of probability in the audience by catapulting its protagonists to fame in a few pages, underlines Du Bois's idealism.

Although Du Bois mercifully eschews the tragic mulatto motif, he informs his romance with the concerns for gentility and "cultured" diction that hinder his predecessors. Moreover, he resorts to overplotting in order to incorporate historical events and issues. Otherwise he offers a rich contribution to Afro-American historical romance, having selected the literary mode appropriate to his utopian solution for Post-Reconstruction despair. Furthermore, he anticipates recent black historical literature: its commitment to reclaiming African history, its embrace of supernatural knowing, its return from the urban North to the agrarian South to keep in touch with folk roots, and, above all, its quest which ends in triumph. Du Bois, in fact, has greatly influenced the thrust of Afro-American literature, and *The Quest of the Silver Fleece* is emblematic of that influence.

Du Bois shifts the action of his romance from rural Alabama to Washington, D.C., and back again; in this way he contributes to the fiction of the great migration. But Du Bois cares as much for the political relationship between the two regions as he does for the disenchantment of his main characters with Washington. The reader first encounters the Eastern speculator's attitude toward the South's two great resources — cotton and blacks — in the person of John Taylor, a Wall Street clerk, who enters business for no other reason but to profit from black labor. First, Taylor uses his sister Mary as a wedge to obtain an interview with Colonel S. John Creswell, a cotton baron who runs the Farmer's League in Alabama. Taylor then proposes an alliance between his brokerage firm and Creswell's political influence with an eye toward controlling the Southern cotton market. Further sealing the combination, Harry Creswell marries Mary Taylor, and Taylor marries Helen Creswell, Harry's sister. Despite the ensuing collaboration, Taylor and Colonel Creswell differ, and their difference is significant thematically. Always described in mechanistic language, Taylor is "cool and steel-like," with "a disquieting, relentless element" in his "unimpassioned" voice.[3] He despises lying, drinking, and gambling; at the same time, he devotes his life to business speculation, in which he is completely ruthless. In contrast, Creswell, "a stately, kindly old man," though willing to defraud his black tenants and to "gamble and drink 'like a gentleman' . . . would never willingly cheat or take advantage of a white man's financial necessities" (81, 412–13). With Taylor and Creswell, Du Bois contrasts Northern entrepreneurs and Southern Bourbons. Their dealings convey a sense of the vast economic forces controlling the cotton industry, forces that overpower and exploit the helpless sharecroppers, both black and white.

As the only romancer of post-Reconstruction to lay bare the plight of lower-class blacks, Du Bois reveals the sharecropping system to be very little different from slavery. The Christmas season illustrates the system's duplicity. Colonel Creswell, one of "the lords of the soil," converses with his clerks about the proper way to distribute the wages to one sharecropper: "Well, he's a good nigger and needs encouragement; cancel his debt and give him ten dollars for Christmas." Creswell perceives that another farmer, having raised a bountiful crop, is trying to move away from the plantation. To ensure his servitude, Creswell advises, "Keep him in debt, but let him draw what he wants" (183). Similarly, when Zora and Bles, the romance's protagonists, raise a good crop, Harry Creswell cheats Zora out of her money and leaves her twenty-five dollars in debt. Through these and other scenes, Du Bois fictionalizes the manipulation of the sharecroppers that takes place in part because the landlords are dishonest, in part because the workers themselves are too ignorant to understand the system and too acculturated to question it. Only through the "talented tenth's" messianic power that Du Bois celebrates in *The Souls of Black Folk* (1903) can the uneducated be saved from such exploitation. Therefore, when Bles and Zora return from Washington, they organize the people to fight against the sharecropping system.

In contrast, the political corruption that Bles and Zora confront in Washington appears indomitable. Du Bois goes further than Griggs and Chesnutt in depicting the horror and complexity of post-Reconstruction politics. His distance from his material is such that he achieves an almost naturalistic work; unlike Griggs and Chesnutt he rarely editorializes but simply presents scenes and characters responsible for the corruption. On a quest for wealth, power, and status, all are enmeshed in a web of intrigue and backstabbing that coolly dispenses with those incapable of playing by the rules. Caroline Wynn, an educated mulatta, has become a senator's mistress to further her own interests. Eager to marry a politician, she suggests to the senator that Bles, her suitor, be given an office. Mrs. Vanderpool, a wealthy and influential woman, agrees to promote Bles for treasurer, in hopes of securing the French ambassadorship for her husband. When Bles speaks against the Republican party for refusing to support an education bill, however, the position of treasurer goes to Sam Stillings, a former friend of Bles. Seeing her chance, Caroline jilts Bles to marry Sam. Further complicating the unbelievable tangle of coincidence, Mary Taylor Creswell, whose husband Harry has been suggested for the French ambassadorship instead of the dissolute Vanderpool, is in turn framed by Mrs. Vanderpool for having deliberately given a prize to a sculpture submitted by Caroline. When the press discovers that the prize has gone to a black, Creswell loses the appointment.

In all these machinations, Du Bois reveals that he, like Chesnutt, sees historical process as resulting from human needs for security, wealth, and status and from humanity's ability to learn the methods to satisfy those needs. Aptheker delineates the positive aspect of this view of history when he summarizes Du Bois's essay "Mr. Sorokin's Systems." "The historian," Du Bois held, ". . . must believe that creative human initiative, working outside mechanical sequence, directs and changes the course of human action and so history . . . it is man who causes movement and change."[4] And for Du Bois, as for Griggs and Chesnutt, education represents the primary means for the individual to effect change. But the type of education acquired is of great significance. To analyze the educational situation for black America during post-Reconstruction one must acknowledge Booker T. Washington. Chesnutt and Washington were good friends. Although Chesnutt disagreed with Washington's insistence on industrial education, their friendship prevented Chesnutt in his published writings from disparaging Washington's ideas. Both Chesnutt and Griggs reacted to Washington's rejection of higher intellectual aims, his elevation of industrial work, but neither openly denounced him as did Du Bois. In "Of Mr. Booker T. Washington and Others," Du Bois enunciates his view that not only had Washington's educational and political theories sped disenfranchisement and withdrawal of aid to black colleges, but these same blacks could not survive without the voting privileges Washington discounted. Furthermore, Washington's insistence on self-respect conflicted with his insistence on silent submission. Finally, though Washington deprecated black colleges and supported common-schools, neither his own Tuskegee Institute nor the common-schools could stay open without teachers, who had to attend black colleges. Du Bois thus exposes the fundamental contradictions of Washington's thought.[5] Accordingly, he organized the Niagara Movement in 1905 to fight discrimination, segregation, and Washinton's accommodationist policies.

The Quest of the Silver Fleece, too, works with Washington's ideas, illustrates the effects they had on the whites controlling school funding. Much of the romance concerns the conflict between Sarah Smith, a white teacher desperately seeking funds for her school for black students, and Mary Taylor Creswell, who cherishes the theory that culture and the masses are incompatible. She advised Zora to become a cook or maid; though she herself teaches in the black school, she refrains from encouraging her pupils' ambitions and envisions their proper vocations as servants or farmers, "content to work under present conditions until those conditions could be changed" (130). Moreover, she believes "that the white aristocracy should team up with northern philanthropists to institute gradual changes in the present system." In fact Mary means well, but she foolishly fails to perceive that the "local aristocracy" has no intention of changing conditions. Rather, they systematically thwart any attempts to improve or maintain the schools. Harry Creswell, in particular, tries to encourage his workers to drop out, and when Northern philanthropists wish to endow the school with $150,000, he explains to John Taylor: "See here! American cotton-spinning supremacy is built on cheap cotton; cheap cotton is built on cheap niggers. Educating, or rather *trying* to educate niggers, will make them restless and discontented — that is, scarce and dear as workers" (160). To Du Bois, as to Griggs, the schools established for blacks belie the doctrine of progress. In fact, Du Bois shows that Southern whites deliberately maintain inferior schools to buttress their economic system. And Eastern speculators like Taylor quickly acquiesce when they see that their profits depend on this spurious logic. Thus, Du Bois undercuts the idea that black education necessarily leads to joy. In its place he offers a radical educational concept, joining Griggs in the mythmaking process. Only when Zora returns from Washington and reclaims a swamp whereupon to build a separate community with a school free from the strictures of the Cotton Combine does education attain any meaning for the blacks. But though the plan is a separatist one, like Griggs's Imperium, it comes about with the help of whites. Without Sarah Smith, Zora would never have escaped the self-defeating world symbolized by the swamp, for Sara both befriends and supports her when she would have given up. And without Mrs. Vanderpool's ten thousand dollars, given because through Zora she realized that culture and the masses are not incompatible after all, Zora could not establish the separate community. Finally, Zora endeavors to unite poor whites and blacks. For Du Bois, as for Chesnutt, the fates of blacks and whites intertwine, and when Sarah meditates that perhaps Zora is "the chosen one," the teacher alludes to a messianic figure who will alter the course of history and serve all humanity, not just black humanity.

Du Bois uses the genre of romance with both greater and less success than his contemporaries. Regrettably influenced by the Genteel Tradition, he strives to convince his audience that his characters are respectable. Initially, Bles and Zora appear as rather rough-hewn farm laborers. As time goes on they aspire to speak white English, acquire education, and dress decorously. But they draw back from "white" habits such as drinking and smoking. Although the black tenant farmers drink too, Du Bois makes clear that whiskey represents an opiate given them by whites who wish to maintain docility and ignorance. Also scorned are novels and candy, correlates of liquor for the white female. And Bles's early apprehension that Caroline seems "white" is borne out by the decadence she embodies. The new mythology, then, for Du Bois, is equated with educated, tasteful, unindulgent behavior.

Moreover, lack of discrimination in sexual matters elicits a kind of gothic horror, predicable not only with regard to the Genteel Tradition, but also in light of an essay from *The Souls of Black Folk* entitled, "Of the Quest of the Golden Fleece." Here Du Bois takes pains to enumerate the varieties of sexual behavior engaged in by the sharecroppers in the Black Belt. No more than 9 percent, he avers, are "lewd and vicious." In fact, he continues, 10 percent are highly respectable, the other 80 percent "fairly honest and well meaning," but inheritors of a loose or non-existent family structure.[6] To be sure, conditions during slavery did not encourage fidelity, but scholars such as Herbert Gutman and Eugene Genovese offer proof that a majority of slaves enjoyed tightly-knit families. In any case, Du Bois's intention, both in his romance and in his essay, is to suggest that the alleged immorality that the sharecroppers embrace results directly from their former bondage and the lack of self-respect it engendered. For this reason, Zora's former prostitution to Harry Creswell deserves the horror with which Bles regards it, as do all the lurid activities that take place in the cabin of Zora's mother Elspeth. Elspeth, "filthy of breath, dirty, with dribbling mouth and red eyes," lives rent-free on the Creswell swamp by trading the sexual favors of her daughter (96). As Harry Creswell's former mammy, she represents a grim counter-stereotype, symbolizing as she does the subterranean terrors of slavery.

Ultimately, Du Bois decries the beastliness of slavery and its attendant practices rather than sexual "promiscuity." Thus to accuse Du Bois of sexual conventionality ignores the degree of debasement involved in the miasmic atmosphere of the death-like swamp and Elspeth's cabin. As Arlene Elder points out, Elspeth has sold Zora and herself into moral slavery, an aspect of the swamp that must be anathematized.[7] To be sure, Du Bois's mythmaking involves denunciation of ignorance and "promiscuity" in favor of education and fidelity. But after all, a black man born so soon after the Civil War could scarcely be expected to present his "talented tenth" otherwise. Obviously, the Genteel Tradition influenced *The Quest of the Silver Fleece,* influenced the way Du Bois delineated his mythic history. And where it functions to present the audience with new heroes, so too does the miraculous element of romance allow for modes of action that attain a level of fantasy.

The Quest of the Silver Fleece might well be entitled *The Legend of the Silver Fleece,* presenting as it does two sharecroppers, one of whom moves to Washington and shortly thereafter is being considered for appointment as United States treasurer. Nearly as surprising is the upward mobility of Zora, who after accompanying to Washington the influential Mrs. Vanderpool, acquires a gift of ten thousand dollars and returns to Tooms County, Alabama, to organize the masses to build a free community. Both attain this rapid upward mobility through their wiles and, like the characters in other black historical romances, elucidate for their audiences the possibilities for blacks. Miraculous too is Zora's ability to mesmerize the black people with one powerful speech—to gain their respect and admiration and to wean them away from a corrupt preacher. Exhorting them to abandon the opiate of religious faith in the hereafter, Zora points out that work for themselves, for the here and now, should replace their slavish devotion to master and preacher. With this episode, Du Bois ushers in the attitude toward the black church articulated by James Baldwin's *Go Tell It on the Mountain,* Eldridge Cleaver's *Soul on Ice,* and Malcolm X's *Autobiography.*

Du Bois's use of romance for mythmaking moves beyond the conventions employed by Sutton Griggs and Charles Chesnutt. For him, as later for Arna Bontemps and William Attaway, romance draws its poetic quality from a love of nature and a sense of the setting as a force both supernatural and mythic, as what Richard Chase calls an "enveloping action."[8] Characters interact with the setting, are conscious of it as a force to contend with. Bles and Zora's love of cotton typifies the characters' love of nature. The reader first encounters this attitude when the narrator remarks that for Bles, cotton is "a very real and beautiful thing, and a life-long companion . . . ." As Bles describes to Mary Taylor Creswell the manner in which cotton grows and flowers, "the poetry of the thing [begins] to sing within her, awakening her unpoetic imagination . . ." (31). As a result, she recounts the story of Jason and the Argonauts. According to Greek myth, Jason arrived at Iolcus in Thessaly to claim his share of the kingdom from his uncle, Pelius. The latter told Jason that his share would be awarded when he brought Pelius the Golden Fleece from its owner Aeëtes, the Greek king. Though Aeëtes agreed to give the fleece to Jason, he forced Jason to face additional obstacles so difficult that Jason overcame them only with the aid of Medea, Aeëtes' daughter. When Aeëtes did not keep his word, the witch Medea helped Jason destroy the dragon guarding the Fleece. Seizing the desired object, Jason and Medea fled the country. To inhibit Aeëtes's pursuit of them Medea cut her brother's throat, dismembered his body, and strewed it in Aeëtes path.[9]

Mary is disturbed indeed when Bles parallels Jason's theft of the Fleece to the Creswell's exploitation of blacks, their thievery of the cotton from their rightful owners: those who have grown it. Zora, too, views the myth differently from Mary. When Bles tells Zora the legend, she wonders whether Elspeth is the witch. Zora suggests here that just as Medea helped Jason and betrayed her own father, sacrificed her own brother, so too has Elspeth prostituted her own daughter to the Creswells.

Because Du Bois emphasizes the Greek myth, one apprehends that for him, and for Bles and Zora, cotton possesses a similarly mythic significance. Early in *The Quest of the Silver Fleece* Bles and Zora clear a portion of the swamp, obtain some seeds from Elspeth, and vow that the cotton will grow because they will "love it into life" (p. 72). Encouraged by their love, the cotton crop is more magnificent than any ever seen. As a result, the two of them burst into joyous song, "a low, sweet melody of [Zora's] father's fathers" (128). Because Zora has claimed her great-grandfather is an African king and because she and Bles identify with Aeëtes rather than Jason, their song functions as a paean to their African heritage. Through growing the silver fleece, they have not only redressed Jason's wrongs but have recaptured their own majestic lineage, a link that the cotton continues to symbolize throughout *The Quest of the Silver Fleece*. When Bles abandons Zora, only her dedication to the fleece prevents her from capitulating to the self-destruction of the tenant farmers. Cotton is "greater than Love" and illuminates "the Way . . ." to transcendence (228-30).

But cotton alone does not contain the germ of transcendence. The cotton that the tenant farmers grow for their landlords remains tainted with servitude. Only cotton grown in the swamp possesses mystical powers. Before this notion is explored, it is necessary to understand the way the swamp functions. Throughout Du Bois's romance, characters (Zora in particular) regard the swamp as a force with which they must interact. Often, the swamp is personified through groans, moans, and shrieks. The creatures who inhabit the swamp emphasize its gothic duality. According to twelve-year-old Zora, the swamp teems with "little fairies . . . that hops around and sing, and devils—great ugly devils that grabs at you and roasts and eats you . . ." (19-20). Although these creatures receive no mention after Zora matures, they give way to gnarled fingers that strangle Zora when she despairs, forcing her to descend into hopelessness.

But the swamp is more than a cruel and menacing force with which Zora must wrestle. For Du Bois, the swamp symbolizes the dual nature of reality. Not only does it shriek and groan; it possesses a "low, seductive voice" that apprises Bles and Zora of the splendor available if only they learn to tap it (70). Full of magnificent dreams, the swamp embodies a positive as well as a negative force: "The golden sun was pouring floods of glory through the slim black trees, and the mystic somber pools caught and tossed back the glow . . ." (76). Early in the romance the reader becomes aware that the swamp contains both ruinous and regenerative power. Representing the dehumanization of slavery that blacks must transcend, the swamp also contains the seed of a new identity. Whereas other post-Reconstruction romances seek to escape the horrors of slavery, Du Bois wishes blacks to confront and transfigure those horrors. In "The Conservation of Races" (1897) Du Bois maintains that blacks should not seek "a servile imitation of Anglo-Saxon culture, but a stalwart identity which shall unswervingly follow Negro ideals." Rather than eschewing all vestiges of their "vast historic race," black heroes must emerge Phoenix-like from the ashes of their past.[10] Such emergence reaches full expression at the romance's conclusion when the entire swamp is cleared to produce the fleece that liberates the tenant farmers from their former "masters." For Du Bois, then, setting functions not only as a force to reckon with but a force that allows the characters to attain heroic stature; for without the silver fleece and the swamp, both suggesting a potentially ideal world, there would be no quest.

Du Bois interlaces the quest motif with Marxism. A Marxist interpretation of the Jason and the Argonauts legend introduces the notion that workers are exploited by those in control of the means of production. Early in the romance, Zora insists to Mary Taylor Creswell that she will never work except to help those she loves (presumably, the people). Somewhat disconcerted by this view, Mary rushes off, leaving behind a pin that Zora quickly seizes. When Mary accuses her of stealing, Zora inveighs against the greed of a woman who has five pins but begrudges even one of them to a young girl with nothing. Moreover, she contends, people do not own what they neither need nor use. A Marxist view emerges again when Bles and Zora grow the secret cotton crop already alluded to, symbolically repossessing the fleece from the thieving landowners. Du Bois thus denies the value of private ownership, be it of a pin one does not need or of a surplus of natural fiber rightfully due workers who produce it.

Du Bois's debt to Marx surfaces most clearly in the chapter entitled "The Cotton Mill." Just as Du Bois exposes the link between capital and political influence, he reveals the lords of cotton's manipulation of the masses. When discussing the new mill's advent, Taylor and Creswell agree to play off white mill workers against black field workers in order to keep wages down. When white mill workers complain about wages, the capitalists threaten to hire black workers. The fear this threat inspires redoubles the hatred of the poor whites toward the blacks, yet one white woman maintains, "Durned if I don't think these white slaves and black slaves had ought ter get together . . ." (395).

Of all early black romancers Du Bois is the most eclectic. His conception of history can best be described as an attempt to reconcile a cluster of opposites. The empiricism gleaned from William James, his Harvard professor, struggles with romanticism. Darwin's theories fuse with New England transcendentalism: "It is, then, the strife of all honorable men of the twentieth century to see that in the future competition of races the survival of the fittest shall mean the triumph of the good, the beautiful, and the true . . . ."[11] From Marx he gains an empathy and a solution for the plight of the masses, but this solution is to be initiated by members of the "talented tenth." Du Bois lived through and saw with great clarity the same events that bewildered his contemporaries: political corruption, black disenfranchisement, Jim Crow laws, mob rule. He realized that education, even of a member of the "talented tenth" such as Caroline Wynn, often led nowhere; for he himself experienced the alienation of the educated blacks who felt themselves socially and psychologically incompatible with the working class. But at the time he writes *The Quest of the Silver Fleece,* he stands apart from those who come before him. For Du Bois is not mired in pessimism as are Griggs and Chesnutt. Instead, *The Quest of the Silver Fleece* demands that the reader embrace a triumphant myth: the potential of Bles, Zora, and those like them to lift the Veil separating them from the good, the beautiful, and the true.

William Attaway's *Blood on the Forge* (1941) explores many of the same conditions and themes as *The Quest of the Silver Fleece.* But *Blood on the Forge* possesses a more realistic flavor than *The Quest of the Silver Fleece.* Attaway attends closely to commonplace detail, and he presents his characters' speech, manners, and mores with unflinching truthfulness. Finally, *Blood on the Forge* mythologizes the power, wisdom, and spontaneity of uneducated black folk. From Attaway's perspective, the working class is endowed with special qualities that this audience must acknowledge. Living close to their instincts, Attaway's folk sense their oppression, making them ideal agents of revolt. Strength and stamina, faith in supernatural and intuitive wisdom, and appreciation of nature and of physical pleasure comprise the heroism of folk culture. Attaway voices his belief in the proletariat's childlike innocence, but he must finally enunciate the deterministic view that living close to one's instincts may lead to violence, and when that violence is improperly directed, it will destroy. Nevertheless, *Blood on the Forge* concludes by celebrating the warmth and power of those impoverished blacks who, despite their anguish, maintain transcendent vision.

Attaway bases his romance on the myth of pastoral innocence. His central characters re-enact the Afro-American journey from south to north, with the Northern industrial setting suggesting monstrousness, and the Southern agrarian one suggesting dissipated beauty. Because the South has lost its promise, Attaway's heroes do not return there, as do Bles and Zora; however, they cherish nature, and this union with nature allows them to survive. Precepts of naturalism, the Harlem Renaissance, and Marcus Garvey underlie Attaway's narrative. The romance's legendary qualities enable him to create a trinity: three brothers, each of whom clearly stands apart from the others without narrative probings into motivation that would spoil the simplicity of Attaway's mythmaking. Their names, Big Mat, Melody, and Chinatown, suggest their separate ideological functions at the same time as they testify to the creativity of naming in black culture. As folkloric characters, each has a distinct role. Big Mat represents monumental strength, Melody intuitive wisdom, especially as embodied in black music, and Chinatown childlike spontaneity; all three reflect closeness to nature. This joining of nature and romance gains intensity when underscored by the oral narrative, which weaves the poetry of black speech into a complex texture without sacrificing the authenticity of folk culture. Unlike most black historical fiction, *Blood on the Forge* largely excludes positive images of women from its mythmaking. Attaway's naturalism relegates women to victim roles, thus limiting the scope of his mythology. Otherwise, *Blood on the Forge* is an excellent work. Attaway's evocation of folk culture passionately insists on the wonder and beauty of simple pleasures and convincingly denounces technology's exploitation of the land, and of human resources, in the pursuit of profit.

Blood on the Forge introduces the reader to such exploitation through the Moss family: Mat, Melody, and Chinatown, three half-brothers who work land whose barrenness parallels that of Hattie, Mat's wife. Conditions for the Moss brothers resemble those depicted in Du Bois's romance. When their mother dies while plowing and is dragged miles through the rocky Kentucky clay by a mule, Mat mangles the animal with a piece of flint to assuage his grief. As a result, the landlord Mr. Johnston claims their share of the crop for two years, leaving them totally destitute. Their plight is further emphasized by the hog intestines they must depend on for food, and by Mr. Johnston's callous explanation of his preference for black labor: "niggers ain't bothered with the itch; they knows how to make it the best way they kin and they don't kick none."[12] But unlike Du Bois's abject sharecroppers, Attaway's possess a nascent sense of rebellion, despite Mr. Johnston's opinion. Even without a spiritual leader such as Zora, they grasp the reality of their situation. Chinatown reflects, "We just niggers, makin' the white man crop for him. Leave him make his own crop, then we don't end up owin' him money every season" (6). After this awareness prompts Mat to physically retaliate against a riding boss, the three decide to follow a Northern jackleg's advice and travel north to the Pennsylvania steel mills.

Attaway skillfully exploits the tension between the Moss brothers, looking forward to life in a new world where the land is not "tired," and the jackleg, enticing them north for the purpose of breaking a strike. *The Quest of the Silver Fleece* fictionalizes the great migration, but *Blood on the Forge* explores the dynamics of exodus with greater complexity. Blacks, driven by the lynch mob's increasing terrorism and repeated crop failure, have migrated north. Northern industrialists, motivated by a need for labor previously filled by European immigrants whose influx has been stemmed by World War I, rather than by racial tolerance, pursue and welcome them. Driven by the fear that "the riding boss [will] live to lead the lynch mob," Mat and his brothers desert the worn-out land and thus become tools for further exploitation of the masses (34). *Blood on the Forge*'s excellence proceeds in part from Attaway's ability to recreate not only the migration's historical conditions but the chilling sense of betrayal the Moss family experiences from the very moment they are herded "like hogs headed for market" into the boxcar that will discharge them into the world of the steel mills (45). Phyllis Klotman likens this journey to the slaves' middle passage in crowded ships' holds, another journey to a miserable, alien existence.[13]

Like Du Bois, Attaway celebrates the pastoral. The narrator communicates this affinity for nature: "The mules saw [Big Mat and Melody] a long way off and laughed like mules laugh when they have been lonely" (26). When the Moss brothers arrive at the steel mills, they respond touchingly to the word "mule" after they learn it denotes a steel-hauling engine: "That word mule — it sounded like home" (61). After several months in the North, Mat's longing for home is satisfied somewhat by long walks in the hills, away from the dehumanizing machine. In every instance, home is associated with nostalgia for nature; thus does Attaway skillfully contrast Northern industrialism with Southern pastoralism. Soon after their arrival in the North, the Moss brothers join the collective silent voice of the steel workers who wonder, "what men in their right minds would leave off tending green growing things to tend iron monsters?" (51). As the men become acculturated, they put up stronger defenses against this initial sense of the steel mill as a monster, defenses that are, nevertheless, continually undermined by Smothers, a black man crippled by a mill accident. According to Smothers, "it's wrong to tear up the ground and melt it in the furnace. Ground don't like it." When humanity trifles with nature, Smothers continues, the steel will retaliate (62). Through Smothers, Attaway fuses two elements of romance: the sense of the marvelous and that of the setting as a force, or more properly, two forces. Clearly, Smothers possesses supernatural, visionary powers, allowing him to foresee that, enraged by humanity's assault, steel will eventually avenge itself through the very tools of humanity's destruction. Thus steel and technology represent twin enemies to the steel workers. Although the workers deride Smothers' prophecies, the reader knows their derision masks fear that Smothers speaks the truth.

That truth manifests itself in the swift, inexorable deterioration of the three central characters. Indirectly, the mill destroys them through alcohol, the controlling image of dissolution. Whereas earlier black writers assume a prejudice against whiskey on the audience's part, Attaway explores alcoholism's causes and effects. "Corn" has many functions: it provides almost the only entertainment in a desolate environment; it stimulates the workers exhausted by twelve- to twenty-four-hour shifts to begin work again. Sadly, corn also helps to blunt the workers' longings to escape their misery: "Of course the hot-metal workers had to keep liquored up. There was always a craving in them that wasn't to be satisfied" (78). Attaway, like Du Bois, envisions alcohol as an opiate that prevents the proletarian from acting with self-interest. Further, he emphasizes that liquor aids in releasing violence, an effect he ultimately deplores. The destructive potential of alcohol, then, serves as a main theme in *Blood on the Forge*. Fortunately, naturalism invests Attaway's preoccupation with psychological power, and realism restrains him from narrative intrusion. As a consequence of that restraint, Attaway allows Chinatown to innocently describe the deadly seductiveness of corn: "When I die don't bury me. . . . Jest pour me back in the jug" (103). Thus, through alcohol, the steel mill affects the Moss brothers indirectly. But setting acts directly on the characters as well, severely interfering with Melody's and Chinatown's identities. Clearly, music represents Melody's essence; it provides him with his only defense against pain. When Melody discovers he can no longer create new songs, he half-intentionally smashes his hand at work, an act that both vents his anger toward the job that has robbed him of his music and allows him an excuse not to be able to play. His own responsibility for the accident notwithstanding, Melody has obviously been victimized by the steel mill; thus has he interacted with the setting.

To a much greater extent does Chinatown's accident illustrate Attaway's use of the setting as an enveloping action. In the chapter preceding the accident, Smothers has attained the role of oracle, his prophecies gaining credibility as events point toward doom. Mat's affair with a fifteen-year-old Chicana, a prostitute with whom Melody is also infatuated, has splintered the Moss family. When Mat suspects another man of "creepin' on" him, he tries to kill the suspect and lands in jail. In the mill, an accident Melody experiences leads the men to believe the furnace jinxed. Chinatown, sent to take over Melody's spot, feels an inchoate fear: "The wrong . . . was in the air about him. . . ." He listens to the sounds from the mill. Although the men resist Smothers' chant "steel's gonna get somebody," their fear that this time he may be right sets the mood for him to recount the story of his accident. Evident throughout *Blood on the Forge*, the oral narrative comes into play with particular effectiveness here. Punctuated by "a soft chant that was like little explosions in among [his] words . . . Goddam . . . Goddam," the oral tale told by Smothers captivates his audience with his conviction that steel is determined to avenge itself on the men. His own refrain, "roll steel git him . . . roll steel git him . . . ," is picked up by the haunting steel voices that link the present fearsome moment with the past one. Just as the steel laughed and talked at the time of Smothers' tragedy, so does it threaten the men today (177). And when subsequently Melody senses that a monster is trying to unchain himself, the flash that follows claims fourteen men, including Smothers, leaving only one other besides China-town alive. Chinatown's survival is a mixed blessing. Blinded by the explosion, China has been acted upon by the setting, has in fact been nearly defeated by the steel: "He had been a man who lived through outward symbols. Now those symbols were gone, and he was lost" (190).

Setting functions as an enveloping presence in both *The Quest of the Silver Fleece* and *Blood on the Forge,* and closeness to nature is reflected in both, but Attaway's romance diverges sharply from those of his predecessors with respect to characterization. To be sure, Du Bois wrote about the common folk; but for those folk to be heroic, they were to become educated and genteel. Speaking of the older Du Bois in 1935, the controversial E. Franklin Frazier questioned Du Bois's "sympathetic understanding" of the black masses. Descending from two generations of free blacks and educated at Harvard, Du Bois seemed to Frazier an eternal aristocrat, alienated from the working class. "The voice of Du Bois," Frazier continued, "is genuine only when he speaks as a representative of the Talented Tenth."[14] Ironically, some Marxist historians scoff at Frazier today in much the same way as he scoffed at Du Bois forty years ago. Nevertheless, one must admit that Frazier's assessment of the author of *The Quest of the Silver Fleece* contains a germ of truth.

According to the conventions of the romance delineated by Henry James, the hero may be "a morbidly special case."[15] In modern literature the hero may be as remorselessly violent as Bigger Thomas and command identification, even adulation, from his audience. The Moss men depart from previous heroes to such a degree that one is surprised to realize only thirty years have elapsed since the previous historical romance's publication. All three brothers demonstrate the influence of Attaway's hobo days, the Harlem Renaissance, and Marcus Garvey. A Jamaican black, Garvey exerted untold influence on black American literature. He began his Universal Negro Improvement Association in 1914 in Jamaica, bringing it to the States in 1919 and recruiting over a quarter of a million members in the U.S. by 1920. His program consisted chiefly of the plan for all blacks to emigrate to Africa, but that plan had less impact on blacks than did Garvey's rejection of the middle class aspirations of Du Bois and other NAACP members. Particularly did he appeal to urban migrants who viewed that organization as elitist, and who, being dark-skinned, faced greater obstacles in assimilating. But Garvey did more than articulate the grievances of the black masses. Addison Gayle writes, "For Garvey to be black meant to be the inheritor of a tradition which reaches beyond the Pharoahs, to cultural artifacts that extol the dignity of the human spirit."[16] Exhibiting Garvey's influence, the Moss brothers are neither educated nor aspiring to be so. Not only is black English employed, it is played with, elevated to poetry. The men's passions ennoble them. Distance between Attaway and his predecessors is perhaps best illustrated by the early episode in which the brothers wait eagerly for their chitterlings, the air "steamy with a hot-manure smell, done-chitterling smell" (30). Gone are the preoccupations with clothes, furnishings, courtly attitudes toward women. In fact the recurring image of the young prostitute Anna in the mud-encrusted "dance-hall dress" that for her symbolizes affluence lays the ghost of elegant attire. And Mat's misogyny culminates in one of the most graphically depicted beating in all black literature.

Chinatown and Melody are emblematic of two Renaissance values, Chinatown representing child-like sensuality, Melody intuitive romanticism. China's purely ornamental gold tooth ("there had never been anything wrong with his teeth") and his adoration of red pop and corn manifest his hedonism (2). Women exist for him solely to give pleasure; they represent simply "good times." Capable of inspiring laughter wherever he goes, China is completely absorbed in the moment, rolling "like a pony in the dust, tickled over how he had tricked Melody" after telling a joke (41). In the world of historical romance, he is the prototype of exuberance and physicality unfettered by analysis.

Like China, Melody is a non-rational being. Although reflective, he intuits most of what he knows; he has not lost touch with spiritual matters that defy rational understanding. With his music he gives birth and form to these matters, but when he loses his songs his impotence is complete. When he first encounters Anna, he can perform neither sexually nor musically but knows "he is on the edge of something" (87). He has slept with prostitutes before, but Anna is the first to call up his artistic sensibility; thus his sexual impotence symbolizes his inability to come to grips with the inner urgings once actualized by his music. He and

Anna do have a sexual encounter later in the romance, yet neither is satisfied because it leads nowhere, fails to rescue Anna as she begs to be rescued. In the emasculating presence of the machine, Melody cannot perform the messianic function he might have in a pastoral setting. Despite his impotence, Melody invests *Blood on the Forge* with its primary romantic impetus. His yearnings, though they bear no fruit, remind the reader of those things that, according to Henry James, one "never *can* directly know. . . ."[17] Who else but Melody would attend a dogfight "to feel the lives of those people burning together in a single white flame"? (111). Fifteen years earlier Melody would have served as a paradigm of artistic sensibility. By 1941 the Depression had severely impaired that sort of characterization. Yet, like Chinatown, Melody is part of a new mythology for the audience. Uneducated and unheroic in the traditional sense, he serves to remind the reader that though oppression may render black folk somewhat ineffectual, it will never extinguish that flame that burns within Melody, nor will it completely defeat China. The concluding scene leaves the audience with China listening closely to something no one else hears. Stripped of his sight, China begins to perceive the less literal world. The reader thinks of the conclusion to *The Grapes of Wrath:* despite apparent defeat, the proletariat partakes of a larger vision that eventually must triumph.

Of the three brothers, Mat comes the closest toward embodying the messianic role. Usually dubbed "Big Mat," he bears some resemblance to Bigger Thomas in the capacity for violence that erupts repeatedly throughout *Blood on the Forge*. Initially, the reader hears of this violence through the image of Hattie: "She was Big Mat's wife. The marks on her told that much" (2). Attaway makes the reader aware of the destructiveness of this violence; yet the other characters exalt Mat's power. To the steel men, "Black Irish's" strength and endurance endow him with mythic stature; in their eyes he stands trimphant before the machine's humiliating potential. When Big Mat finally abandons the idea of bringing Hattie north, he becomes "drunker than any man had ever been before" (117) and at a dogfight rushes in to avenge a blow struck at Anna by the owner of a dog she is trying to rescue. "One swing of his arm sent Bob Dank halfway across the barn, knocking people down like straw stubble" (114). As a result of Mat's heroics, Anna instantly recognizes

him as destined to deliver her from the status of peon. Satisfying all Anna's fantasies, Mat is "a big man with muscles like a bear on the mountain . . . [with] a pine tree on his belly, hard like rock all the night" (122).
Here Attaway communicates that for the steel workers, power is unques-
tionably worshipped. Even when Mat beats Anna, she declares, "it is
right for the man to beat the woman" (154).

Other characters' exaltation of Mat's power turns to an equivocal
end, however, during a riot. Because of his immensity and power, Mat
is deputized to terrorize the union strikers, becoming very much like
Bigger in his apprehension that whereas all his life he had been emas-
culated, "now he was a boss. . . . After all, what did right or wrong matter" (232). At first, Mat, like Bigger, cannot understand the exhilaration
he experiences from being boss, cannot fathom what it signifies to him.
Ultimately he realizes that deputization represents a potent medicine for
his shattered ego. "That medicine was a sense of brutal power. . . . That
the cure might be deadly was too deep a thought for him. The only
thing he felt was a sense of becoming whole again" (250). When Mat's
power is unleashed, he enters a realm where pure violence takes over,
where cruelty becomes the ultimate goal. Brought to "complete kinship
with the brutal troopers," Mat is at the mercy of his instinct, an instinct
the narrator decries for its misdirection (252). As in Bigger's case, Mat's
aggression is fleeting, ending when a union member fells him with a
pick ax. His death, requiring countless blows of the ax, attains mythic
stature. Beginning to perceive his class interests, Mat, who has striven
to prove himself master rather than peon, reaches an epiphany just before his death: "It seemed to him that he had been through all of this
once before. Only at that far time he had been the arm strong with hate.
Yes, once he had beaten down a riding boss. . . . Had that riding boss
been as he was now? Big Mat went farther away and no longer could
distinguish himself from these figures. They were all one and all the
same" (274). With this Marxist sentiment, Attaway tempers the cruelty
of Mat, in much the same way that Wright does with Bigger, and writes
a romance that will embrace both black and white labor. Thus for Attaway, as for Du Bois, Marxism enters significantly into the conception
of history and into the mythology to which he contributes.

Attaway's romance gains much of its power from the importance of setting and from the author's willingness to present realistic, even "morbidly special" characters; however, without his skillful use of oral narrative, *Blood on the Forge* would be far less powerful. Communication among characters often shows the influence of the oral tale, as in the passage with Smothers cited earlier. Often this communication takes the form of singing or chanting. Early in the romance, China and Melody play a wishing game. "'China' [Melody] half sang, 'you know where I wish I was at now?'" (9). At other times, too, characters "sing" or "chant" rather than speak. Through calling attention to this device, one common to black speech, Attaway elevates their dialogue, invests it with ritual significance. Other ritualistic touches include the refrains varied from one passage to another such as the mournful "We just niggers, makin' the white man crop for him" (6) and later "Make you forgit you just a nigger, workin' the white man's ground" (27). Fusing repetition and song, Attaway makes transcendence available to his audience without intruding on the folk sensibility.

Other oral devices include epithets and similes to establish characterization. Particular epithets are used especially with China, whose "golden grin" and "slant eyes" are emblematic of the laughter the reader comes to associate with him. Attaway varies the formulaic epithet, too. Until the accident, China nearly always grins or laughs when he isn't singing or chanting his speech. Once he "[clucks] his gold tooth" (20). In a typical passage, the narrator explains, "his gold tooth shone . . . his slant eyes . . . made laughing his natural look" (3). Characterization also develops through similes; a few are trite, but most are strange and original, even when they merely embroider the hackneyed. Mat's face is described as "an old piece of harness leather left a whole season to blacken and curl in the sun and rain" (25). Melody's infatuation with Anna derives in part from his perception of her face, "broad as a spade but good to see" (81). A little later he glimpses her legs, "beautiful as fresh-split cedar" (86). As these examples show, most of Attaway's similes appeal on some level to nature. Describing the deputies called up to break the strike, Attaway narrates, "the mounted troopers wielded their clubs like men with scythes, felling grain." Later, when the troopers have brutalized the union members and their families, they glare at the victims "like men regretful at the finish of an orgasm" (253).

Attaway's use of the oral narrative provides the audience with satisfying recurrences by way of refrains, chants, and epithets. Further, the oral narrative brings about identification through demotic language and images, earthy yet unusual figures of speech, and folk characters whose grandeur derives from qualities attainable to the audience. The oral narrative devices function for Attaway in *Blood on the Forge* in much the same way as they do for Bontemps in *Black Thunder:* they record the rhythm and form of common speech while at the same time revealing its poetic beauty. For Attaway, as for Bontemps, oral narrative techniques are integral to mythmaking. As do all protagonists of oral narratives, Melody, Chinatown, and Mat embody the audience's values to a certain degree, most readers rejecting their violence, but the influences of the Harlem Renaissance and naturalism allow for a frankness of characterization eschewed by Du Bois. Not only does Attaway depict blacks without gentility or erudition, his three protagonists exhibit sexual and spiritual impotence, unabashed hedonism, and misdirected destructiveness. Such characters appear before Attaway's fiction; however, in most cases these characters do not command the readers' primary sympathies.

Whereas Du Bois and Attaway both call upon Marxism and naturalism, naturalism influences Attaway's concept of history far more deeply than Marxism. By the thirties Du Bois had altered his Marxist notions to exclude the possibility that black and white workers could unite, but 1911 saw him fervently assured that to remove the means of production from the capitalists was the first step in freeing the proletariat from its dilemma. In contrast, Attaway, while deploring Mat's violence toward union members, realizes that for many workers, identification with the interests of the union is well-nigh impossible. The black foreman Bo enunciates the problem: "Maybe them guys was fired 'cause I said I seen 'em going into the union place. But hell! I got to keep my job. I got to do what they say. Don't forget I'm the only nigger in the mill got micks under him!" (213-14). Driven by the survival instinct in a brutally competitive battle, blacks must struggle against their foes or be defeated. Tragically, many of the steel workers fail to perceive the real foes. Instead, they merely displace their anger on animals (the dogfights), women, and each other. The strikebreakers epitomize such displacement of anger: "in their faces was a record of hard, undisciplined lives—old scars, broken noses, lantern jaws blue with stubble, lines of dissipation. They look[ed] brutal because they had been brutalized" (223). And as a result of the brutalization, they kill and maim those who are acting in their interests.

Ultimately, Attaway is romantic enough to believe that Mat's participation leads to an apocalypse, just as China's blindness finally allows him to "see" beyond the literal. Attaway's characters may not consciously make the right choices, may be temporarily swayed by Bo's exhortation that there are no absolute rights or wrongs. Still, they yearn to unite with truth. Thus, the final chapter shows Melody and Chinatown leaving behind the red clay hills of Kentucky and heading to Pittsburgh. Uncertain as their quest may be, Melody and Chinatown, devoid of the traditional props of education, devoid even of grand heroics, represent Attaway's contribution to the mythmaking process. Armed with mutual love and a vision of "the Strip: a place where rent was nearly free and guys who knew how to make out would show them the ropes," the Moss brothers epitomize the collectivist notion of heroism (276).

5   Retreat into the Self

Ralph Ellison's *Invisible Man* and
James Baldwin's *Go Tell It on the Mountain*

The study of post-Reconstruction romancers showed that
the exceedingly oppressive political climate accounts for both the dormant literary period preceding Sutton Griggs's and Charles Chesnutt's
works and the tenor of their works as well. Frances Harper's *Iola Leroy*,
as has been noted, has close affinities with William Wells Brown's romance. In much the same way, the fiction produced between *Blood on
the Forge* (1941) and Ralph Ellison's *Invisible Man* (1952) derived largely
from Richard Wright's *Native Son*.[1] Robert A. Bone speculates that the
works of the Wright school, those of assimilationist nature (*e.g.*, Willard
Motley's *Knock on Any Door*, 1947, and Zora Neale Hurston's *Seraph
on the Suwanee*, 1949) and *Invisible Man* result from the diminishing oppression in the forties and early fifties.[2] It is possible, however, to look
at those years and arrive at very different theory.

On the surface, conditions appeared to be improving dramatically.
In 1940 both the National Defense Advisory Committee and President
Roosevelt spoke out against discriminatory hiring practices. Soon after
the President's message to Congress, the Office of Production Manage-
ment established a Negro Employment and Training Branch in its Labor Division. These events appeared to set the climate for black liberation, but historian John Hope Franklin was not alone in believing that
these gestures were "purely rhetorical."[3] Other apparent advances followed. Under pressure from Brotherhood of Sleeping Car Porters president A. Philip Randolph, Roosevelt, on June 25, 1941, issued Executive
Order 8802 for the purpose of prohibiting discrimination in defense in-

dustries. At the time, the document was regarded as one whose significance equalled that of the Emancipation Proclamation, a comparison which later proved ironic. For just as emancipation failed to lead to full freedom for blacks, so too did this executive order fail to combat discrimination. Opposed by most white employers, Order 8802 became a largely symbolic, unenforced order. Roosevelt's death in 1945, coupled with a South Carolina incident in which twenty-eight men were exonerated despite their participation in a lynching, served to underscore the apparent hopelessness of the black plight. Franklin describes the almost total despair of blacks in 1945 in *From Slavery to Freedom.*

As the forties passed into the fifties, reform continued on an unclear path, perhaps heightening discontent more than a rigid adherence to class structure would have done. Every effort toward improving the status of blacks was met with backlash. Although the Truman administration's report, *To Secure These Rights,* demanded the end of discriminatory hiring practices in the Army, the Truman administration did not properly enforce this demand.[4] And even when discrimination was abolished with respect to military jobs, segregation still existed in the U.S Army. As late as 1951, 30 percent of U.S. field troops in Korea were segregated, and segregation continued in other areas of life as well. In 1950 the Supreme Court abolished Jim Crow cars on interstate railroads, but separate waiting rooms were built to reinstate the caste sysem. And despite a diminution of segregation in residential housing, a Cicero, Illinois, mob stormed a house purchased in 1951 by a black couple. Franklin reports that whites "broke windows, mutilated the exterior, and shouted vile epithets at the couple."[5]

In short, though conditions had undeniably improved since post-Reconstruction, the sense of desperation in both whites and blacks echoed that of the earlier period. Much as post-Reconstruction white Southerners strove to reinstate a more familiar system, white United States citizens of the mid-twentieth century seemed incapable of allowing unequivocal rights to Afro-Americans, so that every law or statement intended to improve the conditions of blacks was accompanied by a harsh reinstatement of the old order.

The difficulties experienced by Griggs and Chesnutt in their attempts to present heroes, their vacillation between militancy and accommodation, and the solace they found in ambivalence or resignation have been discussed, as have been the shattering reality of oppression in Du Bois and Attaway and the partial antidotes to this oppression provided by Marxism that shored up their concepts of history. With the disengagement from Marxism and the political equivocations of the forties and early fifties, back writers struggled desperately to create a new mythology, just as Harper, Hopkins, Griggs, and Chesnutt had done. It is natural to consider, then, whether the Wright School, the assimilationists, and Ralph Ellison's and James Baldwin's works reflect not simply the deterioriation of white supremacy, but a realization of the conflict between symbolic and real legislation for blacks. No doubt this realization combines with the disorientation and despair characteristic of the period.

With these notions, the reader can view *Invisible Man* and *Go Tell It on the Mountain* with an eye toward their similarity to each other and to the tradition of black historical fiction. Ellison and Baldwin mythologize history, as the writers treated earlier have done, but with a much different mythmaking process. Their era forced them into the white literary mainstream, as it had forced the Wright School to revert to naturalism and the assimilationists to flee from protest. Both Ellison and Baldwin write fiction that returns to the distant past, thus qualifying their works as traditional historical fiction that deviates from the romantic mode that previously typified black historical fiction. Both Ellison and Baldwin eschew ideological concepts of history, as do many writers of the late twentieth century. Finally, both counter the reductive view of blacks offered by sociologists and fleshed out in Richard Wright's Bigger Thomas.

Ellison ushers in a new era, one in which writers begin to insist that black mythmakers, by definition, must take a hard look at history in order to shape their future visions. To Ellison, the Afro-American writer must re-evaluate history through a destruction of the false promises offered by white culture before he or she can invent a mythology. Ellison's mythic vision, which is at root humanistic, aims to focus his audience on the cultural heritage black and white Americans share; the Afro-American background, however, as *Invisible Man* presents it, does not reach back into African culture but into the Western intellectual heritage. Wisdom, according to *Invisible Man,* lies not within the pastoral

South, or Africa, or, indeed, any specific locale other than the mind of the American, who, through self-examination, can re-envision this country's original ideals. What distinguishes Ellison from earlier writers are his retreat from the separatism of Griggs and his disavowal of ideology, be it the capitalism embraced by Brown or the Marxism of Du Bois and Attaway. But like all writers examined here, Ellison views myth and history as closely linked.

Rather than bringing myth and history together by way of romance, Ellison synthesizes several modes, contributing to *Invisible Man*'s complexity and reinforcing his insistence that blacks have much to contribute to American culture. His picaresque hero weds Western literature and black folklore to mythologize Afro-America's extraordinary talent for survival. To accentuate his belief in laughter's healing powers, Ellison employs oral narrative. Lest the audience feel that Ellison's comic bent is meant to deprecate the possibility of black heroism, he gives his fiction an epic scope, at the same time investing his protagonist with introspective capabilities. Thus does he suggest blacks' intellectual power to come to grips with history and invent the future. Ellison's primary limitation lies in his assimilationist tendencies, not the least of which is his refusal to recognize the "infinite possibilities" of Africa as well as America, or to consider deeply the origins of the music and folklore to which he is indebted. That severe limitation aside, *Invisible Man* remains a work of genius that inaugurates an attitude toward history central to Afro-American literature more than thirty years after its own publication.

Repeatedly, black historical writers have debunked the myths of white America. From descriptions by Brown, Bontemps, Harper, and Hopkins of the abuses of slavery through Griggs's and Chesnutt's explosion of the separate-but-equal concept to Du Bois's and Attaway's castigation of urban migration, each writer has undercut the good life white America supposedly offers. *Invisible Man*, however, is the first comprehensive deconstruction; and at least seven critics have explicated the progress through history made by the protagonist of *Invisible Man*.[6] Taken together, these studies amply chart the manner in which the protagonist's encounters with various situations outline not only the roles offered blacks from post-Reconstruction to the forties, but also the extent to which each role fails to measure up to its mythic promise. It is profitable, however, to compare the fictionalization of history in *Invisible Man* and the works studied earlier in this book.

In the Prologue, where the narrator invites us to look at slavery, his presentation is largely symbolic (in this sense, rather like Hopkins's and Du Bois's writing). Ellison's narrator has smoked marijuana, heightening the "unreality" of his vision, and the girl standing on the auction block is so slightly mentioned as to pass unnoticed by some readers. This slave, who has a voice like the narrator's mother, is a mulatta; remembering the presentation of mulatto characters by earlier black writers, one wonders whether this woman is more beautiful to the narrator because she is the "color of ivory."[7] In his vision, the narrator later confronts a former slave, torn between hatred and love for her master, the father of her sons. Her struggle enunciates the narrator's own ambivalence: should he embrace blackness and act out his violence against the oppressor or should he accept his American identity, thereby forgiving his oppressor? This ambivalence hearkens back to Du Bois's remark in *The Souls of Black Folk* that "one ever feels his twoness—an American, a Negro; two souls, two thoughts, two unreconciled strivings; two warring ideals in one dark body."[8]

The protagonist's participation in a civically sponsored Battle Royal, in which he and several of his high school classmates are forced to endure a series of humiliations, including a horrifying scramble for fake coins tossed on an electrified rug, warns the reader of the limitless degradation that has been and will be required in the black's struggle for civil rights. The episode concludes with the invisible man delivering a parody of Booker T. Washington's Atlanta Exposition Address. When the invisible man takes Norton, a trustee of the college to which the protagonist's speech has earned him a scholarship, on a tour of his college town, this trip propels them into the world of the sharecropper explored earlier by Du Bois and Attaway. The episode involving Trueblood, the black tenant farmer whose impregnation of his own daughter has earned him the approbation of white townsfolk eager to reassure themselves of blacks' "animalism," contains themes and techniques explored in earlier historical fiction. The reader may observe, for example, his living in former slave quarters, his joyous sensuality, and his folk wit. To the initiated, in fact, Trueblood may gently parody the heroes of *Black Thunder* and *Blood on the Forge*.

Trueblood's incest is presented through oral narrative. In one sense, the story is a formula episode; the fall of the innocent storyteller is inevitable, and Ellison engages audience interest through Trueblood's incantatory piling up of detail. The pace of the sentences is rapid as a result of heavy reliance on mono- and di-syllabic words, yet the episode maddeningly delays the culminating event through such seeming digressions as the pseudo-Freudian dream and through repetition and elaborate, yet demotic, figures of speech. Repetition combines with outrageously satiric metaphors and similes, as when Trueblood sets the scene for the action: "'It was dark, plum black. Black as the middle of a bucket of tar. . . . It was black dark'" (42). Later, Trueblood speaks of trying to disengage himself from his daughter: "'There I was, tryin' to get away with all my might, yet having to move *without* movin'. I flew in but I had to walk out. I had to move without movin' . . . '" (46). As in much oral narration, similes are the primary figures of speech, but to emphasize the pure joy of the telling Ellison embroiders and expands even simple comparisons. Similes combine with lengthy coordinated sentences to create a marvelous conjunction of simplicity and poetic sensibility in the following passage:

> . . . you up in the second-story window and look down on a wagonful of watermelons, and you see one of them young juicy melons split wide open a-layin' all spread out and cool and sweet on top of all the striped green ones like it's waitin' just for you, so you can see how red and ripe and juicy it is . . . like when you watch a gal in a red dress and a wide straw hat goin' past you down a lane with the trees on both sides, and she's plump and juicy. . . .
> (43)

Through the repetition of coordinates and the personification of the "young, juicy" watermelon, later to be implicitly compared to the "plump, juicy" girl, Ellison's narrator achieves a humorous effect akin to the wicked glee that informs the yam-eating incident in which the protagonist embraces his heritage by declaring, "i yam what I yam" (201). The natural affinity between the oral narrative and myth emerges clearly in Trueblood's narrative which, like those in *Black Thunder, Imperium in Im-*

perio, and *Blood on the Forge,* enriches the mythology offered to Ellison's audience, celebrating the common folk while embroidering the conventions of the oral tradition.

As with the Trueblood episode, the protagonist's confrontation with dispossessed, educated blacks hearkens back to post-Reconstruction fiction. The veterans at the Golden Day, a tavern and house of prostitution, have realized that their education has not allowed them to enter the middle class; rather, it has further alienated them from both blacks and whites, thus leading to their "madness." Following up this thinly veiled warning with a campus ceremony, Ellison further underscores for the protagonist the hollowness of his educational endeavors. A speech given at the ceremony echoes the earlier parody of Booker T. Washington in its reference to the college founder, who escaped bondage to begin "erecting the scaffolding of a nation" by building a college for blacks (96). Oblivious to the "opaque glitter" of the speaker's glasses, oblivious to the symbolic implication of the speaker's "sightless eyes," the invisible man, who remains deeply impressed by the speech, is crushed when Dr. Bledsoe ousts him from academia. At the turn of the century Griggs and Du Bois exposed the duplicities required of black educators, who functioned as tools of the dominant whites. Bledsoe serves a similar function: "I've made my place . . . and I'll have every Negro in the country hanging on tree limbs by morning if it means staying where I am " (110). Expelling the protagonist, he offers some advice: "You let the white folks worry about pride and dignity—you learn where you are and get yourself power, influence, contacts with powerful and influential people—then stay in the dark and use it!" (111). Like Pharoah in *Black Thunder,* Jerry in *The Marrow of Tradition,* Caroline in *The Quest of the Silver Fleece,* and Bo in *Blood on The Forge,* Bledsoe has reached his position through equivocation and ruthlessness—and to those characteristics he will continue to adhere. In *Black Bourgeoisie,* E. Franklin Frazier inveighs against the failings of the black nouveau riche, deploring their obsession with wealth and status, their hollow intellectual lives, and their tendency to displace self-hatred onto other blacks, especially when that tendency leads black politicians, for example, to compromise demands for better conditions with personal ambition.[9] Bledsoe represents the fictional equivalent of those Frazier criticizes.

As the protagonist moves to New York and goes to work at Liberty Paints, Ellison begins to elucidate the tragic disappointments of the Great Migration. Here the invisible man meets Kimbro, a "slave driver" (151) from the white working class, and Lucius Brockway, who proudly characterizes himself as the machine inside the machine and even drinks from a white mug to prove his allegiance. Brockway, who works in the recesses of the factory (which no doubt symbolizes the American industrial economic system), intends to stay like Bledsoe "in the dark," safely unnoticed in the grotesque interior of the system. Although the invisible man regards Brockway skeptically, the protagonist's rejection as a scab by the union he briefly encounters forces him to join Brockway in the bowels of capitalism. Even that niche fails to provide security, which is made clear when a factory explosion hurtles the protagonist into an uneasy rebirth in the factory hospital. In this work, organized labor provides no more support for the protagonist than it has done in earlier black fiction (*Blood on the Forge,* for example), and capitalism has literally exploded for him, leaving him to fall back on the folk roots of Buckeye the Rabbit and Mary Rambo. When the protagonist is released from the hospital and rescued by Mary, the well-meaning boarding house owner, the reader may assume that he has symbolically returned south. But his return to the people, unlike those characters of earlier, more romantic black fiction, is not successful.

While living with Mary, the narrator's speech decrying eviction enables two black tenants to move back into their "dark little apartment that smelled of stale cabbage" (213). When he returned to Mary's boarding house, which also smells of cabbage, and decides to accept a profferred job with the Brotherhood, the historic connection between the evicted tenants and Mary is underlined by the cabbage smell. Likewise the symbolic distance between the individual's poverty and the Brotherhood's affluence is heightened by the contrast between the cabbage eaten by Mary and the evicted tenants and the cheesecake that Brother Jack buys for the protagonist when he offers him the job. At the point that the Brotherhood demands the invisible man move out of Harlem to meet the needs of Harlem's residents, it is immediately clear that the Brotherhood has no real interest in the people. To be sure, urban migration propelled blacks into the political arena, making it possible for them to shape part of U.S. history rather than remaining outside it; and this fact has been treated by such writers as Du Bois (Bles in *The Quest of the Silver Fleece*). Nevertheless, the invisible man, like earlier politically manipulated black characters, finally apprehends the Brotherhood's corruption. Preparation for his political disaffection begins early and, as do the other blind alleys he explores, creates a good deal of dramatic irony. From Jack's assertion that the evicted tenants are relics, "dead limbs that must be pruned away . . . or the storms of history will blow them down anyway" (221) to the warning note "this is a white man's world" (289) to Jack's reminder that the protagonist was "not hired to think" (355), Ellison provides a surfeit of foreshadowing, intensifying the comic opacity of the protagonist. Finally, when the invisible man confronts Brother Hambro, his mentor, and learns that the black brothers "will have to be sacrificed," the full horror of the Brotherhood engulfs him (378). "My God, what possibilities existed!" he thinks later. "And that spiral business, that progress goo. . . . And that lie that success was a rising *upward*" (385). One may be tempted to interpret this passage as a rejection of Marx's theory that society inevitably evolves toward the elimination of classes, but such an interpretation does not take into account Ellison's own statements about *Invisible Man*. In an interview at West Point, Ellison vigorously denied that the Brotherhood should be construed as the Communist party. "I did not want to describe an existing socialist or communist or Marxist political group," he insists, "primarily because it would have allowed the reader to escape confronting certain political patterns, patterns which still exist and of which our two major political parties are guilty in their relationships to Negro Americans."[10] Clearly, Ellison, like many post-Depression writers, believes blacks have been betrayed by all political parties, and he has used this belief as he has fictionalized the political disenchantment of the forties and early fifties.

The final scenes of *Invisible Man*, in which the protagonist confronts Ras the Exhorter and flees to his cellar, parallel the conclusions to earlier works examined here. Ras, the street orator, is a man whom he must reject as a role model, not only because of Ras' "refusal to recognize the beautiful absurdity of [his] American identity" (422), but also because he sees that Ras is only another tool being used to engineer the destruction of Harlem. Moreover, like Josh Green and Big Mat, Ras will finally bring about his own destruction, though it is significant that he dies at the hand of the black protagonist rather than the white oppressors. For this episode, scholars have accused Ellison of betraying fellow Afro-Americans, but it is clear that the invisible man's spearing of Ras represents to him the murder of his own violent impulses. The action is scarcely laudable, but it is nonetheless necessary for the narrator's emotional survival. Ellison, like Griggs, Chesnutt, and Attaway, ultimately shrinks from a violent solution. The protagonist's equally necessary escape into his cellar has been read by some critics as a gesture of defeat, similar to that of Dostoevsky's Underground Man. But Ellison himself sees the conclusion differently, maintaining that the protagonist, "by finally taking the initial step of trying to sum up the meaning of his experience . . . [has] moved to another stage of his development."[11] In another interview, Ellison elaborated on this point: "If there's any lesson for him to learn, it's that he has to make sense of the past before he can move toward the future."[12]

To fully elucidate the genre of *Invisible Man* would be somewhat redundant: the work has been called variously an epic, a picaresque, and a romance.[13] It would appear, however, that Ellison fuses the three genres. The search for identity, the quest that encompasses the black American historical experience, is appropriately handled through the epic, to which Ellison acknowledges some debt, and the epic's elevated tone and protagonist are appropriate to Ellison's mythmaking process. The grand design of an epic, however, is a bit serious for the twentieth century, and Ellison tempers the form by employing the picaresque. Through making his central character blind, foolish, but astoundingly wily, he brings the epic tradition down to earth. Eleanor R. Wilner has compared the protagonist to Brer Rabbit because though the rabbit of folklore is victimized, he exploits his vulnerability to trick his tormentors, living like the classic picaro, forced to desperate and quick use of his wits and emerging from each comic reversal virtually unscathed.[14] John, a kindred victim-hero from black folk culture, is at different times the slave who outwits his master or the sharecropper who outmaneuvers his boss. Ellison's narrator represents an amalgamation of these various heroes. In discovering the extent to which Ellison employs the romance, the reader might recall that in black historical fiction preceding *Invisible Man,* the writers sought to create romances with characters who possessed miraculous powers. Ellison's protagonist, though he shrugs off the role of leader, is resilient; Ellison does not allow oppression to crush his narrator. Distancing himself from the innumerable defeats Afro-Americans have suffered, Ellison celebrates survival.

But to read *Invisible Man* solely as a fusion of epic, picaresque, and romance fails to take into account the characterization of the protagonist, who is surely more fully developed than would be the protagonist of a work of any of these traditions. Such a reading also ignores Ellison's allusion to the similarities between *Invisible Man* and *Notes from Underground*, a similarity based on the confessional mode as later delineated in Peter Axthelm's *The Modern Confessional Novel*. The protagonist in these two works are clearly comparable: each is nameless, each speaks from underground, and each begins by identifying himself ("I am an invisible man" (3). "I am a sick man. . . . I am a spiteful man").[15] Axthelm's defining element of the confessional form demonstrated in *Notes from Underground* raises further parallels. Dostoevsky's confession has two parts, one expository, one in which the protagonist recounts various events. Likewise, *Invisible Man* begins with a long narrative, moves to re-enacting the story, then returns to narration. The protagonist of *Notes from Underground*, Axthelm states, pits himself "against the external world." His "self-discovery . . . is achieved through an understanding of his relations with others."[16] In these respects, the two works are undeniably similar. But ultimately, *Invisible Man* should not be read as pure confession any more than it should be read as pure epic, romance, or picaresque. Unlike the protagonist of *Notes from Underground*, the invisible man is not obsessed with suffering, with hyperconsciousness. He cannot be said to suffer from inescapable pain. The reader cannot imagine the invisible man proclaiming, as does the Russian, "Every decent man of our age must be a coward and a slave" (217). And finally, Ellison's protagonist, though anti-heroic, declares, "Despite the Brotherhood, I believe . . . in action" (11). The under-ground man, in contrast, is ultimately passive, inert. In short, Ellison uses the confessional tradition to *augment* the other genres. Through it, he can enrich the characterization of picaresque, romance, and epic in order to impart the notion that one must look inward to discover reality. Introspection provides the anodyne to the vicissitudes of the world of the forties and early fifties, a time in which, according to Chester E. Eisinger, uncertainty and dissatisfaction were dominating principles.[17]

In the period between 1941 and 1953, writers were urged to produce literature carefully democratic and anti-fascistic. For Ellison, however, it is not enough to repudiate the Communist party and extol democracy. Democracy as he presents it in *Invisible Man* is facile and formulaic, making promises it cannot fulfill. Just as Norton quotes Emerson with no genuine understanding of him, so have Americans failed to retain the original democratic spirit, failed to transcend ideologies. Ellison seeks to inform the notion of democracy with new life, to call for a recrudescence of faith in America's infinite possibilities. The chief significance of *Invisible Man*, Ellison says, is "its attempt to return to the mood of personal moral responsibility for democracy which typified the best of our nineteenth-century fiction." He goes on to define that fiction as those novels that are "imaginative projections of the conflicts within the human heart which arose when the sacred principles of the Constitution and the Bill of Rights clashed with the practical exigencies of human greed and fear, hate and love."[18] In returning to this "mood of personal moral responsibility for democracy," Ellison wishes to create fiction that laments what he perceives as the sterile, mechanistic qualities of both quasi-democracy and Marxism. Ideologies must give way to a humanistic conception of history and the black's place in it.

Such a concept of history, or more properly such a return to innocence, can accrue for Americans, black or white, through literature. An artist who recreates history can help readers understand the past, just as the invisible man comes to understand his past, both personal and racial. In his remarks before the 1977 MLA, Joe Weixlmann stated that the literary and social concept developing in American literature is "the untrustworthiness of past historical accounts." Weixlmann listed several novels that typify this trend, with *Invisible Man* first on the list.[19] Arna Bontemps no doubt initiated the trend; however, Ellison represents a turning point, since Baldwin, and later Ernest J. Gaines, Alex Haley, William Melvin Kelley, Toni Morrison, and many others have shared this impulse to reinterpret the past. Like the invisible man, the audience, according to Ellison, must realize that history is a boomerang that "moves in a parabola. . . . There is implicit in the image the old idea that those who do not learn from history are doomed to repeat its mistakes. History comes back and hits you."[20] Ellison adheres to three principles. First, despite Marx, history may repeat itself, may be reversible. Second, history is not a cyclical forward movement, evolving inevitably toward utopia. Third, and perhaps most significantly, history is not explicable through abstract theory. Theory, Ellison believes, is limiting. Instead, history represent "another form of man trying to find himself and come to grips with his own complexity, but within the framework of chronology and time."[21] The history Ellison fictionalizes, then, strives toward the mythopoeic.

History in *Invisible Man* is mythic in at least two ways. First, the epic qualities of the protagonist's quest elevate both his life and black history far beyond the literal. Second, the events and characters do not directly parallel history. Ellison has insisted on this point many times; yet some critics continue to draw exact parallels between Ras and Marcus Garvey, the Founder and Booker T. Washington, the Harlem riot and the riot of 1943. Ellison seeks to prevent such facile correspondences by referring to Garvey and Washington as separate people in the novel, totally apart from Ras and the Founder. Further, he makes no reference to the Depression, though the novel probably takes place during that time. John F. Callahan has suggested that Ellison makes these distinctions in order to use both differences *and* associations in history and fiction.[22] Ellison's own statement in *Shadow and Act* lends further support to the idea of the fusion of history and myth in the novel.

> When I started writing *Invisible Man* I was reading Lord Raglan's *The Hero*, in which he goes into figures of history and myth to account for the features which make for the mythic hero and at the same time I got to thinking about the ambiguity of Negro leadership during that period. This was the late Forties and I kept trying to account for the fact that when the chips were down, the Negro leaders did not represent the Negro community.[23]

In an interview at West Point, Ellison again describes the influence that *The Hero* had on his novel: "the human imagination finds it necessary to take exemplary people – charismatic personalities, cultural heroes – and enlarge upon them. The myth-making tendency of the human imagination enlarges such figures by adding to their specific histories and characters."[24] The result of the synthesis of myth and history in the novel is to Ellison "a conquest of the frontier; as it describes our experience, it creates it."[25]

The names Ellison and Baldwin couple in literacy criticism in much the same way as do the names Hawthorne and Melville, Emerson and Thoreau, Fitzgerald and Hemingway. And, indeed, similarities between Ellison and Baldwin abound. But before exploring some of these similarities, it is necessary to consider some differences. Ellison was born in 1914 in Oklahoma City. At that time his father owned and operated an ice and coal business. From Ellison's given name, Ralph Waldo, the reader may infer the family's literary bent. After three years at Tuskegee studying music, Ellison left college for a summer job in New York and never returned. Although from time to time he was out of work and, by his own admission, slept nights in St. Nicholas Park below City College, today he lives elegantly. Critic Richard Kostelanetz's description of Ellison's clothing and apartment calls up memories of Griggs and Chesnutt, their concern with the material: "He dresses well, in clothes of conservative cut, and sensitively, sometimes condescendingly, notices how others dress. . . . The Ellison's apartment is scrupulously kept, and filled with the best of everyting, all so tastefully appointed that it could well adorn certain fashion pages."[26]

James Baldwin, on the other hand, was born in Harlem in 1925 and spent much of his boyhood supervising his eight younger brothers and sisters. Unlike the Ellisons, the Baldwins were not disposed toward literature but toward fundamentalist religion, and they lived in poverty. "It's my melancholy conviction that I've scarcely ever had enough to eat," confesses Baldwin.[27] Whereas Ellison came to writing rather late, penning his first review and short story at twenty at the urging of his friend Richard Wright, Baldwin began to write plays, poetry, and short stories at age ten. Instead of attending college, Baldwin moved to Belle Mead, New Jersey, with his friend Emile Capouya immediately after high school graduation. Today in Paris he lives simply, not expensively, and apparently plans to remain an expatriate. The faith in democracy that Ellison espouses even today contrasts sharply with Baldwin's distrust of America.

Baldwin transmutes the messianic myth into that of an artist-priest whose visionary powers allow transcendence of oppression so that she or he can ultimately change history. To Baldwin, the personal and racial past are inseparable; therefore, to grasp racial history, one must first confront personal history. Beyond knowledge lies change, and within each sensitive intellectual lodge the tools for transforming history. *Go Tell It on the Mountain*, like *Invisible Man*, exemplifies distrust of collective effort in favor of individual action. Moreover, although Baldwin's work anticipates the urge to explore and reconstruct history, an urge permeating Afro-American literature of the sixties, seventies, and eighties, *Go Tell It on the Mountain* does not reckon with African history or culture.

The introspection Baldwin demands of his leaders prohibits him from employing the romance, with its de-emphasis on subjectivity. Instead, he turns to the confessional mode to convey his protagonist's guilt, confession, and transcendence. By using flashbacks disguised as prayers to present personal histories, Baldwin underscores the spiritual dimensions of those histories, at the same time focusing on the points of congruence between the personal and racial past. Finally, one must applaud Baldwin's recognition of the centrality of religion in black life and his ingenuity in employing a fictional mode that clearly suggests spiritual and religious concerns.

In a sense, Baldwin's entire canon might be called confessional, but critics have done surprisingly little to illuminate Baldwin's use of the form. Most refer to *Go Tell It on the Mountain* as an autobiographical novel, based on the author's now legendary conversion to the ministry. But to term a novel "autobiographical" tells only part of the story; to some extent, most fiction may derive from the writer's life. The term autobiographical, though it does link episodes and characters to their creator, fails to elucidate much about the way the artist transforms these elements into art. Moreover, authors often augment or alter the actual when they transmute it into fiction. Baldwin, for example, as quoted by Fern M. Eckman, says that Richard, John Grimes' biological father, is "completely imaginary,"[28] but at least one critic has theorized that Richard's characterization is unsuccessful because Baldwin was too close to his material to achieve aesthetic distance.[29] Looking at *Go Tell It on the*

Mountain as confessional probably discloses more about Baldwin's transformation of life into art than viewing the work as autobiography.
Axthelm offers two essential qualities of the confessional mode: the
protagonist's obsession with self-discovery and the suffering en route to
this discovery. These two qualities are very clear in John Grimes's experience in *Go Tell It on the Mountain,* and further study of theory demonstrates more confessional elements in the novel. In "The Confessional
Tradition and Selected Confessional Literature: 1821–1914," Harvey A.
Kail distinguishes between two confessional modes, the secular and the
religious. The latter mode includes, according to Kail, five characteristics:

(1) a conversion and/or calling
(2) a confession of sin (*confessio peccati*)
(3) a confession of praise (*confessio laudis*)
(4) a pattern of separation, initiation, and return
(5) a peculiar intimacy between confessant hero and audience (confessor).[30]

With these characteristics in mind, the reader can consider *Go Tell It
on the Mountain* as a confession.

Central to the novel is John Grimes's conversion on the threshing
floor. Such a conversion scene is, according to Kail, obligatory in true
confessional literature.[31] Because this scene comes at the end of *Go Tell
It on the Mountain* and is primarily meaningful as a culmination of the
preceding episodes, it seems sensible to begin studying the novel by
looking at John's absorption with his sin, a conviction contributing to
the book's anguished tone. Scholars have regarded John's masturbation
as the "sin" for which he feels most guilt, the sin provoking him to be
"saved," and it is clear that sexual guilt is pivotal to John's psychic distress. For John, sex is inescapably connected with horror, from his first
view of two people copulating "in the basement of a condemned house."
When the woman demands fifty cents, the man threatens to cut her with
a razor. John never watches again because he is afraid; still, he sometimes hears his parents in their bedroom, "over the sound of rats' feet,
and rat screams, and the music and cursing from the harlot's house
downstairs."[32] Perceived as degrading, such accompaniment helps to
mutilate John's perceptions of sex. Additional pressures reinforce his
association of sex with evil. When two young and presumably innocent

church members are discovered "walking disorderly," the paternalistic minister warns them that whether or not they are innocent of sexual contact, sin is "in the flesh," and he orders them to discontinue their relationship (15-16). Perhaps most instrumental in producing John's sexual guilt is Gabriel, his cruel stepfather, who uses fundamentalistic religion as a weapon to beat back his own lasciviousness. Gabriel's attempt to vanquish the memory of his affair with the "harlot" Esther, an encounter that produced an illegitimate son, leads him to visit his shame and anger on John. Also illegitimate, John unwittingly testifies to Gabriel's cowardice at abandoning both Esther and her son. But John's discomfort and guilt derive from other "sins" as well, though until his conversion he cannot be said to confess them, since there is no confessor until the conversion scene. Secretly, John takes pride in the intelligence his school principal praises him for, hates Gabriel, and relishes the thought that when Gabriel is on his deathbed John can use his intelligence to curse him. Because Gabriel is a minister, John refuses to accept God because he cannot "bow before the throne of grace without first kneeling to his father" (20).

During John's conversion he comes to grips with his guilt and makes his *confessio peccati*. He experiences a welter of hallucinations, including an ironic voice that urges him to abandon the temple for the world. Further stimulated, he comes to confess his sins: He is "the Devil's son," whose blackness represents to him shame, ugliness, and degradation, and whose evil provides him with the courage to revile his father: "I hate you. I don't care about your golden crown. I don't care about your long white robe. I seen you under the robe, I seen you!" (226). John's confession of viewing his father's "hideous nakedness" (224) seems to him blasphemous, for this sight has led John to realize that Gabriel, whom he has previously associated with God, is a sexual being. Soon he perceives that Elizabeth, his mother, and his aunt Florence share his sin. Such knowledge comes about in his vision of Elizabeth, "dressed in scarlet," looking over her shoulder "at a cloud of witnesses," and his aunt, "gold and silver flashing on her fingers, brazen earrings dangling from her ears" (227). Although John has not read the prayers of the saints, he understands on an unconscious level some of what has passed. But whereas a reader can probably winnow out the good from the bad in the prayers,

John envisions the past as completely horrifying. For John to convert, he must transcend the suffering that blacks have endured beginning with slavery, must transcend the shame he feels. But he must also transcend sexuality; for crippled by an entirely negative view of sex, he cannot differentiate between the "evil" sexuality of the prostitutes on the street and the "holy" sexuality of marriage. If sin is "in the flesh," how can sex between his parents, to the accompaniment of the curses of those same "evil" prostitutes, represent something holy?

As previously observed, *confessio laudis*, or confession of praise, often follows *confessio peccati*. This part of the confession comes after John's conversion in the series of statements he makes to his father, the most significant being: "I'm going to pray God . . . to keep me, and make me strong . . . to stand against the enemy . . . and against everything . . . that wants to cut down my soul" (236). In the religious mode, the conversion is typically followed by a calling to the ministry. Thus most scholars read John's final statements, "I'm ready . . . I'm coming. I'm on my way" as a harbinger of the ministry of Baldwin's persona (253). It is impossible, however, to interpret this call in a completely positive manner. The narrator gives many suggestions that John's conversion is inconclusive, among them John's ambivalence during his confession of faith when his voice shakes, "whether with joy or grief he could not say" (236). Other signs that John's conversion is not altogether joyous include his father's lack of pleasure at the event, the cat who watches John and the saints with "malevolent eyes," the intermittent ambulance sirens, and one parishioner's grim admonition, "The Devil rises on every hand" (238–39).

Go Tell It on the Mountain, then, conforms to several characteristics of the confession. The confessions of sin and faith and the conversion that may be viewed as culminating in a call to the ministry are obviously integral to the work. *Go Tell It on the Mountain* contains other confessional elements, among them the protagonist's obsession with self-discovery, his suffering en route to this discovery, and his sense of his own evil. When initiated, John reverses his decision to live separately and differently from his community and attempts to return to the flock. But his return is, finally, equivocal. Although John may be said to return on one level, his conversion is spurned by his father and perhaps destined to lead to even further alienation.

One additional element of the confession, the intimacy between confessant and confessor, exists to some extent in *Go Tell It on the Mountain*. In most confessional literature, the reader acts as confessor, with the narrator speaking directly to that reader. First-person narration, however, is not crucial. The confession may be filtered through another consciousness, as in Thomas Carlyle's *Sartor Resartus* or James Joyce's *Portrait of the Artist as a Young Man*. Thus the multiple selective third-person point of view should not constitute an obstacle in classifying Baldwin's work as a confession. What is important is the presence of a confessor or confessors. Although Gabriel may not "hear" John's confessions of sin, in an objective sense, these confessions are addressed to him; he serves as the confessor. Likewise, though John addresses his confessions of faith primarily to Gabriel, his step-father's taciturn response does not negate his role as confessor. The failure of intimacy in the confessions derives from Gabriel's inability to help establish the closeness John desires. In contrast, John's veiled confession to his friend Elisha is a testament to their intense comradeship.

Both Baldwin and Ellison proclaim their indebtedness to Dostoevsky, the father of the modern confessional novel. Knowing this, the reader is not surprised to find that they decide not to rely entirely on the romantic genre of earlier black writers, with its de-emphasis on character development. Also significant in their use of the confession is the shared debt to Wright. *Native Son,* primarily a naturalistic novel, attains much of its power from depth of characterization, as does all effective naturalism. A great deal has been made of Ellison's statement that the person who wishes to write sociology should not write a novel, and the Baldwin/Wright controversy stirred up by Baldwin's essay "Everybody's Protest Novel" has engendered its own school of criticism. Yet emerging from the controversy is the evidence that Baldwin and Ellison alike seek not to bury Bigger but to complicate him. John and the invisible man are, like Bigger, products of urban migration. The despair they feel at the unfulfilled promises of the North is no less intense than Bigger's. But Marxism failed to satisfy the demands of black writers by the mid-forties and early fifties, and without that ideology, Ellison and Baldwin turned inward. Further subjectivity allows them to counter Bigger Thomas at the same time they reject external answers. With the confessional mode they exorcise demons, while suggesting that self-discovery is, like salvation, a continuous process, that one initiation leads to another. Hence, the invisible man's series of reversals, each of which teaches him that oppression will continue to recur in different forms, unless, through self-examination, humanity discovers the way to reform democracy. Likewise, at the conclusion of *Go Tell It on the Mountain* John's conversion is only partly redemptive; organized religion offers fleeting sustenance. Other initiations will follow.

The scholarship on *Go Tell It on the Mountain* provides a thorough study of the way in which "The Prayers of the Saints" fictionalizes history; so it is only necessary here to consider how Baldwin's treatment of history is both similar to and different from those historical works discussed so far. Baldwin, like Ellison, provides the reader with a black history from slavery to the present, though *Go Tell It on the Mountain* does not have the epic scope of *Invisible Man*. But through flashbacks concerning Florence, Gabriel, and Elizabeth, the reader re-lives the black experience. Florence's mother, born a field slave, seems to her the "oldest woman in the world" (76). One of the woman's children, presumably fathered by the master, is taken from her and raised as a house servant. After emancipation she leaves the plantation but remains in the South living very much as she did before, "[doing] washing for the white folks" (79). Her warning to Florence that "Death [rides] mighty in the streets" in the North only whets her daughter's appetite to escape from her dreary environment and move North (79). There is a remote quality to these reminiscences of slavery and post-Reconstruction. The mammoth suffering of the romances of the earlier writers is in Baldwin's work veiled, understated. It appears that Baldwin, though willing to fictionalize these painful periods, prefers not to engage the reader's imagination too deeply, for fear he will diminish the impact of the later suffering of urban disenchantment. Baldwin also ignores the disappointments of education, labor unions, and politics that have been fictionalized by Ellison and the others; it is enough that his characters endure the grinding poverty that seems to be the legacy of their field slave ancestry. Harlem and the black church are the world, and they substitute for any treatment of Jim Crow in its various guises. For Baldwin, simplicity is essential. In this brief passage, one apprehends all the anguish of the Great Migration.

"[Gabriel] had once had a mighty reputation; but all this, it seemed, had changed since he had left the South" (55).

Both Ellison and Baldwin, then, fictionalize a century of black history, and for both John and the invisible man the personal and racial past remain inseparable, functioning as tools to self-understanding. Baldwin enlarged on this view in 1971 in his dialogue with Margaret Mead, *A Rap on Race*: "If history were the past, history wouldn't matter. History is the present, the present. You and I are history. We carry our history. . . . We act on it. And if one is going to change history—and we have to change history—we have to change ourselves. . . ."[33] For Baldwin, as for Ellison, history cannot be controlled by political or religious ideologies. The black church, like the various United States political parties, has not provided true leadership. Although Baldwin's later writing is far more militant than it was in *Go Tell It on the Mountain,* by 1971 his notion of the individual's place in history remained the same as that conveyed by his first work. And, like Ellison, he believed in adjusting the myths presented in previous histories: "the liberation of this country . . . depends on whether or not we are able to make a real confrontation with our history [which] has been criminally falsified by white, Anglo-Saxon Americans, who now find themselves prisoners of their own falsehoods and myths. . . ."[34]

Ellison and Baldwin use history to serve as a focal point of fiction; but neither believes, as later writers have, that this history needs to include Afro-American beginnings. Ellison has said that he knows he is part African but believes that most of his heritage is American. His portrayal of Ras pinpoints his conviction that there is something silly about the "primitive," particularly in the riot scene when Ras dons his West Indian costume. To be sure, the time was not ripe in 1952 for a serious presentation of a West Indian or African chieftain; but Ellison emphasizes the incongruity of this costume in the middle of Harlem. Baldwin confesses that particularly as a child he felt a certain degree of shame with respect to Africa: "It was contemptible because it appeared to be savage . . . I wanted not to be identified with that." Part of his shame, he explains, derived from his hatred for his father, his rejection of his father's attitudes. "My father thought of himself as a king, and he would have said . . . we were descended from kings in Africa." It would be erroneous to assume that Baldwin completely rejected Africa, however, for he continues, "In church I imagined myself as an African boy, dancing as I might have danced thousands of years ago. It really was a mystical experience and it did something permanent to my sense of time."[35] Despite Baldwin's ambivalence toward Africa, a deification of African characters clearly would have been impossible in the early fifties. U.S. history books appeared to be predicated on the notion that black African heritage should remain as unexplored as possible. Baldwin writes: "These were the only books there were. Everyone else seemed to agree."[36] A black writer who would mythologize must intuit at least some of the limitations enforced by the time. And obviously Baldwin, like Ellison, wishes to continue in the tradition of mythmaker. John Grimes may grow up in a ghetto similar to the one that nourished Bigger Thomas, but Baldwin insists that John defies the dehumanizing forces that crippled Wright's protagonist. "To be a Negro in this country and to be relatively conscious is to be in a rage most of the time," Baldwin has said; "the first problem is how to control that rage so that it won't destroy you."[37]

On one level, *Go Tell It on the Mountain* repudiates the limitations of Bigger Thomas. Baldwin strives to assure the audience, both black and white, that though Harlem produces, for example, the antisocial behavior of Roy, John's brother, it also begets John's earnest strivings for truth. Much of John Grimes's sense of worth derives from his school principal's assurance that he's a "very bright boy," and his gentleness, sensitivity, and intelligence put him in touch with higher realities that will allow him to transcend the negative effects of his environment. During his conversion, John's perceptions are lyrically rendered, suggesting that he is a potential artist-priest whose early environment will empower him to create rather than destroy. The confession is ideal for portraying John's mythic potential because Baldwin believes that only by becoming acquainted with inner turmoil can blacks understand the meaning of personal and racial suffering and transmute it into a paen to survival. John will not triumph through denying suffering or through laughing at it. Rather he will explore suffering without allowing anguish to engulf him.

Invisible Man, like *Go Tell It on the Mountain,* counters *Native Son.* Ellison's protagonist, absorbed in a grand quest, enriches Wright's assault on an oppressive society so that the assault attains mythic stature. Although Ellison has been castigated for embellishing his protagonist so that he is palatable to the white literary establishment, Addison Gayle, a black nationalist, has felt able to defend Ellison: "Despite its assimilationist denouement . . . the novel remains a remarkable one and anticipates much of the creative direction of the coming years. The heroism and courage of the racial past, the pomp and pageantry to be found in racial customs . . . and the struggle of men and women to escape the limiting definition of outsiders – this is the fruit of *Invisible Man*."[38] Ultimately, both Ellison and Baldwin claim literary antecedents, and both draw also from Afro-American history and culture. Ellison's knowledge of music, black cultural heroes, and history coalesces to produce *Invisible Man*. Likewise, Baldwin fuses music, history, and doctrines of the black church in creating *Go Tell It on the Mountain*. Obviously each work emerges from the black American experience. Each must be regarded as a product of the same forces that shape Ann Petry's assimilationist *Country Place* (1947) and the raceless novels of Willard Motley and Frank Yerby. But Ellison and Baldwin respond to the period not by denying racial matters, as did Motley and Yerby, but by plunging into the white literary mainstream. As a result, their work reverberates with the themes and techniques characteristic of that "mainstream." Disenchantment with radical politics pervades not only *Invisible Man* but Norman Mailer's *Barbary Shore* (1951) and Saul Bellow's *Dangling Man* (1944). Like Baldwin and Ellison, Bellow depicts through the confessional form the internal world of his rootless protagonist. Joel Knox, of Truman Capote's *Other Voices, Other Rooms* (1948), is forced to enter an adulthood as terrifying and as surrealistically rendered as those of the invisible man and John Grimes. Equally horrifying is the world revealed by William Demby (*Beetlecreek*, 1950), a black writer of considerable merit. The preoccupation with adolescent loss of innocence that typifies Ellison, Baldwin, and Capote is also central to Carson McCullers's *The Member of the Wedding* (1946), Jean Stafford's *The Mountain Lion* (1947), and J.D. Salinger's *The Catcher in the Rye* (1951). Such concern with initiation delineates the mood of fragmentation and disillusionment, the search for values, for autonomy, of the period Robert Lowell called the "tranquilized fifties." Although Ellison and Baldwin cannot properly be called "tranquilized," the formful beauty of their work contrasts sharply with the ugly realities they reveal. Their writing embodies a strong conviction that American society in the fifties inescapably thwarts the self. Published before desegregation irrevocably altered the social climate, each work struggles to speak ethically and persuasively, to reach both black and white readers. Confronted with the conservative Eisenhower era, the best each writer can offer is a carefully crafted, perilous affirmation of the self.

6   The Passage Back

William Melvin Kelley's *A Different Drummer*
and Alex Haley's *Roots*

The eleven years that elapsed between publication of *Go Tell It on the Mountain* and *Roots* (1976) were so significant as to alter completely the texture of the black experience and the fiction depicting that experience. Meaningful legislation, beginning with the Supreme Court's decision to desegregate the public schools in 1954, unleashed the long-thwarted expectations of black Americans and allowed, perhaps for the first time, the contemplation of genuine equality. Possibly the most important step in changing the temper of the times was the establishment of the Civil Rights Commission in 1957. This action reflected the tendency toward social justice and prepared the ground for later legislation: The Civil Rights Act and the Anti-Poverty Act, both passed in 1964, and the Voting Rights Act of 1965, the latter of which sealed the fate of disenfranchisement. With the election of Richard Nixon, the mood shifted from militance to gradualism. The subsequent election of Ronald Reagan plunged much of the nation into profound pessimism, as the Reagan administration dismantled many social programs of the sixties, attempted to overturn all of the civil rights policies of the past twenty years, and continued to widen the gap between rich and poor. Nevertheless, there is no going back to the degree of legally sanctioned racism prior to 1954—one hopes.

To recapitulate here the events and climate since 1954 is unnecessary. With respect to black American history, however, it may be useful to recall that the years from 1954 to 1968 included the establishment of the Southern Christian Leadership Conference, the Student Non-violent Coordinating Committee and the Black Panthers, the increasing impact of the Black Muslims (founded in 1930) and the Congress for Racial Equality (founded in 1942), and the NAACP's consequent loss of hegemony. Perhaps more pertinent to this study than the freedom rides, sit-ins and March on Washington, events not fictionalized in the two romances to be discussed, are the emergent leaders of the period (Martin Luther King, Malcolm X, Eldridge Cleaver, Angela Davis, Stokely Carmichael) and the temper of optimism and militancy that occasioned the terms "Black consciousness," "Black pride," and "Black power."

In accordance with growing equality, Afro-Americans have begun to view black history as a pageant to be celebrated rather than denied. Proceeding from this desire to celebrate are several traditionally historical literary pieces, works that fictionalize the distant, rather than the immediate, past: Margaret Walker's *Jubilee* (1966), a depiction of slavery and post-Reconstruction, Ernest J. Gaines's *The Autobiography of Miss Jane Pittman* (1971), a treatment of the century immediately following Emancipation, Ishmael Reed's *Flight to Canada* (1976), a study of slavery and escape, and Charles R. Johnson's *Oxherding Tale* (1982), a picaresque narrative about the "peculiar institution." In conjunction with Kelley's and Haley's romances these works erupt into full-fledged fictionalization of slavery, using black history to fortify the mythmaking process. Numerous writers conjure up inner history, among them John Wideman in *Hurry Home* (1970), Toni Morrison in *Song of Solomon* (1977), and David Bradley in *The Chaneysville Incident* (1981). Octavia Butler's *Kindred* (1979) catapults her protagonist back to her ancestral plantation through time travel. Varying in mode and technique, these and numerous other works underscore the growing desire to explore, to revise, to mythologize that which was once avoided.

Repressive conditions were in part responsible for directing Ellison and Baldwin into the "mainstream" of American fiction in the early fifties; predictably, when that crisis was over and a new era of racial autonomy was announced, many black fiction writers were freed from the need to prove themselves to white academicians. When John A. Williams decries the "literary ghetto" to which he feels he has been consigned and calls for the integration of black literature into American letters, he asks less for assimilation than for acknowledgment. Amiri Baraka and Addison Gayle have taken a much different position, embracing the black aesthetic as an approach divorced from white literary critical concerns, one that primarily revolutionizes the audience's consciousness. Wherever Kelley and Haley stand on this issue, both return to the romantic mode used by black writers from Brown to Attaway, and both develop the romances in a "popular" vein. Both extol oral history as a vehicle for revising official history. For both of them, "black history" and "white history" are inextricably bound, just as are the fates of black and white Americans. Finally, and most significantly, both Kelley and Haley believe that Africa is the locus of black American heroic origins.

A Different Drummer, first published in 1959, reflects the period's optimism. Kelley's use of romance to present action freed from the requirements of external reality creates a fable that is in part highly improbable, in part gruesomely realistic, but that is, finally, positive in its vision of the future. Kelley, like Bontemps and Attaway, invents messiahs who are intuitive and unschooled rather than rational and educated. His revolution is engineered by a man whose diminutive stature signifies the potential of those without apparent economic or physical power. But unlike Bontemps and Attaway, Kelley turns back the clock to reveal the positive values inherited from the mother country. Kelley invites his audience to jettison Western theorizing for a radical revising of history based on those qualities he sees as innate in black folk culture: monumental strength, apocalyptic vision, and regenerative humor. Renewing the separatism fictionalized by Sutton Griggs, Kelley plays with the romance's inherent improbability to envision a mass exodus, one that is both representative of the mental state he wishes his audience to acknowledge, the autonomy of black culture, and believable within the context of the romance. To underscore Afro-American history's legendary qualities, he calls upon black folk tradition, including the oral narrative with comic dimensions. At the same time, he accentuates historical ambiguities by manipulating time and point of view. Kelley's technique veers toward allegory at times, especially in the direct relationship he establishes between the mass exodus and black cultural autonomy, and in these allegorical moments he may sacrifice black life's political complexities; however, he wants to make sure his audience does not misread his signs. Despite the resultant simplicity, Kelley excels in rendering a vision of black consciousness, and his work remains one of the best in the canon, the astonishing achievement of a man of twenty-three.

In unfolding this fable, Kelley first present the reader with a quasi-historical document, an excerpt from the *Thumb-Nail Almanac*, 1960, detailing the exodus of all blacks from a mythical Southern state in 1957, an exodus that spells out the romance's extraordinary quality. Rather than a geographical state, the scene of *A Different Drummer* represents, as one scholar notes, "a state of a mind, a state of being, the state that occurs when one group of men denies full human rights and identity to another group."[1] Following the pseudo-official document, the reader receives Faulknerian interpretations of that history by various characters. That is to say, in trying to define the meaning of and motivations for the mass exodus, the characters reveal their individual views of reality, and, in particular, of Tucker Caliban, the man responsible for inaugurating the exodus.

Mister Harper, the oral interpreter of history for the white sharecroppers who daily assemble on the porch, postulates that Tucker Caliban's role can be attributed to "blood." In presenting the story of Tucker's heroic ancestor, the African, Mister Harper spins a tall tale ("can't a story be good without some lies").[2] From Kelley's point of view, these "lies" are integral to mythmaking, sanctifying the virtues of "primitive" strength, independence, and courage, enlarged to suit the mode of the tall tale. Kelley displays with dexterity all the familiar oral narrative devices. The frame allows him to make use of a white teller and audience, thus extending the story's scope: the African is a paradigm for the entire town of Sutton, not the black community alone. Further, because one episode involves the tricking of a white trickster (the auctioneer), the "white frame" provides irony. The betrayal of a leader by one of his followers (an incident which by 1959 had become a formula episode in black fiction) is here embellished beyond simple predictability by Kelley's outrageous parody. After offering to slap the African on the cheek to identify him, the auctioneer's assistant confesses his motivation, "I'm an American; I'm no savage" (29). Self-parody invests other devices of the oral mode, such as demotic language and similes, with new life. Recounting the dialogue between the slave ship's captain and the auctioneer, Mister Harper explains, "You understand, they spoke different in them days, so I can't be certain exactly what they said, but I reckon it was something like: 'How do. How was the trip?'" (18). Similes, used liberally throughout *A Different Drummer*, are particularly effective in this section because, as in the tradition of white Southwestern humor, they refuse to treat the subject matter terribly seriously. Mister Harper reports anachronistically that the African's head was "as large as one of them kettles you see in a cannibal movie" (21) and that in making his escape he gathered up his chains "like a woman grabs up her skirts climbing into an auto" (24). With Kelley, as with Ellison, the fusion of self-conscious humor and the oral narrative serves to endear him to a more sophisticated literary audience than had read most of his predecessors, but because *A Different Drummer* keeps such a technique on a relatively simple level, Kelley caters to "popular" tastes in a way that Ellison does not.

Although Kelley employs many so-called Faulknerian devices, including manipulation of time, multiple point of view, interplay of characters from one romance to the next, and concern with the deterioration of white aristocracy, he shies away from complex characterization. In this sense *A Different Drummer* embodies popular romance convention to a much greater extent than Faulknerian works. All characters, from the colossal African to the diminutive Tucker Caliban, possess far more ideological than psychological depth. For Kelley, these are folkloric characters, destined to grapple with external, rather than internal, truths. It is enough that the African emerges from the ship's gangway to stand "two heads taller than any man on the deck" (21), slices off the head of the auctioneer, wearing a green derby, with such force that his derby sails half a mile to cripple a horse, frees numerous slaves, attracts twelve followers and manages to elude his captors for months. Unrealistic he may be, but his legend represents perhaps the first attempt by a black fiction writer to mythologize his African heritage, to imbue it with totally positive significance.

But the African's impact reaches beyond the immediacy of his heroism. Without his blood and his legend, Tucker Caliban would not have effected his quiet rebellion but would remain simply a short, taciturn black man, content with living up to the sacrifice for which his father is eulogized. Tucker, though a bit more "realistic" than the African, nevertheless attains characterization primarily through symbolic scenes.

At the age of two, he constructs "something even bigger than himself" out of blocks. "Then he crawled back to it, balled up his fist and punched at it just once and destroyed it completely. He cut his hand doing it, but didn't cry at all. You had the idea, the way he did it, that he wasn't playing" (143). As an adult, Tucker rejects the paternalism of the NAACP (called the National Society for Colored Affairs), saves enough money to buy a portion of the land on which his ancestors were enslaved so he can free himself and his family, but then realizes he must abandon rather than transform the land. Salting his land, shooting his livestock, shattering the grandfather clock given as a symbol of faithful service, and burning his house, he leaves Sutton, and every other black citizen in the state magically does likewise.

The response of Sutton's whites emphasizes the mythic significance of these actions. When Mister Harper receives news that Tucker is salting his land, he gets to his feet, for the first time in thirty years, feeling as he does that here at last is an event worthy of his interest. Innumerable citizens witness Tucker's destruction of his property, querying him about what he is doing. His refusal to acknowledge their queries or, for that matter, their presence, renders them subservient to him. The whites' rapt attention during the black exodus underscores their fearful respect for black power, a response dating back as early as Gabriel Prosser's revolt. It is important to realize that for the first time the rebellion succeeds; the whites are completely powerless to retaliate. Obviously, Kelley dramatizes passive resistance, and direct action is simultaneously dramatized.

As with the tale of the African, self-parody allows Kelley to exalt these actions further without becoming heavy-handed. Bennett Bradshaw, the Marxist-turned-preacher, calls Tucker's destruction of the clock "gloriously primitive" (71) and later inquires "Don't you feel you're on the site of some significant event . . . ? Isn't there something here that taps in you an epic vein, reminiscent of the Bible or the Iliad?" (125). Summarizing the events' meaning, he remarks, "Thus begins a legend" (131). Bradshaw is a rather ludicrous figure, but the reader responds to the truth of his words. In fact, Kelley's humorous treatment of Bradshaw enhances the mythmaking process, allowing the preacher to articulate notions a narrator might not.

Obviously, Tucker's actions make him heroic, in the romance tradition. To understand the nature of that heroism, the reader must remember that Tucker is not physically larger-than-life but "seven-eighths life size," suggesting that "the little man" is perfectly capable of effecting change (177). Not only that, but Tucker is not "a sophisticate drawing inspiration from Plato [full of] the unique thunderbolts of thought that come to men of genius," but a fundamentalist, whose actions are unencumbered by rationalism (127). "You only gets one chance," he states; "that's when you can and when you feels like it. When one of them things is missing, ain't no use trying" (182). Given the political climate in 1957, blacks *feel* they want to rebel; what's more, they *can*. And it is here that Tucker differs from earlier heroes of black historical romance. He is not the first to act on instinct, but he is the first to live in an era in which rebellion can significantly alter the course of history. Writing of the intermixture of history and myth in *A Different Drummer*, James R. Giles has noted that Tucker cannot be seen as a traditional leader of the masses, in the sense of Bennett Bradshaw. Rather, "through understanding the legacy of the African, Tucker Caliban has unleashed a spontaneous folk revolution. Myth has shown the way to future salvation."[3]

Another character whose significance is primarily ideological and symbolic but who achieves near-heroic stature is Mister Leland, the tenderly-presented visionary son of a white sharecropper. Taught early that blacks should be respected, Mister Leland is the only character Tucker trusts enough to confide in about his activities. When the boy asks him why he destroyed his property, Tucker responds, "You ain't lost nothing, has you?" (55). Although Mister Leland fails to grasp Tucker's implication that he is trying to recover his lost heritage, Tucker's trust in him and Mister Leland's perceptions in the romance's final scenes suggest that Kelley sees this child as the embodiment of hope for the South, perhaps for all the United States. Simultaneously, the atavistic element of poor whites, certain that they have found the real leader of the exodus, are in the process of tormenting Bennett Bradshaw, perhaps lynching him. Misinterpreting the mob's noises for a "party" honoring Tucker's return, Mister Leland envisions a reunion the next day when Tucker will joyously share with him both the leftover party fare and the knowledge that he has found what he had lost. The implication, of course, is that in Mister Leland's eyes, though he does not yet realize it, a time will come when Sutton's white inhabitants will welcome back the black expatriates, when the lost Eden will be redeemed. Presenting his redemptive vision through a child's eyes, Kelley enunciates the virtue of instinct rather than rationalism. And that Mister Leland is a working-class white should not be ignored, for at the same time he experiences his revelation, Dewey Willson, III, and Mister Harper, the fallen aristocracy, are bemoaning their powerlessness in the face of the lynch mob. Giles illuminates Mister Harper's role when he points out that, though he comprehends the significance of the African legend, his cynicism renders him impotent to put that knowledge into action.[4]

Kelley's faith in the redemptive power of the masses, which Mister Leland's vision enunciates, is further amplified by Bradshaw himself. An "Ivy-educated" intellectual, founder of the Resurrected Church of the Black Jesus Christ of America, Inc. (174), Bradshaw is a self-described relic of an outworn epoch. He has accepted a chauffeur-driven limousine from a parishioner and is otherwise mildy corrupt (humorously sketched out when he "buys" Mister Leland in order to extract the truth about Tucker's motives). His allegiance to the black bourgeoisie must not be totally misconstrued, however. Bradshaw is not really evil, merely incapable of the type of leadership needed in contemporary society. Kelley sheds light on Bradshaw's meaning in an article called "The Ivy-League Negro," in which Kelley divests himself of the responsibility for political leadership by virtue of the fact that he feels little kinship with the black masses. Educated at Harvard under Archibald MacLeish and John Hawkes, Kelley admits to feeling more comfortable with educated than with uneducated people, though he extols the masses' authenticity. Kelley views educated blacks as devoid of leadership potential because they are inescapably alienated from the masses, "too refined" to involve themselves with the masses' struggle.[5] Tucker's wife Bethra learns from Tucker that her education has drained her faith in the primacy of emotion and her power to act independently, without social sanction. Finally, a leader's function is not to exhort but to assist followers in locating "the courage within themselves" (149). The black rebellion is ostensibly "spontaneous" (191), but some form of leadership is necessary. Lack of education, however, does not guarantee knowledge of moral principles.

The reader knows this to be so from the mob scene; following the dictates of Bobby-Joe, a false messiah, the white sharecroppers externalize their despair rather than mobilize their courage. As Mister Harper asserts, the sharecroppers "ain't got what those colored folks have " (198). If the reader can believe in Mister Leland's vision, perhaps eventually the sharecroppers will arrive at the greater consciousness Mister Harper perceives.

Kelley's concept of history in *A Different Drummer*, though it champions the masses' potential, cannot be called truly Marxist. As has been shown, only the uncorrupted element of the white working class partakes of a redemptive vision. In fact, beginning with post-war disenchantment with communism, black literature has eschewed historical theory. Theories of humanity's place in history, from the doctrine of progress to determinism to Marxism, have served only to entangle blacks in a destructive rationalism, leading to despair. *A Different Drummer* illustrates clearly the effect of an overabundance of rationalism in David Willson, whose entire life has been vitiated by his failure to act on his liberal principles, on Dewey Willson II, his son, who dreams of being paralyzed from the waist down, on Mister Harper, who has sat in a wheelchair for thirty years, on Bennett Bradshaw, who relies on role playing to justify his existence, and on Father John, an old black man whose life has been meritorious only in terms of sacrifice to his oppressor. Ellison and Baldwin pave the way for Kelley's devaluation of old ideologies, yet neither of their historical works whole-heartedly endorses rejection of rationality. Not until *A Different Drummer* does a black writer feel free to strip away Western rationalism and seek to recover the purity of his African heritage, one that weds instinct and action. Rather than avoiding the past, Kelley feels, blacks must intuit its meaning, must act on it. Perhaps in the process white Americans too will allow themselves to trust their instincts, hearkening back to the lessons of Ralph Waldo Emerson and Henry David Thoreau.

According to Ihab Hassan, mock romance is a prevalent mode of contemporary American fiction.[6] Through the use of parody Kelley helps establish this tradition. *A Different Drummer*, while possessing all the virtues of the black historical romance, achieves a polish that no previous romancer reflects, with the exception of William Attaway in *Blood on the Forge.* By devising a tall tale rather than a straightforward oral narrative, Kelley gently pokes fun at the "primitiveness" of the concepts he sanctifies. With Bennett Bradshaw ("why not call me Uncle Tom . . . ? At least it is an old and respected name in some circles") (125) and other characters, he playfully ridicules the stock figures and formula episodes that typify the black historical romance. It should not be inferred from this analysis that Kelley intends to diminish the mythic history he presents, however. Rather, *A Different Drummer* represents a distillation of all that has gone before.

Begun in 1964, Alex Haley's *Roots* did not emerge until 1976, the author's self-named "birthday offering" in the bicentennial year. While different in scope and execution, Haley's work has much in common with *A Different Drummer.* Unlike Kelley, however, Haley has done little to modify the conventions of the historical romance, but he has done an enormous amount toward revising Afro-American history for a large audience, particularly when one takes into account that the romance underwent a transformation into a serialized television program viewed by 140 million people, making it "the highest-rated miniseries of all time,"[7] according to George Keramidas, vice president of Television Research for ABC. Haley's failure to document his sources properly, a failure that caused a legal scandal involving Harold Courlander, has no doubt deservedly damaged his reputation. Partly in response to this furor, critics have largely ignored *Roots.* In his *Black Fiction: New Studies in the Afro-American Novel Since 1945,* editor A. Robert Lee considers as one entity novel and television production, labeling it "defused and neutered costume history."[8] Admittedly, Haley's literary talents fail to approach those of many of his contemporaries, and, as with many works appealing to a wide audience, art and politics suffer. Nevertheless, *Roots* represents quite an achievement. Selling hundreds of thousands of copies in only a few years, *Roots* is a cultural phenomenon, the first black romance to attract the notice of virtually the entire nation, proudly offering revisionist historical fiction and demanding that Afro-Americans embrace their own potential heroism. Other black writers may eventually nudge *Roots* into obscurity, but the literary critic should take into account Haley's profound influence in the realm of cultural history. Published in the same year as Herbert G. Gutman's *The Black Family in Slavery and Freedom, 1750–1925,* Haley's work corroborates much of Gutman's data.[9] Haley, however, is not an historian; he has labeled *Roots* "faction," and the "truth" of the history, like the truth of Truman Capote's *In Cold Blood* and other non-fiction novels, is embedded in the fictive world Haley portrays.[10]

Roots might be called a hymn to oral history. By insisting that his audience acknowledge oral history's significance, Haley reinforces certain Afro-American ideals submerged under a deluge of myths promulgated by the "official" history that whites have written. He demonstrates the close connection between black Africa and black America, and at the same time announces the power and beauty of such African retentions as the naming process and the extended family. Finally, Haley wants to secure his audience's acceptance of black heritage and to ensure faith in the cultural values lodged therein.

The strategy Haley employs for his mythmaking includes the bold design of the romance, allowing him to depict his ancestors as emblematic of Afro-American heroism: intelligent, strong, proud, resourceful, charismatic, and courageous, despite every effort to undermine those characteristics. The romance, which never demands complicated psychology, allows Haley plenty of space to recreate stylized figures who can remain just as remarkable as they appear in his family's oral history. Romance enables Kunta Kinte, the African, to embody the dignity which lies at the heart of the black experience; it makes way for the glamorous allure of Chicken George without decrying his ethical lapses; and it mythologizes a procession of later ancestors, whose heroism might slip away on closer scrutiny. With the exception of Kunta and Chicken George, Haley's heroes and heroines are not deeply memorable. His dialogue reveals little of the poetry of black speech, and when he permits genealogy to subsume plot, the latter part of *Roots* assumes the quality of reportage rather than fiction. Still, *Roots* continues to captivate readers hungry for the appeal of romance coupled with history, and for that reason, Haley has succeeded in enhancing Americans' awareness of Afro-American history.

Given the laws prohibiting slaves from writing, black history would have completely evaporated, were it not for the narratives of escaped slaves such as Frederick Douglass and William Wells Brown. But beyond those narratives lies other history never recorded, history whose disappearance has led to numerous myths. One of the most damaging of these myths is that Africans possessed no culture before coming to the United States. The oral tradition begins in Africa when the *griots*, those "walking archives of oral history," go from village to village delighting people with tales of their ancestors.[11] Like all oral historians, the *griot* seeks both to entertain and to teach, and his or her function is adopted by each of the successive generations of Haley's family, from the celebrated Kunta Kinte, the African, to Alex himself, who, unlike his mother, does not recoil at "all that old-timey slavery stuff" (664). Without these oral narratives, Haley would have had no knowledge of his forebears. Thus does he underline the significance of the *griot* tradition to his mythmaking.

In accordance with this tradition Haley recreates family history by means of romance, an appropriate mode for his "faction." Given the assumption that he is working from actual events, the reader might think that his ability to make use of the improbable, of the miraculous, of the mythic would be limited. Haley, however, successfully fuses the real and the romantic. Not all characters partake of the miraculous, but each generation boasts a centrally significant character who transcends his or her oppression and receives acclamation. In no case does Haley fully reveal the inner life of any character. Most are individualistic; though Haley does employ formula characters, his major figures do not fall into this category. No doubt the most memorable character is Kunta Kinte, as colossal as the African from *A Different Drummer*. Because Kunta is a real person, however, Haley must devise means to mythologize him beyond the merely legendary. Kunta Kinte does not stand "two heads taller than any man" as does the African, but from birth he is remarkable.

Underscoring his magnitude is Kunta's "distinguished lineage" (3). Named for his grandfather, who in times past saved the village from famine and served as the holy man, Kunta is destined to become great. For in Juffure, the Gambian village where Kunta is born, a child's naming is attended by all villagers, who pray to Allah to give the child "the strength and the spirit to deserve and to bring honor to the name" bestowed (3). When named after a leader such as Kairaba Kunta Kinte, the child is doubly blessed. Kunta's greatness develops as years pass. He is the youngest boy in the village ever to be allowed to accompany his father on a trip; he never lies, and he quickly acquires the two principal traits of the Mandinka tribe: "dignity and self-command" (21). These traits prove essential to his survival. Captured by slave traders, Kunta endures the hideous Middle Passage. Despite the three months in which he must lie chained on his back, covered with sores, excrement, and vomit, his resistance lowered by starvation, he goads himself into survival by a promise to avenge his suffering and manages to remain among the two-thirds surviving cargo. After four attempts to escape his master, he submits to bondage only after his foot suffers mutilation. Shoring up his legendary presentation is his admission that he feels ashamed to prefer slavery to death. Were he not disabled, he could survive in the wilderness, unlike the "domesticated" blacks.

Kunta's pride in his African heritage is reinforced by his refusal to learn English. When he finds his self-enforced alienation from the other slaves unbearably lonely, however, he learns to communicate. In time he becomes the local *griot*, the "best-informed source of news and gossip" in slave row (297). But no matter how acculturated he becomes, he never severs his ties with his homeland. And it is in this sense that Kunta serves as the keystone of Haley's mythmaking process. The most meaningful night in his life consists of a visit with the only other African in the county. All the slaves refuse to discuss Africa, partly because their masters forbid such discussions, partly because they have come to accept the myth of the primitive and wish to forget their origins. Going one step further, some slaves deny having descended from Africans at all. Kunta always maintains his dignified reserve, never forcing stories of his homeland on his fellow slaves. But when his wife Bell grudgingly indicates an interest in his past, he astonishes her by writing in Arabic (slaves assume Africans are not literate) and pronouncing the Mandinka names for various objects around the hut, demonstrating that the African standard of living is considerably more advanced than she had supposed. Subsequently, the Mandinka words he teaches his daughter, Kizzy, repeated through the six succeeding generations, enable Haley to learn Kunta's tongue and thus to unravel his own African history. But despite Kunta's success at instilling pride in African language and society, he can never convince Bell and Kizzy of the slavocracy's corruption, a truth his psychological distance from North American culture affords him. The danger in Kizzy's being raised as a house servant is foreshadowed by the African proverb, "in the end, the cat always eats the mouse it's played with" (347). Although Kizzy bears an African name meaning "stay put," she acts out the truth behind the proverb when she is sold for forging a traveling pass for her lover so that he can escape. Kizzy acts primarily to illustrate the tragedy of those slaves whose intelligence victimizes them, her great facility for language serving only to refashion her from literate house maid to grinding field slave, sexually exploited by her new master. Finally, she functions ideologically. Kunta, though more fully developed than Kizzy, also serves a symbolic function. Unlike most of the other slaves, he never accommodates, always retains a sense of himself as noble, the descendant of a great leader, a cut above his associates. For his audience Kunta is the distillation of West African culture.

In fictionalizing Chicken George, Kizzy's son by her sexually exploitive master, Tom Lea, Haley's use of romance succeeds well. Even as a young boy, George displays remarkable creativity in story-telling and mimicry, the heir to the African *griot* tradition. And as a fortune-teller predicts, George continues to be extraordinary. After George's four years of training, Lea boasts that George will become "the equal of any white or black . . . trainer in Caswell County" (470). When Lea is offered four thousand dollars for George, he refuses, sensing George's value exceeds that sum. George's monetary value might be seen as a device to exalt him in Lea's eyes; Haley, however, suggests that George's real value lies in his talent, even though that talent is compromised. Only when he decides to save his earnings as a means to buy the freedom of his family does he apprehend the only value inherent in the oppressor's money.

Chicken George, however, never really understands cockfighting's total corruption. For Tom Lea, cockfighting has brought wealth and status, elevating him from poor white to slave owner, but though attended by glory, the sport exploits animals in the same way the plantation owners exploit people. When George vows one day that a particularly beautiful gamecock that struts in front of him at that moment must never be trained but must remain free, the reader assumes that George recognizes the sport's inherent evil. Unfortunately, such is not the case. Having identified completely with the power Lea has attained through cock-fighting, Chicken George has also become infatuated by his own legendary qualities. Caught up in the American Dream, he gives Lea two thousand dollars, the money he has saved to buy his family's freedom, to put up for a fight with a moneyed Englishman, Sir C. Eric Russell. Lea's losing all forces George to realize that he has squandered ten people's freedom. He fails to realize, however, that his fatal error has been his identification with Lea, his faith in the American Dream and, most horrifying of all, his trust in the integrity of a man who has earned his money through exploitation. When Lea sends George to England and sells his family to meet the debt, George registers astonishment.

Notwithstanding the corruption of George's occupation, Haley treats this occupation as a great adventure, and George's opacity is forgiven. Further, his fame follows him to England, reinforcing George's romantic presentation. A picaresque hero, he furnishes his audience with vicarious excitement and a sense that they can elude defeat. Haley treats George's sexual escapades with the same tolerance as he presents his delusions of grandeur. Even though *Roots* appears in its final pages to be modeled on the post-Reconstruction romance, the handling of George's infidelities reflects today's liberalized mores. His "tomcattin'" is regarded with considerable amusement, though Haley never presents it explicitly. If there is something disquieting about the jaunts on which he and his white father embark after the cockfights, an uneasy suggestion that George is a chip off the old block, these affairs prove harmless and do not interfere with his marriage to any extent. Finally, George is a lovable rogue, attired in green scarf and black derby, who appalls assembled guests with the sexual innuendo of his wedding speech: "De Lawd is my shepard! He done give me what I wants!" (506). And his somewhat foolish scheme to move his family to a new town after Emancipation finally works out well, thus reinforcing his mythic quality.

Only one of George's eight children serves as a significant figure in the romance. When just a child, Tom is recognized as the smartest of the children, as more a man than his father (545). Unlike George, Tom is serious, responsible. Instead of cockfighting he chooses blacksmithing. When the family obtains their freedom and the whites prohibit Tom from building a blacksmith shop, insisting he go to work for a white employer, this twist of fate enables Haley to contrast Chicken George's out-moded accommodationist stance with Tom's militant position. Refusing to compromise with the whites, Tom asserts, "Things don't never get better less'n you makes 'em better" and devises a rolling blacksmith shop (650). So ingenious is his idea that not a single man, woman, or child fails to gape at his invention. Tom's business being an immediate success, in no time the entire family establish themselves as "decent Christian folk" who pay their bills, demonstrate industriousness, and otherwise contribute to mythmaking (651).

At this point, Haley begins to rely more heavily on the mode of romance to speed *Roots* to a conclusion. The narrative gives way almost entirely to plot as characters rush through a succession of courtships, marriages, births, and deaths. Perhaps Haley touches so lightly on these years because he feels other writers have already amply chronicled the events between Emancipation and 1921 (his birthdate). Perhaps he did not wish to overemphasize the good fortune his family apparently enjoyed during those years at the expense of diminishing the impact of earlier suffering. Whatever the case, romance dovetails neatly into the truly miraculous lives of the Murrays, Palmers, and Haleys. Tom's daughter's decision to marry wins her parents' thorough approval, for her fiancé is "de bes catch in Henning" (657). When Henning's ten leading white businessmen approach Tom, offering to cosign to pay off the bankrupt lumber company's debts so that Tom, renowned for his acumen, can run it, this arrangement results in Tom's eventually becoming one of the town's most prominent citizens. His brothers' pivotal role in building the town's first church and school further ensures the family's prominence.

Mythic qualities emerge in the next generation, when Haley's mother Bertha distinguishes herself just as much as did Tom. Continuing Kunta's and Bell's regard for literacy, Bertha amazes her parents by being the first in the family to attend college. As a person whose "ready wit . . . got quoted often around town," Bertha surprises no one when her college performance is exemplary (660). The entire black community attends church the day she brings her beau, Simon Alexander Haley, and their wedding represents the first social event in town attended by both blacks and whites. That Haley has reason to exalt his family's remarkable deeds is without question. And his selection of events to accentuate their heroism plants him firmly in the romantic mode employed by black writers from William Wells Brown to Kelley. Finally, romance works well for Haley's mythologizing purposes. The elevation of suffering as proof of virtue, the legendary quality of the characters, the sense of adventure, the fast-moving plot and the occasional use of melodrama are highly appropriate for his self-described "symbolic saga of all African-descent people" (681).

Haley, like Kelley, champions Africa, views it as the source of much that black Americans should come to value in themselves. He laments, "We have been a people characterized by being ashamed of our past. We have rarely looked at it, even though there may be living grandmothers who came on slave ships as late as 1850."[12] With *Roots* he hopes to counter the myths about Africa blacks and whites share. His primary concern has been to transfigure the concept of the primitive, a word our culture has traditionally viewed as synonymous with "savage." Through detailed presentation of Kunta's life in Africa, he consecrates aspects of the culture from which black Americans derive.

Kunta's early years are the antithesis of savagery. He has many books that belonged to his grandfather, and he is well educated. Religion plays a central role in Kunta's life from the beginning. At birth adults remind him that Allah represents the only thing greater than himself. Above all, the Mandinka must value himself or herself as an individual, and pride and dignity will proceed from that self-love. But such self-worth does not devalue others' needs. Tightly-ordered, Mandingo society demands respect for family and friends. Among other things, Kunta learns never to force another to speak when he or she does not wish it. Africans do have slaves, but such enslavement is either voluntary or the result of a criminal offense. In the course of his narrative, Haley takes pains to describe various rites of passage. Many may at first seem trivial, but all carry great meaning for the West African in that they reinforce the significance of each individual at the same time as they welcome him or her into the community. For Kunta, these rites culminate in the rigorous initiation into manhood: four months in the wilderness in which he becomes acquainted with his tribe's rules of conduct. From perfecting his hunting abilities, he gains respect for the close relationship between humanity and nature, a relationship that negates waste of natural resources. As a warrior, he learns that Mandinkas never initiate battles but are excellent warriors if driven to fight. Further demonstrating their pacifism is the prohibition against fighting among themselves. Learning absolute subservience to his community's rubrics, designed for everyone's good, Kunta arrives at knowledge of his union with family, tribe, Africa, and the natural world. The significance of Kunta's manhood training, accompanied as it is by circumcision, is tragically enlarged because it is so soon followed by the nearly total emasculation of his enslavement, and by the literal castration that he mercifully avoids by choosing to lose his foot instead. By fictionalizing West African culture, Haley divests his audience of numerous misconceptions and provides anthropological insights as well. At the same time, he reveals that a society less technologically advanced than the United States may surpass it in many ways. Obviously, Haley's contribution to the mythologizing of Afro-American history is considerable.

In the transition to Western society, fortunately, Haley's family has preserved some aspects of African culture. Haley lavishes great care on descriptions of food. Not only does he enshrine meals as a form of celebration, communion, and recreation, but he shows that a great many American dishes derive from African cookery. In the United States, Kunta becomes a gardener, thus putting into practice the love of the land acquired in his youth. Dropping rocks into a gourd each new moon not only enables him to keep track of his age but also allows him to remain in touch with the harmonious relationship with nature symbolized by designating months as "moons." In time, he lets Kizzy drop rocks into the gourd, and her delight echoes that of Kunta when as a child he accompanied his father on a significant journey. When Kizzy is sold, grief so overwhelms Kunta that he shatters the gourd against the hut's floor. Paralleling the 662 moons he has lived, the ricocheting pebbles serve as an immensely powerful image of the havoc his master's perfidy has caused.

Kizzy provides Kunta's primary meaning. As his only child, she is the sole recipient of his lineage. Anyone who loses his or her only child, with no hope for another, surely experiences a sense of annihilation. But when one has been wrenched from own's homeland, robbed of all cultural and familial ties, and forced to engage in work that has little personal value, the loss is far greater because a child provides the only source of continuity. The scene enlists the reader's sympathy on still another level: to an African, reproduction represents the pinnacle of achievement. For Africa is a kinship-dominated society, and, as Paul Bohannan notes, this factor triples the importance of parenthood because "rights to the most important aspects of life are dependent on kinship. . . ." In such a society, he continues, "most of one's status derives from kinship factors. Only on the birth of a child does a woman become truly a kinsman in her husband's group. Only on the birth of a child is a man assured of the 'immortality' of a genealogy position in his lineage, or even of security of esteem among the most important people of his community."[13] For Kunta, Kizzy serves as the last vestige of his culture, and she too has been stolen from him. But this loss is not as total as it might have been because Kunta's sense of the family's significance passes down from Kizzy through each generation until it reaches its apotheosis in Haley's decision to fictionalize his genealogical history. As early as 1892, Frances Harper mythologized the black family. Pivotal to *Roots*, and to Haley's mythmaking, is not only the celebration of the black family, but also the assurance that this celebration stems from African kinship. That *Roots* emerged in the same year as Gutman's *The Black Family in Slavery and Freedom, 1750–1925* probably shows that Haley was not influenced by Gutman, although he may have read other studies published previously. Lawrence Levine, Sterling Stuckey, John Blassingame and others argue with the premise that the black family has been the fragmented, unstable unit theorized by E. Franklin Frazier's *The Negro Family in the United States* (1948) and Daniel P. Moynihan's *The Negro Family in America* (1965). Whether Haley was aware of these studies is not at issue here, but it is interesting to view *Roots* as the "factional" cousin of these historical works, even if Haley is unaware of the relationship.

The importance of the family to Haley's mythmaking emerges symbolically through the characters' emphasis on the naming process. As pointed out earlier, the entire African community attends Kunta's birth and naming. When he has his own child, he struggles to convince Bell of the necessity of giving her an African rather than a "toubob" name "which would be nothing but the first step toward a life-time of self-contempt" (342). In addition, as the father he must not only choose the name, but must whisper it to the baby three times before he tells anyone else what name he has chosen. Thus is Kizzy's naming the initial gesture toward preserving his beloved heritage. With each child born in *Roots* much is made of the name to be chosen, particularly during slavery. In fact, one of Gutman's central arguments for the black family's solidarity and continuity during slavery is the use of relatives' names.[14] When given by the slaves to their own children, such names repudiated the tie to the white family, a tie represented by the surname forced on the slaves. One of Kunta's greatest indignities is his toubob name, Toby Waller, an appellation he refuses to acknowledge. Given the significance attributed to the naming process, the reader can appreciate the depth of Kizzy's degradation when, upon her producing a son fathered by her master, Tom Lea forces her to allow him to name the baby. Not only is this ordeal a terrible transformation of Kunta's insistence on the father's right to name his child, but Tom's choice of "George" exacerbates Kizzy's humiliation, the original George being a slave Lea "jes' plained worked . . . to death" (440). Kizzy, however, refuses to allow this abasement to daunt her and vows she will "never regard George as other than the grandson of an African" (438). Partly as a result of her vow, George transcends his name and follows in the footsteps of those legendary African slaves who "prospered beyond their masters" (53). For in their final confrontation, George tricks the destitute, alcoholic Lea, thus allowing George to obtain his freedom papers. Named after Lea himself, George's son Tom also transcends his name and prospers beyond his master. And when George's wife gives birth to her first girl, they name her after her grandmother Kizzy, who exults, "ain't done lived in vain" (539). Bohannan comments thus on grandparenthood's importance in African society: "Only on the birth of a grandchild is a person in a position to be truly sure that his name and spirit will live in the history and genealogy of his people. This factor, combined with that other factor that is so true everywhere—that grandparenthood allows a perfect and rewarding position for summing up the meaning of the life cycle—makes grandparenthood enviable, and elderhood the finest estate."[15]

With this analysis in mind, the reader can better understand the impact of Kizzy's birth and name. Procreation furnishes the quintessential experience in *Roots*. Further, each birth, with the exception of George's, is solemnized by the ritual of narrating Kunta Kinte's legend. And whenever a family member wants to marry, he or she must bring the intended around for inspection. In one instance, Tom refuses to give his daughter permission to marry a man because her beau is mulatto and therefore unworthy of the family's pride in its African ancestors, who believed "the more blackness a [person] has, the more beautiful she is" (29). Although obviously closely related to courtship and procreation, sex is never explicitly presented. In our era, in which fairly explicit sex is almost obligatory in the popular historical mode, it is worthy of notice that Haley carefully circumvents such a device. Underplaying sexual realism, Haley not only widens his audience to include the most self-consciously "respectable" element, but provides a counter-reality to such exploitive pot-boilers as Kyle Onstott's *Drum* and *Mandingo*. Finally, lack of sexual explicitness allows Haley to de-emphasize George's infidelities, enhancing his paradigmatic quality and demonstrating the family's endurance despite all threats. Although the Frazier/Moynihan school claims that the matriarchal structure has led to internal instability, even to anti-social behavior on the children's part, Haley shows that the matrifocal unit need not be destructive. George's family's stability derives in part from his wife Matilda. George resents her strength but does not suffer fears of emasculation. In addition, the children grow and prosper. Only one son reveals any signs of anti-social behavior, and that behavior never develops to any extent; *Roots* is a long way from *Native Son*.

Buttress for what might have been a crumbling edifice comes from another of African culture's legacies: the extended family. With the aid of Aunt Malizy, Uncle Pompey, Sister Sarah and Grandmother Kizzy, Matilda cements the familial unit. The closeness between the four adopted family members and George, Matilda, and the eight children affirms another aspect of African culture that Americans might profitably study. Since American culture has only recently abandoned the extended for the nuclear structure, it is unnecessary to look to African kinship patterns for guidance. Nevertheless, Haley should be commended for reminding his audience of the security that may accrue from an extensive family structure. Given the deification of a modified kinship system, the reader is forcibly struck by the anguish inflicted on George's family when

Tom Lea refuses to include Grandmother Kizzy and the other adopted family members in his sale of George's family. Tom persuades Lea, however, to let them buy the others from him when they re-earn the money George has unwittingly squandered in the chicken fight. After being sold, Tom and the others insist, "we ain't jes' here workin' for 'nother massa, we workin' to git our fam'ly back togedder" (585).

The reader must not underestimate the mythic significance of Haley's treatment of the black family. While agreeing that slavery demolished wholeness by splitting up families, and that the matrifocal structure does exist, Haley also demonstrates that the spirit of African kinship has transcended mere structure to create supportive, loving relationships. Further, such a spirit of African kinship has continued into the present generation; raised by his parents and grandparents, Haley also enjoyed summer-long visits from various aunts, who often sat on the porch swapping "snatches and patches of . . . the long, cumulative family narrative that had been passed down through the generations" (664). Social psychologists insist that the family serves as society's building blocks. The unit, if genuinely stable, vital, and affectionate, will tend to produce people possessing these same qualities. Rather than allowing slavery's splintering effects to doom them, the black family has adapted to them in part by incorporating the African kinship qualities. Such a theory, borne out by his own ancestry, both negates the damaging myth that the black family produces anti-social behavior and calls for allegiance to a group that can furnish a positive identity.

Haley, then, like Kelley, champions his African heritage and reveals its vestiges in black American culture. For Haley, as for Kelley, such recovery of heritage does not lead to a separatist ideology, as it did for W.E.B. Du Bois in his later years. Instead, Haley envisions a unification of blacks and whites. As Kelley views an enlightened element of the working class as embodying the qualities necessary for such unification, so does Haley. When Ol' George Johnson, a sixteen-year-old white vagrant, wanders onto the Murray property begging for work, Matilda, Tom, and the rest of the family take him in. Despite his role as that dreaded entity, a cracker overseer, his extreme gentleness makes it necessary for them to teach him to "growl and' cuss an' soun' real mean" when the master appears to prevent him from losing his job (639). Behind the master's back, however, the Murrays consider Ol' George and his scrawny wife, unbelievably named Martha, as family. After Emancipation, when the Murrays decide to move to Tennessee, Ol' George asks if he and Martha may accompany them. Although some of the blacks object (a dozen families go with the Murrays), in the end they decide that George "can't help it if he white" and the Johnsons join the exodus (647). In Tennessee, when Ol' George experiences most of the same post-Reconstruction discrimination as the Murrays, they fully accept him into the fold. The virtue of George, and presumably any white of any class who would share in Haley's redemptive vision, is that he is not ashamed of his identity. Acceptance of one's heritage occupies a central place in Haley's mythmaking. *Roots* explores and exalts black history, but Haley hopes that "whites too may become more interested in their genealogy" and may acknowledge the intricate knotting of their past with that of blacks. That recognition, Haley continues, "reflects the real potential of harmonious relationships between blacks and whites in America."[16] Central to these relationships is the vitality that blacks offer whites, the sense that blacks have enriched Western culture. Just as Mister Harper declares in *A Different Drummer* that the whites "ain't got what those colored folk have" (198), so does Haley suggest that without the black Murrays, Ol' George and Martha Johnson would perish. And during the Middle Passage, Kunta perceives that on many occasions "the toubob were at their happiest when they were close around the black ones" (193). One thinks of Baldwin's reflections that "the interracial drama . . . has not only created a new black man, it has created a new white man, too."[17]

Haley's vision of the historical connection between blacks and whites does not constitute a Marxist view of history, however. Like Kelley, Haley eschews ideology, contents himself with creating a black cultural artifact. And as such an artifact, *Roots* documents the seventies as perfectly as his *Autobiography of Malcolm X* did the previous decade. With the disappearance of SNCC and the quiescence of the Panthers, CORE, and SCLC, black activism has cooled considerably. *Roots* obviously contrasts with the urge for revolt typified by Kelley's era and reflects the return to more traditional values. In accordance with this traditionalism, his retrieval of the family, that theoretically "dying" institution, is as well-timed as his introducing *Roots* during the bicentennial, a year dedicated to celebrating American history. That this celebration took a largely commercial form does not signficantly detract from Haley's insistence on deifying history from a black perspective ignored and maligned for two hundred years.

Roots typifies its era further. Clearly, it reflects the current, though perhaps temporary, decline of black separatism. As August Meier and Elliott Rudwick point out, the NAACP has re-emerged as a dominant political force, emphasizing litigation and affirmative action over militance, equality over nationalism. With the increasing moderation of the Black Muslims and of Imamu Amiri Baraka, who as early as 1974 insisted "it is a narrow nationalism that says the white man is the enemy," the dominant trend has been toward entrance into the mainstream without sacrificing cultural autonomy.[18] Despite Haley's faith in maintaining this double vision, one Du Bois ultimately found untenable, *Roots* is a long way from *Clotel*'s sanguineness. If *Roots* seems the legacy of Brown's romance as surely as Haley's optimism seems heir to the doctrine of progress, the reader might reflect that Americans have become a bit more realistic — or cynical — since 1853. Few people may have read Robert Heilbroner's *The Future As History*, yet a great many would understand and accept what he calls "the ambiguity of events," the phenomenon whereby an achieved goal thought to symbolize social progress brings in its wake "a new set of problems stemming from that very advance itself." Writing in 1960, Heilbroner warned against facile optimism or pessimism for the future. Rather, he insisted, Americans must realize that social equality, though our first priority, is a long way off.[19] Two decades later, Americans seem to have grasped this idea. Despite advances, Afro-Americans in every part of the country face such a welter of problems as to call into question the very word "advance." For an enormous number of poor, unskilled, and unemployed black people, life offers little more than it did a century ago. Police and Klan harassment are still realities for many. In Chattanooga, Tennessee, Klansmen shot four elderly black women and injured a fifth in 1980. After a local all-white jury found two of the men innocent and the third served only three months in prison, a federal jury awarded $535,000 damages to the women. While this ruling deserves applause, it fails to address the fact that the trial revealed head Klansman William Church's plot to kill George Key, president of the Chattanooga NAACP.[20] In a 1981 San Leandro, California, incident, Klansmembers burned crosses on a lawn, threw a sledgehammer through the front window, spray-painted their insignia on the garage door, and left a note containing racial slurs on the porch.[21] During the summer of 1985, a crowd of some twenty white Chicago youths attacked two young black men with bricks and baseball bats, brutally wounding the victims and destroying their car. Numerous residents of the predominantly white neighborhood observed the scene from porches and windows, none bothering to phone the police or volunteering to identify the assailants. When questioned later, white observers defended their inaction by remarking that such incidents occur frequently in Chicago.[22] In the face of such events, Haley seeks to empower his audience with a belief in their racial and cultural ability to confront and transcend both present and future injustice by carrying on the African tradition of transmitting his family history and assuming the messianic role of mythmaker.

7   Ancestral Quests

in Toni Morrison's *Song of Solomon* and
David Bradley's *The Chaneysville Incident*

The revolutionary aspects of the late sixties and early seventies give way a decade later to what appear to be traditional views toward politics, religion, and the family. Bewildered by severe economic distress and rampant military escalation, black and white Americans of the late seventies and early eighties wrestle with ways to shape their world, ways that on the surface look like old solutions. The belief in radical revolt, while still very much alive on some fronts, is less visible than a belief in electoral politics. Religious faith and spirituality reattain widespread legitimacy. In the black community, the disfavor cast upon the church in the sixties and early seventies begins to be eclipsed by a return to the church as a social and political nucleus, emphasized by that institution's increasing attempts to reinforce movement into the political mainstream. At the same time, Americans gravitate toward the family as a refuge and manifest a renewed interest in family history. Yet these ostensibly traditional views take new turns. Not only does Judeo-Christian religion hold sway; more and more Americans become attuned to supernatural, transcendental, and psychic experiences. Moreover, the concept of the family has undergone innumerable transformations, not least of which is the questioning of conventional sex roles. Finally, white historians begin to acknowledge what Afro-American fiction has maintained all along: that personal history can amplify—or alter—official history.

Emerging from this era, Toni Morrison's *Song of Solomon* and David Bradley's *The Chaneysville Incident* invite the audience to investigate the relationships between North American and West African culture, with a particular emphasis on spirituality and religion, the supernatural, and family history. In fusing the Judeo-Christian and African naming traditions with the notion of ancestor worship, Morrison and Bradley underscore and amplify a deification of heritage. Despite the increase of formal experimentation in black fiction, these two writers demonstrate that the romance still offers exciting possibilities for illuminating Afro-American history. While Morrison's hero, Milkman Dead, typifies the ideological tendencies of the traditional romance protagonist, Bradley's John Washington elucidates the complex psychology of the mythical hero journey. Without question, *Song of Solomon* and *The Chaneysville Incident* represent the culmination of the Afro-American historical romance tradition spanning the years between 1853 and 1981.

The similarities between these two works mark them as companion pieces focusing on a theme of extraordinary magnitude: the African-American must acknowledge and explore the complexity of black history and culture that is symbolized by the term "Afro-American." In the process, the Afro-American must reclaim fundamental aspects of his or her heritage: ancestor worship, the supernatural, and African religion and folklore. Both authors come to terms with the close relationship between myth and history through allowing their heroes to embark on the archetypal quest for selfhood, during which Milkman Dead and John Washington reconcile themselves with their personal histories. Differences between Morrison and Bradley lie less with their mythology than with their fictional strategies. Morrison, a quintessential romancer, fine tunes the convention of one-dimensional characterization by merging the African naming tradition with Judeo-Christian and classical associations, investing *Song of Solomon* with an epic quality. Improbability, the germ of romance, allows for her delightful forays into black folklore and magic. Although the result occasionally may appear stylized, *Song of Solomon* is, on the whole, stunningly realized. Bradley, who also plays with the naming tradition, felicitously conjoins it with the oral narrative. Unlike Morrison, however, Bradley synthesizes romance conventions such as the mythical hero journey (John's quest taking place over three days that span centuries) with the conventions of the psychological novel, so that the quest entails a journey into John's creative imagination. John's recountings of regional history, essays which Bradley smuggles into the narrative with varying degrees of success, may distract from his central theme, but they never undermine the astonishing power and complexity of *The Chaneysville Incident*. Despite differences in approach, Morrison and Bradley have created remarkably complicated fictional worlds, wherein the mythmaking qualities of the black historical canon have coalesced with African philosophy, religion, and folklore.

Morrison and Bradley move beyond the mythmaking conventions of their literary precursors to employ one of the most ancient mythical conventions: the quest motif. Structuring both *Song of Solomon* and *The Chaneysville Incident*, this motif, which Northrop Frye has called the "major adventure, the element that gives literary form to the romance," allows Morrison and Bradley to interweave history and myth at the same time they draw on Afro-American and African philosophy, folklore, and legends.[1] Invested with the particulars of the Afro-American experience, the quest motif takes on entirely new significance. While several black historical writers, among them Du Bois and Ellison, have employed the quest to some degree, Morrison and Bradley are the first writers considered here who make full use of the monomyth, as defined by Joseph Campbell in *Hero With a Thousand Faces*.[2] As Dorothy H. Lee has amply demonstrated, *Song of Solomon* takes its protagonist, Milkman Dead, on the mythical hero journey. During Milkman's preparation for adventure, his friend Guitar functions as a guide who provides the hero with his initial tools for his quest toward selfhood.[3] Milkman journeys from his family's sterile, materialistic world, ostensibly to recover the gold his father and aunt Pilate have left in a cave in Shalimar, Virginia. This journey catapults him into a terrifying but transforming underworld, where he is divested of the accouterments of civilization and undergoes a number of trials. Two of these, a fight and a hunt, initiate him into the Shalimar community at the same time as they attest to the hero's stamina and courage. Having gained acceptance in his ancestral home, Milkman finds he can unravel the particulars of his personal history, in part through decoding the children's rhyme which shares its title with Morrison's romance, and return to the Northern community with his boon: knowledge of his family history. Although Milkman's final confrontation with Guitar may lead to his own death, Milkman's great-grandfather Solomon, that "flying African," has bequeathed him a secret which liberates him from the loss of physical body and teaches him the meaning of transformation: "If you surrendered to the air, you could *ride* it."[4] Morrison tailors the monomyth to Afro-American history because she, like her predecessors, has a strong commitment to the mythmaking process. For the audience, knowledge of one's history will furnish not only pride but power. Milkman's journey, as Lee writes, empasizes that "in order to go forward . . . one must go back—examine the past rather than ignore it."[5]

Through use of the monomyth, Bradley, too, illustrates a firm conviction in the power one gains from personal history. His narrator, John Washington, leaves the urban North to return to the rural setting he came from. Like Milkman, John leaves home with a tangible goal: to bury his old friend, Jack; but he too finds himself completely obsessed by the desire to unbury his family history. During most of his quest, John's state of mind might be described as mad, in the sense of a transcendent awareness that ignores the distractions society attempts to impose. Bradley's opening passage suggests the Call to Adventure, as John receives a telephone call from his mother conveying John's boyhood mentor's wish that John come to his bedside before Jack dies. Lest the reader underestimate the nature of this call, John, the narrator, underlines its mythic significance: "Sometimes you can hear the [telephone] wire, hear it reaching out across the miles; whining with its own weight, crying out from the cold, panting at the distance, humming with the phantom sounds of someone else's conversation. . . . whining, crying, panting, humming, moaning like a live thing."[6] With this haunting passage, reflective of Bradley's love of the oral narrative, John draws us into his vaguely supernatural vision. Ignoring, or perhaps compelled by, the midnight hour, he takes the next bus, thus beginning his quest; both reluctant to answer the Call to Adventure and driven to do so, John spurs himself on with hot toddies. John's departure from his adopted home, urban academia, takes him back to a region whose mythic significance is underlined by the names of it various locales: the County, the Town, the Hill.

After Jack's funeral, John realizes he has been summoned for reasons more complicated than a burial. He resists the wiles of three trickster figures: the Judge and his son, emblematic of the white power structure, who in archetypal fashion function to dissuade John from completing his journey, and John's mother, who has colluded with this white power structure. Returning to old Jack's cabin, and aided by the tools of historical scholarship, pens and notes that acquire a magical dimension because he believes they will help him untangle his personal history, he begins the second stage of his journey and the second major part of *The Chaneysville Incident*. Like Milkman, John feels driven to merge himself with elemental reality: he abandons all but the most meagre comforts Jack's dwelling provides. During this phase of his quest, John enters a state of mind akin to the holy madness of a mystic, leaving the corporal world almost entirely. Suffering through a number of grueling initiatory trials, including a deer hunt, John finally enters fully into the depths of the underworld: his creative imagination. The final section of *The Chaneysville Incident* begins when John emerges, having gained liberation as a result of immersing himself in his history and fusing that history with African philosophy. Finally, Bradley's hero returns to his urban community fortified with knowledge that transcends the historical facts that academia prizes. Until his quest, John Washington, an historian, has persistently avoided discussing the history of the region where he grew up, an area he has refused to visit for years. Before his quest, Milkman Dead has come to accept the notion that he is incapable of flight, a notion that denies his spiritual link with the past. Consequently, he has become shallow, inhibited, and incurious about his history. Both of these men, having spent years evading their personal histories, end up affirming them, typifying the strenuous journey from denial to celebration of Afro-American history.

Aside from their use of the monomyth, Morrison and Bradley rely on the elements with mythic underpinnings that have characterized the Afro-American historical romance from 1853 to the present. Often, events in *Song of Solomon* are entirely implausible; consider, for example, a scene in which Milkman finds himself walking blocks and blocks in a direction entirely opposite from everyone else on the street. Morrison's surrealism extends to her audacity in creating Pilate, Milkman's aunt, born entirely without help from her mother, who dies while bearing her. That Pilate emerges without a navel testifies to Morrison's desire to develop a character with the power to "literally invent herself."[7] Self-created and self-contained, Pilate exemplifies life itself. Pilate's birth, in fact, demonstrates the degree to which Morrison, unlike her predecessors, dares to move into a mythic realm where characters are not merely superhuman but supernatural. As one might expect with such a character, Pilate's magical abilities are legendary. She is "believed to have the power to step out of her skin, set a bush afire from fifty yards, and turn a man into a ripe rutabaga" (94). Although her imposing stature reinforces her mythic image, in one instance she becomes small and pitiful in order to manipulate the white police to release Milkman and Guitar from jail. More important, she is a conjure woman, bringing about Milkman's conception with a potion. Pilate's connections with magic are emblematic of Morrison's contribution to black literary mythmaking.

Bradley is primarily a novelist, as evidenced by *The Chaneysville Incident*'s multi-faced characters, in whose psychology Bradley is intensely interested. Moreover, whereas events in *Song of Solomon* are often supernatural, events in *The Chaneysville Incident* are ordinarily natural. They may, however, stretch the limits of plausibility, as in the three Forty-Mile treks in the Wilderness. Other elements that reveal *The Chaneysville Incident*'s tendency to hover between novel and romance emerge in the oral narratives about Moses and C.K., John's great-grandfather. For Morrison and for Bradley, the Bible is a useful mythmaking device. Just as Pilate and Milkman's sisters Magdalena and First Corinthians call up Christian associations, so too does the name of John's father Moses. Moses's messianic role surfaces in two narratives in particular, both told by Old Jack with John serving as the frame narrator. As is often the case with messianic figures, this ostensible "hayseed" comes out of nowhere. Moses obtains entry into the male community—a Saturday night poker game—because no one suspects that the stranger is in fact the famed maker of "Black Lightnin'"who has built a reputation for wealth ("all he done was try an' keep the greenbacks from cuttin' off his air") and "meanness" (he has reputedly killed eight government agents investigating his moonshining activities) (52). The game progresses with riveting slowness, the players believing that the stranger's ridiculous losses testify to his stupidity and naiveté rather than his awareness that the game is rigged. The final showdown, in which Moses reveals his identity and predictably defeats "the sneakiest rascals north a the County Jail," elevates his status further (54). Not only does Moses trick the trickster; he leaves most of the take and walks away with a grin. Shooting government agents qualifies him for heroism, but when the trickster is black, the rules demand ultimate benevolence. A man of superhuman powers, Moses nevertheless refuses to abuse those powers.

In the second major narrative about Moses, he employs his power for salutary political ends. Himself a trickster, Bradley dupes the reader into believing this incident to be the one from which the book's title derives. In this episode, Moses and Old Jack seek to prevent the lynching of their friend Josh, who has decided to ask for the hand of a white woman with whom he has fallen in love. Although both Josh and Old Jack are folk heroes, Moses assumes gigantic proportions. Initially, Jack and Moses set out to intercept Josh's request to marry the woman. Tracking Josh involves consummate skill, for not only must they follow him on foot, while he is on horseback, but they have no real idea which direction he has gone. Throughout the narrative, Jack emphasizes the differences between himself and Moses, who "wasn't exactly human." After running nearly forty miles, Jack is "damn near dead," whereas Moses is merely a little winded (95). When they realize they must confront a lynch mob in Chaneysville, Pennsylvania, Jack is completely terrified, whereas Moses appears mildly fearful—for the first time in his life. Moses's messianic reputation is reinforced when he disguises himself as the thirteenth "apostolic" Klan member and, unarmed, frees Josh from the thirty-man lynch mob. The incident illustrates Bradley's firm belief in the oral narrative's mythmaking potential, whereby tricking the trickster can occur on a grand scale; furthermore, since the local and state governments endorse the lynching, preventing it mythologizes the subversion of the corrupt law by the lawless. Not merely a folk hero, Moses is a political demigod. With both works, then, echoes of the Judeo-Christian world underpin the romance.

By preparing their questing heroes to accept the lessons of a rural setting, Morrison and Bradley avow the equation between the pastoral and the wise explored in earlier fiction. Milkman and John are each adopted by a spiritual mentor outside the nuclear family, someone considered disreputable by their immediate kin, who directs them toward values distinct from the materialistic ones offered at home. Just as Pilate teaches Milkman how to soft-boil an egg, Jack teaches John how to build a fire. In each case, the sacramental act speaks for the beauty and simplicity of the natural world. Milkman's parents Ruth and Macon, who suffocate their natural feelings by surrounding themselves with useless objects, stand in opposition to Pilate, who lives close to her instincts through divorcing herself from material possessions. Pilate's rustic home, redolent with pine needles and blackberry wine, contrasts sharply to the Dead's stuffy, pretentious dwelling, where Milkman's sisters devote their lives to making artificial roses. Milkman's father, whose guiding principle is to "own things," drives an elegant car appropriately dubbed a hearse by the rest of the black community because the family derives no sensuous pleasure from it. Pilate, on the other hand, who refuses to install electricity or indoor plumbing, has created an environment into which visitors sink comfortably. Overdependence on the luxuries of modern technology and a mercantile society, Morrison suggests, interferes with spontaneity, prevents inner peace. Taking this argument one step further, Morrison reveals that pastoral simplicity enhances self-knowledge. Milkman achieves wisdom only by retracing the historical process of urban migration, leaving his Midwestern city and returning to his ancestral home, Shalimar, Virginia, where he exchanges his new three-piece suit for ancient hunting garb and begins to view the hills not as scenery but "real places that could split your thirty-dollar shoes" (257). Participating in a hunt for a bobcat, which will be eaten rather than converted to a trophy, Milkman awakens to existential truth: "out here . . . all a man had was what he was born with, or had learned to use" (277). In a pastoral setting, he reaches kinship with nature: "he felt the sweet gum's surface roots cradling him like the rough but maternal hands of a grandfather. . . . he tried to listen with his fingertips, to hear what, if anything, the earth had to say" (279). Only after he achieves total empathy with the bobcat as it is being skinned can he begin to unravel his genealogy buried in the children's rhyme he has heard, but not understood, his entire life.

Bradley, too, places faith in the lessons learned by close contact with nature. John's quest takes him from Philadelphia to rural Pennsylvania, where, stripped of material encumbrances, he begins to reconstruct history in Jack's log cabin, as devoid as Pilate's house of electricity or running water. John also gains confidence during a hunt that parallels his quest. As he trails a deer, he recovers his ability to empathize with his prey, the tracker's strategy inherited from Josh and Moses. Later, this strategy becomes critical in delving for the truth of his past. Morrison and Bradley displace the allure of urban affluence with that of rural simplicity in order to demystify the Great Migration's promises as insistently as do Du Bois, Attaway, Ellison, and Baldwin.

For Morrison and Bradley, more so than for any of their literary precursors, union with nature prepares one to apprehend the agrarian wisdom of Africa, wisdom that has long seemed elusive. In some cases, alcohol is an aid to discovering one's heritage. Whereas black writers since Frederick Douglass have regarded alcohol as a symbol of dissolution, a mask for political reality, Morrison and Bradley invert its customary significance. Wine in *Song of Solomon* and whiskey in *The Chaneysville Incident* are viewed primarily as natural substances. Moreover, they represent the heroic success of those characters – Pilate, Moses, and C.K., John's great-grandfather – whose ingenuity enabled them to circumvent the overwhelming restrictions Afro-Americans have historically confronted. Denied access to political, business, and professional life, blacks have found avenues to income outside those arenas. As the only sources of alcohol in a dry county, C.K. and Moses Washington exert control over powerful whites, turning around the historic manipulation of Native Americans with "fire water." Ultimately, wine and whiskey are gleaned from the earth, offering proof of the agrarian society's rewards. In *Song of Solomon,* the recurrent smell of ginger, equated with Accra and "the sha-sha-sha of leg bracelets," furnishes another link between the pastoral in Africa and in America (184).

This kinship with nature and the wisdom it provides relates closely to acceptance of the supernatural, an acceptance earlier writers toy with, but which Morrison and Bradley move to the center stage of their mythmaking. Morrison observes, "Black people believe in magic. . . . It's part of our heritage."[8] Scholars agree that such belief may represent the most notable African retention in Afro-American culture. Customarily, the form taken to present the supernatural is romance, but Morrison and Bradley infuse the romance with new life through intermingling the supernatural with African philosophy and folklore. These elements have been conjoined in earlier historical fiction, but never have they been so fully incorporated into plot.

Communion with one's ancestors, a concept at the heart of African philosophy, informs both *Song of Solomon* and *The Chaneysville Incident*. The degree to which the Western mind rejects this concept is brilliantly fictionalized in the character of Judith, the white woman with whom John lives. Simultaneously attracted and antagonistic to white women, John has selected Judith as the receptacle for his commingled feelings of desire and rage. Their relationship provides a painful psychodrama that, as Trudier Harris reminds us, acts out historical truths about black men and white women.[9] John appears to love Judith, however, despite his complete distrust of whites in general and despite the influence of Old Jack's misogynistic conviction that all women fall into two categories: bad and dangerous. Further complicating their relationship, Judith is a psychiatrist, one of those people who, from John's perspective, analyze and dismember instinctive ways of knowing. Her reaction to John's firm belief in communion with his ancestors typifies the skeptical, rational, analytic way of thinking: she sees his belief as insane. But as *Song of Solomon* and *The Chaneysville Incident* show, Morrison and Bradley affirm the African concept of Muntu (man or humanity), which includes the living and the dead. As Janheinz Jahn explains, "the dead are not alive, but they do exist." Furthermore, he continues, according to African philosophy, "the departed are spiritual forces which can influence their living descendants."[10] Both *Song of Solomon* and *The Chaneysville Incident* depict this interchange of life force, by which the departed give advice to and empower the living, the living honoring their ancestors in return.

Both Ruth, Milkman's mother, and Pilate maintain posthumous relationships with their fathers. When Ruth's father dies, she fearlessly enters into an embrace with him, an act that forever severs her relationship with her husband. Years later, Milkman investigates one of her midnight excursions and learns that Ruth often visits her father's grave. Sexually and emotionally abandoned by her husband, she turns for strength and guidance to the only person she believes to be interested in her. Pilate and her father have an even closer relationship after his death.

Throughout her life, he offers her advice, acting as her spiritual mentor; his injunction, "you just can't fly on off and leave a body" directs her to return to Shalimar to recover the bones of a man Macon had killed in what he regarded as self-defense (332). These relics, which she calls her inheritance, are later revealed as her father's bones, a legacy fitting Morrison's mythmaking.

Extending the concept of ancestor worship even further, Morrison allows Milkman's personal and racial history to converge with African folklore and philosophy in the song of Solomon. In the last two lines of this children's rhyme, which details his family history, two motifs, naming and flying, intersect: "Solomon done fly, Solomon done gone / Solomon cut across the sky, Solomon gone home" (303). Throughout Morrison's romance, names preoccupy the characters. Macon Dead, disgusted by the cognomen given his grandfather, his father, and himself by an indifferent white man, feels certain that he has another appellation of African origin: "Surely, he and his sister had some ancestor, some lithe young man with onyx skin and legs as straight as cane stalks, who had a name that was real. A name given to him at birth with love and seriousness" (17). Macon's remark is echoed in some form by nearly every member of the Dead family, all the rest of whom, except for Milkman, have Biblical given names. Milkman, having received his nickname when a local gossip discovered his mother nursing him well beyond the socially-sanctioned age, thus has a first and last name given him by those denying his worth, suggesting his lack of identity. No character in *Song of Solomon* possesses an ordinary designation; instead, Morrison links characters with archetypal figures that span centuries and hemispheres: Omar, Circe, Hagar, Guitar, Singing Bird. Fusing East and West, Native American and Afro-American, Christian and Classical tradition, all of *Song of Solomon*'s names resound with association. Milkman's great-grandfather Solomon (or Shalimar, the Eastern-sounding variant) carries an appellation equated with wisdom, the name a caritative from "Shalom," meaning peace or prosperity in Hebrew.[11] But Milkman's great-grandfather has left behind his own legend, one beyond that associated with the visionary king. Having supposedly flown back to Africa, Solomon possessed the ability with which Milkman instinctively indentifies as a child, demonstrating that Milkman has all along intuited the heritage Macon

Dead, weighed down by his own possessions, has forced his son to deny. Milkman's journey home to Shalimar, where he discovers the secret of "those flying Africans," parallels Solomon's flight home to Africa. Even should his friend Guitar kill Milkman in their final confrontation, Milkman, like his ancestors, refuses to acknowledge death's finality, demonstrating his capacity for spiritual transcendence. Thus does Morrison underscore the relationship between the supernatural and natural worlds. At the same time, she emphasizes the continuity of the past and present and the beauty of deifying not only one's heritage but one's ancestors.

The Chaneysville Incident, like *Song of Solomon,* opens with a death but ends by affirming the continuity of life and death. Unlike Milkman, John Washington is initially aware of the mutual dependence between the living and their ancestors. When Jack dies, John understands that he is not "dead" but lives on in an afterworld very much like life. In fact, Bradley's narrator never resorts to the word "dead" at all. He fits out Jack's coffin with the supplies he will need in the afterworld: comfortable clothes, whiskey, tobacco, and a gun. Throughout John's quest, Jack, his spiritual father, as signified by his name, serves as his protectorate. His biological father, too, furnishes John with life force: "Moses had left me more than books and papers; he had left me power" (162). Although John at first believes he seeks the motive behind Moses's suicide, he eventually realizes that his search for truth must delve into history pre-dating Moses's life. Remarkable characters in the Washington family stretch back beyond Moses to Zack, John's great-great-grandfather, a slave who paid an enormous amount toward his own freedom and who suffered execution for his involvement in a slave rebellion. But it is C.K., Zack's son, who becomes the focal point of John's quest.

C.K.'s life, in fact, serves as a paradigm for both Moses and John. Appropriately christened Brobdingnag, C.K. receives his nickname in the form of a brand when he is caught writing the last two letters of his father's name in the dust. C.K. not only highlights Bradley's concern with African naming but reveals those qualities that typify the Washington family's heroism. His history parallels that of Douglass and those other fugitive slaves whose brilliance enabled them to teach themselves to read and write, later becoming abolitionists. As John notes, C.K.'s activities reach beyond those of "a normal man" (426). His first extraordinary action after he escapes from slavery is to write a check, withdrawing the amount paid against his freedom, with interest; soon after, he decapitates his father's betrayer, placing his head on a stake to re-enact the rebels' fates. Unlike most blacks of his day, who were prevented from learning the elements of woodcraft, C.K. becomes an expert woodcraftsman; he develops a passion for learning, reading at uncanny speed; and he makes the best moonshine ever tasted, allowing him to exercise power over the white power structure by manipulating wealthy whites to become dependent on his alcohol. But C.K. desires more than personal glory. He aims for political influence. Becoming a writer, he fuses his story-telling skills with his devotion to justice and devises an ingenious plan. In order to destroy the plantation economy, C.K. transports slaves to freedom, ultimately robbing the Southern slave sysem of $10 million. And, while encoding his strategies for obvious reasons, he writes adventure stories with himself as the hero, advertising to slaves the glorious possibilities of escape, in the manner of Douglass and Brown. Regarded by slaves as a "symbol of hope," a self-taught fugitive who sabotages the "peculiar institution" until he dies leading a group of escaped slaves, C.K. records his history in a journal that Moses passes on to John, thus adding another link to their ancestral chain.

To honor his ancestor, Moses imitates C.K.'s life. He develops his own woodcraftsmanship, celebrating his African heritage; he devours books; he subverts Klan activities by delivering Josh from the lynch mob; and he supports himself by moonshining, not only ensuring his manipulation of dominant whites but establishing himself as a folk hero for the black community, thus simultaneously mythologizing his own life and that of his grandfather. As a final gesture, he takes his own life, dying on the spot where C.K. lies buried. By visiting that spot, as Milkman visits Solomon's Leap, John at last understands Moses's death, a death incurred on a "hunting" expedition, as John has described it ealier. Moses's hunting trip involves no quest for deer, rabbits, or quail, however. "He was looking for a man," John explains. And like any good hunter, Moses "put himself into the mind of the game and headed off after it" (388).

Moses's reunion with his ancestor necessitates suicide, a perfectly plausible act to John if not to Judith, who calls the reunion "a ghost hunt." Having admitted to the possibility that he may re-enact his father's suicide, John surrenders to the supernatural, thus transcending the dependence on Western rationalism that has hindered his ability to discover what happened to C.K. during the last days of his life. In these final pages, the fictional distinctions between Morrison's romance and Bradley's novel/romance become clear. For Morrison, the logical setting for John's encounter with his ancestor would have been the graveyard, where spirits might easily be contacted. But Bradley prepares the skeptical reader for John's subsequent experiences. Thus, John moves from the pastoral immediacy of the graveyard to the marginally "civilized" reality of Jack's cabin, anchored to the Western world by his pencils and notes, before he distinctly hears Jack's voice, advising him about how to track game: "You figure too much, Johnny. . . . You ain't lost him. You jest lost your feel for him. He's still there. Quit tryin' to figure where he's at and jest follow him" (393). Suddenly, as John recreates Jack's storytelling ritual, with himself as the *griot,* he hears the singing of the escaped slaves as they run through the mist. As a child, John has often heard singing when the wind blows, and Old Jack has identified it as the souls of Indians, long before the advent of the white man. John suppresses this perception when he reaches the age when he can explain it away by the laws of physics, laws that symbolize for him the rational knowing he wishes to substitute for Old Jack's "ignorance."

If some readers find John's supernatural perceptions difficult to accept, as does Judith, who can only hear the wind, they can take refuge in Bradley's details. Old Jack's voice and the fugitives' singing may be viewed as mere hallucinations brought on by John's cracking his head on a tombstone, depriving himself of sleep and food, exposing himself repeatedly to the elements, and drinking several too many toddies, the latter of which "violate the limits of sanity" (351). If, on the other hand, readers can accept the conventions of the romance, they will readily grant the existence of these voices and recognize the link between them and the pivotal Chaneysville incident, the "official" details of which are unrecorded and have thus eluded John throughout his narrative. At last John begins to imagine, a feat he has failed to achieve heretofore. Achieving ultimate communion with his ancestor, he enters C.K.'s mind, fictionalizing C.K.'s forty-mile trek through the woods, his repeatedly narrow escapes from Pettis, the slave catcher in pursuit of C.K. and the fugitive slaves he leads, and his restrainedly passionate reunion with Harriette Brewer, his lover. A woman who has been sold into slavery during her activities with the underground railroad, Harriette has killed her own husband rather than betray the fellow slaves she has chosen to liberate. John's recounting of the slaves' personal histories underlines his growing recognition of the role imagination plays for the historian, for it is not so much the details of their lives that concern John. It is the unique courage that infuses them, their refusal to allow themselves to be victimized by the slave system. These are the men and women whose heroism has repeatedly been depicted in the black historical canon. With Bradley's fictionalization of the Chaneysville incident, the actual historical event that as he himself notes, "all along had the power of myth," even before he turned it into fiction, his appreciation of such people's mythic qualities crystallizes.[12]

To inspire the slaves to choose death over recapture, an old man among them narrates a fable personifying whites' attempts to persuade blacks of death's finality. Despite white American dissimulation, black Americans have clung steadfastly to the knowledge crucial to African religion that death "is not an ending of things, but a passing on of spirit, a change of shape," which releases one from the physical body and allows free will for the first time (428). Armed with the truth gleaned from their heritage, the slaves face their deaths as defiantly as did Brown's Clotel, bringing renewed meaning to the lyrics and tune Moses Washington has passed on to his son: "And before I'll be a slave I'll be buried in my grave, and go home to my God, and be free" (430 and elsewhere). Expressing courage and transcendence, this song, like Morrison's song of Solomon, triumphantly mythologizes Afro-American history.

John's final tribute to his ancestors comes when he builds a fire, the ultimate act of power, acoording to Old Jack, who instructs John that what separates humanity from animals is not the ability to *reason*, as Western thought insists, but the ability to make a fire. He notes: "Fire . . . gives a man say. Gives him *final* say. It lets him destroy" (42). The Promethean and Biblical suggestions of John's act, and the peace with which he burns the notes he no longer needs, since they have been transformed by imagination into mythic vision, is shared only part-way with Judith. He hopes she will understand why he has destroyed these notes, but he is unsure. Although Judith's family, the white Virginia "aristocracy," has a history inextricably bound with John's, he has not yet allowed himself to reveal that connection to her. Unlike Alex Haley, who maintains that blacks and whites must celebrate their mutual American heritage, Bradley shies away from easy answers. "There was a lot that I needed that she would never understand. For she was a woman and she was white, and though I loved her there were points of reference that we did not share. And never would" (384). Thus does Bradley insist on the complexity and disparity of Afro-American and Anglo-American historical visions.

Through John's initiation, Bradley urges the audience toward a concept that has inhered in black historical fiction since the nineteenth century: the romance is an excellent vehicle for bringing history and myth together. For not until John Washington moves beyond the concrete particulars of his past to imaginatively reconstruct history can he piece together the facts, achieve total empathy with and deify the ancestor Moses kills himself trying to reach. For Moses, it is necessary to duplicate C.K.'s life; frustrated in his search for his grandfather, he forgets the fundamental law of tracking: the tracker's empathy with his game must not subsume his own identity. Ultimately, the hunter must return to this world. John's time to "go home" has not yet come; rather, he can reach C.K. through making an imaginative leap into history, remaining alive to defy Jack's death, to assume the role of storyteller, to convey not only the historical facts but also the African myth transplanted to America and developed down through the centuries. Unlike Moses, John can return from his passage back to offer the truth of his heritage to humanity. Thus, Bradley suggests that one cannot understand history without accepting the fact that history and myth intertwine. By overturning the racist myths that have falsified black history and wedding facts with African philosophy, the black historian becomes a mythmaker.

Morrison and Bradley have synthesized all the mythmaking qualities of the black historical literary canon with African folklore and philosophy, Morrison basing *Song of Solomon* on the Gullah folktale about slaves flying back to Africa and Bradley underpinning *The Chaneysville Incident* with African philosophy. In almost every feature of these two works typifying black historical fiction, one hears African echoes. The miraculous quality of all the heroic characters—Pilate, Solomon, Moses, C.K., and lastly, Milkman and John—stems not only from their deeds but from the close kinship they have—or find—with Africa. Moreover, these writers' oral narratives perpetuate the *griot* tradition, Bradley through his frame narrations, Morrison through her self-acknowledged strivings to "remove the print-quality of language to put back the oral quality, where intonation, volume, gesture" predominate.[13] At the same time, they reckon with history's complexity through complicated time shifts, revealing the relationship between fact and imagination.

Spirituality permeates black historical fiction, but Morrison and Bradley go one step further, clearly enunciating the interrelationship of Judeo-Christian and African religion. Morrison lures the reader into expecting a fictionalization of the Biblical song of Solomon but replaces Christian associations with African ones. Bradley contends that what have passed in black culture for Christian beliefs have really been Africanisms, especially the concept of an afterlife. Both, then, emphasize the centrality of religion to black life, a religion that reclaims African philosophy and re-envisions Christianity. Bradley, in particular, shuns those destructive tenets of Christianity—for example, the belief that blacks are denied access to heaven. This concern with religion in part explains why these two writers are among the first to acknowledge the degree to which the supernatural functions as a significant aspect of Afro-American culture, to show that the supernatural and instinctive aspects of the pastoral are pivotal to knowing. Communion with ancestors, another manifestation of the supernatural, present in but not central to earlier historical fiction, pervades *Song of Solomon* and *The Chaneysville Incident*. Each writer suggests that ancestors bestow on their descendants will, determination, stamina, and the passion to investigate history. They demonstrate that by recognizing the reciprocity between ancestors and their descendants, Afro-Americans can unlock the secrets of history while honoring those ancestors.

Finally, these two works reveal the mythic possibilities of merging personal and racial history. Each uses an archetypal metaphor, Bradley hunting and Morrison flying, to suggest freedom from the racist inhibitions imposed on Afro-Americans for centuries. Morrison states, "I use [the flying metaphor] not only in the African sense of whirling dervishes and getting out of one's skin, but also in the majestic sense of a man who goes too far, whose adventures take him far away. . . ." Returning to the notion of ancestral reciprocity, she continues, "it is the children who remember it, sing about it, mythologize it, make it a part of their family history."[14] For John Washington, the tracking strategies originating in Africa and passed down through the centuries enable him to cross the boundary between life and death, between one century and another, to "get out of his skin" and re-envision his family's—and his race's—history.

Conclusion

As early as 1853, black writers acknowledged the connections between history, myth, and romance. Beginning with *Clotel*, writers have continued to infuse history with a mythic dimension by way of the rhetorical strategy of romance, thus allowing characters to change history, to become actors in rather than victims of historical process. Black historical fiction examined here is, then, recursive, a fiction that begins and ends with history. Historical particulars, as they appear in this fiction, are accurate, inasmuch as they encapsulate the realities of the various periods: slavery, post-Reconstruction, and the decades leading up to the eighties. Early fiction, for the most part, dwells on historical events contemporaneous with the authors' lives, but as decades pass, fiction increasingly reveals an historical panorama, encouraging the audience to recognize the continuity of the African and American past. Perhaps future fiction will reach back even further into African history. Regardless of the time period or events included, all black historical fiction examined here exhibits a preoccupation with historical events, with these events' effects on the characters, and with a particular concept of history.

In the transformation into fiction, Afro-American history acquires a mythic quality, for this fiction unifies and restructures history into a complicated world informed by the author's ethical vision. It has become a rhetorical commonplace that literature aims at certain reader responses. Black historical writers have created a mythology that focuses the audience on Afro-Americans' potential power, a mythology that encourages a rethinking of Afro-American heritage so that readers can re-envision the past and, thus, the future. This fiction is, therefore, apocalyptic. As such, it employs a number of myths, that is to say themes, images, or character types announcing a world beyond the world historical events would appear to spell out. This combination of myths, this mythology, manifests a distinctly spiritual quality. Pastoral imagery and messianic figures who struggle against oppression prevail. Naming, a pervasive motif, underscores the power to create from both African and Christian perspectives. It would be a mistake to label this mythology strictly Christian, for rarely do writers make direct reference to Christ. Moreover, the fiction rarely posits one deity or messiah; romances often present two such figures, sometimes one male, one female. It is tempting to link this mythology to African religion, which insists on many deities. One might theorize that Afro-American mythology absorbs Judeo-Christian and African myths, developing a parallel mythology not specifically Christian or African.¹ As such, this mythological order remains transcendent, inaccessible to empirical examination.

The natural mode for conveying this mythic history is romance, a mode that allows for the fusion of the real, in the form of historical event, and the divine, in the sense of superhuman characters performing deeds demanding extraordinary courage, intelligence, and stamina, a mode demanding the presence of a state of perfection. Romance does not concern itself with the pedestrian; rather it skates past the boundaries of ordinary living to envision an ideal world. With its starkly heroic characters reminding the audience that good will ultimately triumph, that beauty and adventure inform life, that humanity's kinship with nature reveals spirituality and power, the romance has been persistently derided as naive. Even today, some critics desiring to discount a piece of fiction label it "sentimental romance," implying that its only function is escape. Yet, for decades the romance has dominated American literature, and much "realistic" fiction may be reappraised as veiled romance. Ultimately, romance possesses great possibility for telegraphing to a wide audience their heroic potential, thus constituting a genuinely radical literary form, a rhetorical strategy well suited to mythologizing black history.

One first observes this tendency to select romance as an appropriate strategy for presenting history in the mid-nineteenth century, when William Wells Brown writes *Clotel*. Brown's romance reflects his need to persuade the audience of his characters' "perfectibility," designated by their abilities to attain Anglo-American standards of beauty, intellect, and wealth. Brown and turn-of-the-century writers Frances Harper, Pauline Hopkins, Sutton Griggs, Charles Chesnutt, and W.E.B. Du Bois exhibit the historical effects of slavery and post-Reconstruction, insofar as all six authors strive to counteract racist stereotypes of savagery and inhumanity. Such extremist stereotypes demand extremist response; thus, messianic figures in the early romance largely accentuate genteel manners and minimize folk tradition. When genuine folk influences surface, as in the character of Josh Green, they are generally overshadowed by more conventional rhetorical strategy, in the form of such characters as Dr. Miller. Just as the early writers focus their audiences on the points of congruence between educated whites and blacks, so too they tend to deny correspondences between the Afro-American past and present. Only Du Bois, a transitional figure, suggests a historical continuum by his insistence on transfiguring slavery's legacies.

The twenties ushers in the Harlem Renaissance and with it a desire to cherish those mythic qualities forbidden in the earlier fiction: celebration of sensuality, spontaneity, and intuition, evaluation of folk culture, black English, and African heritage. Yet surprisingly, no historical fiction, as it has been defined here, emerges. Jean Toomer's *Cane,* which concerns itself with urban migration and with the connection between slavery and twentieth-century black life, handles historical matters symbolically and metaphorically. Instead of documenting actual events, Toomer allows the patriarch Father John to serve as the bridge between slavery and the early twentieth century, and *Cane* emphasizes the aesthetic and psychological rather than the historical. For the major writers of the Renaissance, the external trappings of black heritage subsume the nuts and bolts questions of lineage and historical detail. Even as late as the twenties, it must be remembered, historical documentation was sparse; few Afro-Americans could trace their history farther than two generations. During this period, mere celebration of African heritage was a radical act; historical documentation was, by necessity, left for later writers.

Arna Bontemps's *Black Thunder,* notably influenced by Renaissance tenets, did not appear until the mid-thirties, and this romance is a product of the Depression as much as the Renaissance. As such, *Black Thunder* rearranges the romance's rhetorical priorities. Rather than romance serving as a strategy for assuring the audience of black gentility and erudition, it becomes a device for underscoring proletarian power and genius. Bontemps's unabashed delight with his messianic Gabriel Prosser's instinctual wisdom, a wisdom that ensures Gabriel's inauguration of a slave revolt, points up *Black Thunder*'s transitional role in historical fiction. For *Black Thunder* links the Afro-American aesthetic considerations of the twenties with the Marxist prophecies that emerge during the Depression and revoices Du Bois's correspondence between folk culture and politics. Aside from *Black Thunder,* the thirties produced no other yet discovered significant historical romances. Hypothetically, the urge toward political involvement superseded the urge to write reflective historical fiction.

Like the thirties, the forties witnessed a paucity of historical fiction. When William Attaway offers his fictionalization of the Great Migration in *Blood on the Forge* (1941), he provides the major predominantly historical work of that decade. *Blood on the Forge,* like *Black Thunder,* employs mythmaking strategies occasioned by the Renaissance. Attaway, like Bontemps, centers his audience's attention on Afro-American cultural and political power, wasting no time on a refutation of racist stereotypes. Attaway's characters typify the potential of intuitive understanding, the allure of sensuality, and the power of Garveyan ideology; and Attaway mines the romance for further rhetorical strategies to convey these concepts. But unlike Bontemps, Attaway fictionalizes a period closer to his own, and his characters struggle through the decade immediately following World War I, rooting *Blood on the Forge* in the near-present just as firmly as most of its precursors. With Attaway, as with Wright, one sees the impossibility of exploring past history, for *Blood on the Forge,* like *Native Son,* finds questions at the core of determinism, naturalism, and Marxism much more insistent than questions connected with American slavery or African history. Whereas Wright concentrates on the psychological consequences of urban racism and capitalism, however, Attaway wrestles with a concept of history. Still, both delineate the early black writers' reluctance to muse over past history when oppression threatens to obliterate the future.

During the fifties, historical fiction re-emerges with Ralph Ellison's *Invisible Man* (1952) and James Baldwin's *Go Tell It on the Mountain*

(1953), but the romance almost disappears. Clearly, these two historical fictions enter the white literary "mainstream," an entrance dictated in part by the overwhelmingly oppressive decade. And with both Ellison and Baldwin responding on some level to the "sociological" leanings of Wright's Bigger Thomas, it is not surprising that the romance, a genre intermittently in disfavor with white mainstream critics, should be eschewed for modes allowing both psychological complexity and widespread critical applause. Baldwin, who strongly implies that the black intellectual must inquire into his or her personal history in order to shape the future, settles on the confessional mode to convey this notion. Not only does the confession allow space to explore psychic complexities, it brings those complexities to the surface so that the audience can identify with the artist's personal and racial vision. Ellison, who also feels kinship with the confession, insists on an eclectic approach to genre, synthesizing confession, epic, romance, and picaresque. Romance, then, nearly gives way to other fictional modes in the fifties, but myth continues to flourish.

The differences and commonalities between these two mythmakers and the others examined here deserve to be brought into focus before considering those works that follow. Unlike all of their precursors, Ellison and Baldwin examine the black historical panorama, from slavery to their own era, in order to retrieve its mythic power. Unless one explores and understands past history, Ellison and Baldwin maintain, he or she can never become part of historical process. But unlike most of the fiction that comes after Ellison and Baldwin, *Invisible Man* and *Go Tell It on the Mountain* deliberately ignore African history, refusing to acknowledge an historical link taboo among white mainstream critics of the fifties. In contrast to their literary descendants, both emphatically identify with the Western intellectual heritage. Clearly distinguishing them from other black historical writers preceding them, Ellison's and Baldwin's mythmaking strategies emphasize internal quests rather than obviously heroic exploits. Ellison announces the mythology of black survival and transcendence through fusing folkloric allusions with the picaresque mode. His emphasis on black folklore and culture prefigures much contemporary fiction, just as does Baldwin's assurance that personal and racial history must merge.

Not surprisingly, Afro-American fiction of the sixties and early seventies, during which period political activism moves to the fore, begins to take an entirely new direction. Whereas Ellison and Baldwin choose the mainstream as their element, writers who follow them seek to establish literary autonomy. While still devoted to mythmaking, authors begin to turn away from the task of surmounting stereotypes to bring Afro-American heritage in sharp focus. To some extent, these writers, particularly William Melvin Kelley, address Bontemps's and Attaway's concerns: the beauty, wisdom, and power of the masses and the need to engage these qualities in order to revolt against oppression. Unlike the thirties and forties writers, however, black writers of the sixties and seventies take into account the entire scope of Afro-American history. To Kelley and Haley, ignoring African heritage is not only pointless, it is counterproductive. For historical fiction can provide a forum for debate, and insisting that historical voices remain silent deprives both writer and audience of knowledge and, by extension, power. Kelley transforms the romance into the inherently didactic fable, a strategy that enunciates his outspoken political aims as clearly as does his fictional hero, a smaller-than-life, uneducated man almost devoid of the power of speech. With his diminutive messiah, Kelley turns the Du Boisian myth of the "talented tenth" on its head, unmasking the assimilationist tone of Du Bois's concept. Not only does Kelley re-form the thirties working class hero; he makes clear that his modern messiah has inherited his "blood" from his forefather, the African who strides through *A Different Drummer* like a mythical giant. Similarly, *Roots*'s African hero is the agent of Haley's mythmaking, a character who passes down, through the oral mode, African values and traditions. As studiously as earlier writers avoided, and were deprived of, the details of their African heritage, so does Haley cherish African customs, folkways, and mores. Romance serves Haley as well as it served his nineteenth-century literary predecessors, allowing him to turn the attention of his audience to the mythic promise buried in Afro-American genealogy: the edenic quality of the African homeland and the messianic strength of one's ancestors.

The intensive exploration of correspondence between West African and Afro-American culture has somewhat compensated for the diminished urge for radical revolt during the late seventies and early eighties.

Toni Morrison and David Bradley move beyond the natural aspects of the African world sanctified in *Roots* to exalt such African retentions as ancestor workshop, African religion and philosophy, and the supernatural. Morrison and Bradley resort to rhetorical devices identified with both African and Western experience, including the oral narrative, the romance, and the mythological hero journey, whereby the protagonists can return to the rural homes of their ancestors. With the quest motif, these writers underscore the need for black Americans to seek knowledge of their personal histories. The journey back to the pastoral homeland also affords Morrison and Bradley the chance to remind the audience of the spiritual wisdom that inheres in a non-industrial society, thus emphasizing connection with the Africa of an earlier era. At the same time, the process of "going home," symbolizing death for centuries of blacks, links Afro-America's past, present, and future.

Since before the Civil War, black writers have conveyed a significant notion: if history must take myth into account, then romance is the form one almost naturally selects. For romance weds myth, the ideal world, with history, the world of actual events. Moreover, romance permits writers to reveal the duality that Du Bois believed lay at the core of the black American experience. For Du Bois, blacks remained in perpetual conflict, torn between the American and the Afro-American world views. Whether polarities are depicted in violent opposition or whether they are counterbalanced or, perhaps, synthesized into a new vision depends, of course, on the individual writers, all of whom rely on history to shape their contributions to the emergent Afro-American mythology.

Notes

Introduction

1. Darwin T. Turner, "Black Fiction: History and Myth," *Studies in American Fiction* 5 (1977), 110.
2. Northrop Frye, *Anatomy of Criticism: Four Essays* (New York: Atheneum, 1969), 136.
3. Robert B. Stepto, *From Behind the Veil: A Study of Afro-American Narrative* (Urbana: Univ. of Illinois Press, 1979). Stepto does not, however, address himself to most of the works examined here.
4. Claudia Tate, ed., *Black Women Writers at Work* (New York: Continuum, 1983), 185.
5. Ibid., xx.
6. Brander Matthews, *The Historical Novel and Other Essays* (New York: Scribner's, 1901), 18.
7. Turner, "Black Fiction," 110.

1. Celebrations of Escape and Revolt

1. William Wells Brown, *Clotel; or, the President's Daughter* (1853; rpt. Upper Saddle River, N.J.: Gregg Press, 1969), 6. All further references to this work will appear in the text. Arna Bontemps, *Black Thunder* (1936; rpt. Boston: Beacon Press, 1968).
2. Janheinz Jahn, *Neo-African Literature: A History of Black Writing* (New York: Grove, 1969), 17.
3. Catherine Juanita Starke, *Black Portraiture in American Fiction: Stock Characters, Archetypes, and Individuals* (New York: Basic Books, 1971), 89.
4. Stepto, *From Behind the Veil.*
5. Arna Bontemps, *Black Thunder*, 79.
6. John O'Brien, *Interviews with Black Writers* (New York: Liveright, 1973), 13.
7. Ibid., 11.
8. Robert A. Bone, *The Negro Novel in America* (New Haven: Yale Univ. Press, 1965), 31.

9. Herbert Aptheker, *American Negro Slave Revolts* (1943: rpt. New York: International Publishers, 1963), 220.

10. Richard Wright, "A Tale of Folk Courage," *Partisan Review and Anvil* 3 (1936), 31.

11. O'Brien, *Interviews with Black Writers*, 15.

12. "The Popular Mode in Narrative," in James M. Mellard, ed., *Four Modes: A Rhetoric of Modern Fiction* (New York: Macmillan, 1973), 6.

13. O'Brien, 14.

2. Female Paradigms

1. August Meier and Elliott Rudwick, *From Plantation to Ghetto* (New York: Hill and Wang, 1976), 169.

2. C. Vann Woodward, *The Strange Career of Jim Crow* (New York: Oxford Univ. Press, 1966), 70.

3. Ibid., 81–82.

4. Barbara Christian, *Black Women Novelists: The Development of a Tradition, 1892–1976* (Westport, Conn.: Greenwood, 1980), 8–9.

5. Trudier Harris, *Exorcising Blackness: Historical and Literary Lynching and Burning Rituals* (Bloomington: Indiana Univ. Press, 1984), 27.

6. Ibid., 13.

7. Frances Ellen Watkins Harper, *Iola Leroy; or Shadows Uplifted* (1893; rpt. Philadelphia: AMS Press, 1971), 265.

8. Frances Ellen Watkins Harper, "Duty to Dependent Races," delivered to National Council of Women, 23 Feb. 1891, quoted in Bert James Loewenberg and Ruth Bogin, eds., *Black Women in Nineteenth-Century American Life: Their Words, Their Thoughts, Their Feelings* (University Park: Pennsylvania State Univ. Press, 1976), 245.

9. Nina Baym, *Woman's Fiction: A Guide to Novels by and about Women in America, 1820–1870* (Ithaca: Cornell Univ. Press, 1978).

10. Robert Staples, *The Black Woman in America: Sex, Marriage, and the Family* (1973; rpt. Chicago: Nelson Hall, 1978), 153.

11. Barbara Christian, *Black Feminist Criticism: Perspectives on Black Women Writers* (New York: Pergamon Press, 1985), 219.

12. Harper, "Duty to Dependent Races," 224.

13. Pauline Hopkins, *Contending Forces: A Romance Illustrative of Negro Life North and South* (1899; rpt. Miami: Mnemosyne, 1969), 199.

14. Baym, *Woman's Fiction*, 17.

15. Angela Y. Davis, *Women, Race, and Class* (New York: Random House, 1981), 173.

16. Gerda Lerner, ed., *Black Women in White America: A Documentary History* (New York: Random House, 1972), 437.

3. A Necessary Ambivalence

1. S.P. Fullinwider points out in *The Mind and Mood of Black America: 20th Century Thought* (Homewood, Ill.: Dorsey Press, 1969), 75, that in four of Griggs's romances two such heroic figures mirror Griggs's own ambivalence.

2. Sutton Griggs, *Imperium in Imperio* (1899; rpt. New York: Arno, 1969), 40. All further references to this work appear in the text.

3. Hugh M. Gloster, *Negro Voices in American Fiction* (1948; rpt. New York: Russell and Russell, 1965), 57.

4. James M. Mellard, "Prolegomena to a Study of the Popular Mode in Narrative," *Journal of Popular Culture* 6 (1972), 8.

5. Robert E. Fleming, "Sutton E. Griggs: Militant Black Novelist," *Phylon* 34 (1973), 75.

6. Woodward, *The Strange Career of Jim Crow*, 87.

7. Chesnutt Papers, as quoted in William L. Andrews, "A Reconsideration of *Charles Waddell Chesnutt: Pioneer of the Color Line*," *College Language Association Journal* 19 (1975), 144.

8. Journal, May 29, 1880, Charles Waddell Chesnutt Collection, Erastus Milo Cravath Memorial Library, Fisk Univ., Nashville, Tenn., as quoted in J. Noel Heermance, *Charles W. Chesnutt: America's First Great Novelist* (Hamden, Conn.: Archon, 1969), 19.

9. Charles Waddell Chesnutt, *The Marrow of Tradition* (1901; rpt. Miami: Mnemosyne, 1969), 41. All further references to this work appear in the text.

10. Chesnutt Papers, as quoted in Andrews, "A Reconsideration," 142.

11. Helen Chesnutt, *Charles Waddell Chesnutt: Pioneer of the Color Line* (Chapel Hill: Univ. of North Carolina Press, 1952), 21.

12. Woodward, *The Strange Career of Jim Crow*, 16.

13. William L. Andrews, *The Literary Career of Charles W. Chesnutt* (Baton Rouge: Louisiana State Univ. Press, 1980), 180.

14. John Reilly, "The Dilemma in Chesnutt's *The Marrow of Tradition*," *Phylon* 32 (1971), 34.

15. Heermance, *Charles W. Chesnutt*, 137.

4. Visions of Transcendence

1. Arthur P. Davis, *From the Dark Tower: Afro-American Writers, 1900 to 1960* (Washington, D.C.: Howard Univ. Press, 1974), 17.

2. Herbert Aptheker, *Afro-American History: The Modern Era* (New York: Citadel, 1971), 57.

3. W.E.B. Du Bois, *The Quest of the Silver Fleece* (1911; rpt. Miami: Mnemoysne, 1969), 113. All further references to this work appear in the text.

4. W.E.B. Du Bois and Rushton Coulborn, *Journal of Modern History* 14 (1942), 517, as quoted in Aptheker, *Afro-American History*, 54.

5. W.E.B. Du Bois, *The Souls of Black Folk* (1903; rpt. Greenwich, Conn.: Fawcett, 1961), 49.

6. Ibid., 109.

7. Arlene A. Elder, "Swamp Versus Plantation: Symbolic Structure in W.E.B. Du Bois's *The Quest of the Silver Fleece*," *Phylon* 34 (1973), 363.

8. Richard Chase, *The American Novel and Its Tradition* (Garden City, N.Y.: Doubleday, 1957), 23.

9. Larousse Encyclopedia of Mythology (New York: Prometheus, 1959), 210–11.

10. *American Negro Academic Occasional Papers*, No. 2, as quoted in Arnold Rampersad, *The Art and Imagination of W.E.B. Du Bois* (Cambridge, Mass.: Harvard Univ. Press, 1976), 61.

11. "Of the Sons of Master and Man," in Du Bois's, *The Souls of Black Folk*, 124.

12. William Attaway, *Blood on the Forge* (1941; rpt. Chatham, N.J.: Chatham Bookseller, 1969), 18. All further references to this work appear in the text.

13. Phyllis Klotman, "An Examination of Whiteness in *Blood on the Forge*," *College Language Association Journal* 15 (1972), 460.

14. E. Franklin Frazier, "The Du Bois Program in the Present Crisis," *Race* 1 (1935), as quoted in James O. Young, *Black Writers of the Thirties* (Baton Rouge: Louisiana State Univ. Press, 1973), 25.

15. As quoted in Chase, *The American Novel and Its Tradition*, 24.

16. Addison Gayle, Jr., *The Way of the New World: The Black Novel in America* (Garden City, N.Y.: Doubleday, 1976), 116.

17. Henry James, Preface to *The American*, as quoted in Chase, *The American Novel and Its Tradition*, 27.

5. Retreat into the Self

1. The Wright school includes such little-known novels as Lloyd Brown's *Iron City* (1941); Carl Offord's *The White Face* (1943); Alden Bland's *Behold a Cry* (1947); and Willard Savoy's *Alien Land* (1949); as well as the better-known works of Chester Himes (*If He Hollers Let Him Go*, 1945; and *Cast the First Stone*, 1952); Ann Petry (*The Street*, 1946); and William Gardner Smith (*Last of the Conquerors*, 1948).

2. Bone, *The Negro Novel in America*, 160.

3. John Hope Franklin, *From Slavery to Freedom: A History of Negro Americans* (1947; rpt. New York: Vintage, 1969), 578.

4. Meier and Rudwick, *From Plantation to Ghetto*, 270.

5. Franklin, *From Slavery to Freedom*, 609–10.

6. Richard Kostelanetz, "The Politics of Ellison's Booker: *Invisible Man* as Symbolic History," *Chicago Review* 19 (1967), 5–26; Davis, *From the Dark Tower*;

Russell G. Fischer, "*Invisible Man* as History," *College Language Association Journal* 17 (1974), 338–67; Grosvenor E. Powell, "Role and Identity in Ralph Ellison's *Invisible Man*" in David J. Burrows, et al., *Private Dealings: Modern American Writers in Search of Integrity* (1969; rpt. Rockville, Md.: New Perspectives, 1974), 189–94; Harry B. Henderson, *Versions of the Past: The Historical Imagination in American Fiction* (New York: Oxford Univ. Press, 1974), 285–99; John F. Callahan, "Chaos, Complexity and Possibility: The Historical Frequencies of Ralph Ellison," *Black American Literature Forum* 11 (1977), 130–38; Susan L. Blake, "Ritual and Rationalization: Black Folklore in the Works of Ralph Ellison," *PMLA* 94 (1979), 121–35.

7. Ralph Ellison, *Invisible Man* (New York: Random House, 1952), 7. All further references to this work appear in the text.

8. Du Bois, "Of Our Spiritual Strivings," in *The Souls of Black Folk*, 17.

9. E. Franklin Frazier, *Black Bourgeoisie* (1957; rpt. Glencoe, Ill.: Free Press, 1969), 86, 228.

10. Robert E. Moore, ed., "On Initiation Rights and Power: Ralph Ellison Speaks at West Point," *Contemporary Literature* 15 (1974), 184.

11. Ibid., 184.

12. O'Brien, *Interviews with Black Writers*, 75.

13. Stewart Lillard, John Stark, and Charles W. Scruggs explore the epic qualities: "Ellison's Ambitious Scope in *Invisible Man*," *English Journal* 58 (1969), 833–39; "*Invisible Man*: Ellison's Black Odyssey," *Black American Literature Forum* 7 (1973), 60–63; "Ralph Ellison's Use of the *Aeneid* in *Invisible Man*," *College Language Association Journal* 17 (1974), 368–78. Eleanor R. Wilner and Bone demonstrate that the work contains picaresque elements: "The Invisible Black Thread: Identity and Nonentity in *Invisible Man*," *College Language Association Journal* 13 (1970), 242–57; "Ralph Ellison and the Uses of Imagination," in John M. Reilly, ed., *Twentieth Century Interpretations of "Invisible Man*," (Englewood Cliffs, N.J.: Prentice-Hall, 1970), 22–31. Louis D. Mitchell calls the work a romance: "Invisibility – Permanent or Resurrective," *College Language Association Journal* 17 (1974), 380. Stepto, questioning the relevance of any of these genres to Afro-American literature, suggests that Ellison tries to fuse and go beyond ascent and immersion narratives: *From Behind the Veil*, 1967–94.

14. Wilner, "The Invisible Black Thread," 245.

15. Feodor Dostoevsky, *Three Short Novels of Dostoevsky*, trans. Constance Garnett (Garden City, N.Y.: Doubleday, 1960), 8. All further references to this work appear in the text.

16. Peter Axthelm, *The Modern Confessional Novel* (New Haven: Yale Univ. Press, 1967), 13–17.

17. Chester E. Eisinger, *Fiction of the Forties* (Chicago: Univ. of Chicago Press, 1963), 1–20.

18. Ralph Ellison, *Shadow and Act*, (New York, Random House, 1964), 111, 113.

19. Joe Weixlmann, "The Uses and Meaning of History in Modern Black American Fiction," *Black American Literature Forum* 11 (1978), 123.

20. O'Brien, *Interviews with Black Writers*, 73.

21. *Southern Literary Journal* 1 (1969), as quoted in John F. Callahan, "Chaos, Complexity, and Possibility," 130.

22. Ibid., 134.

23. *Shadow and Act*, 37.

24. Robert E. Moore, ed., "On Initiation Rites and Power: Ralph Ellison Speaks at West Point."

25. *Shadow and Act*, 183.

26. Richard Kostelanetz, "Ralph Ellison: "Novelist as Brown-Skinned Aristocrat," *Shenandoah* 20 (1969), 66.

27. Fern M. Eckman, *The Furious Passage of James Baldwin* (New York: M. Evans, 1966), 37.

28. Ibid., 99.

29. Wallace Graves, "The Question of Moral Energy in James Baldwin's *Go Tell It on the Mountain*," *College Language Association Journal* 7 (1964), 219–20.

30. Harvey A. Kail, "The Confessional Tradition and Selected Confessional Literature: 1821–1914," diss., Northern Illinois Univ., 1977.

31. Ibid., 4.

32. James Baldwin, *Go Tell It on the Mountain* (New York: Dial, 1953), 10–11. All further references to this work appear in the text.

33. Baldwin and Margaret Mead, *A Rap on Race* (Philadelphia: Lippincott, 1971), 188.

34. Hoyt Fuller, "Reverberations from a Writer's Conference," *African Forum* 1 (1965), 79, as quoted in Fred L. Standley, "James Baldwin: The Artist as Incorrigible Disturber of the Peace," *Southern Humanities Review* 4 (1970), 18–19.

35. Harold R. Isaacs, "Five Writers and Their African Ancestors, Part II," *Phylon* 21 (1960), 327–28.

36. Eckman, *The Furious Passage of James Baldwin*, 78.

37. "The Negro in American Culture," with Nat Hentoff, Emile Capouya, Lorraine Hansberry, Langston Hughes, Alfred Kazin, WABI-FM (New York), 1969, as quoted in C.W.E. Bigsby, *The Black Writer*, Vol. 2 (Deland, Fla.: Everett Edwards, 1969), 80.

38. Gayle, *The Way of the New World*, 258.

6. The Passage Back

1. Donald M. Weyl, "The Vision of Man in the Novels of William Melvin Kelley," *Critique* 15 (1974), 20.

2. William Melvin Kelley, *A Different Drummer* (1959; rpt. Garden City, N.Y.: Doubleday, 1969), 17. All further references to this work appear in the text.

3. James R. Giles, "Revolution and Myth: Kelley's *A Different Drummer* and Gaines's *The Autobiography of Miss Jane Pittman*," *Minority Voices* 1 (1977), 44.

4. Ibid., 41.

5. William Melvin Kelley, "The Ivy League Negro," *Esquire* (Aug. 1963), 109.

6. Ihab Hassan, *Contemporary American Literature: 1945–1972* (New York: Frederick Ungar, 1973), 1.

7. Telephone interview with George Keramidas, Vice-President, Television Research, American Broadcasting Company, 17 June 1982.

8. A. Robert Lee, ed., *Black Fiction: New Studies in the Afro-American Novel Since 1945* (New York: Barnes and Noble, 1980), 226.

9. Herbert G. Gutman, *The Black Family in Slavery and Freedom, 1750–1925* (New York: Pantheon), 1976.

10. "A Talk with Alex Haley," *NYTBR* (26 Sept. 1976), 2.

11. Alex Haley, *Roots* (Garden City, N.Y.: Doubleday, 1976), 674. All further references to this work appear in the text.

12. "A Talk with Alex Haley," 10.

13. Paul Bohannan, *Africa and Africans* (1964; rpt. Garden City, N.Y.: Natural History Press, 1971), 173.

14. Gutman, *The Black Family in Slavery and Freedom, 1750–1925,* 190.

15. Bohannan, *Africa and Africans,* 173.

16. "A Talk with Alex Haley," 10.

17. James Baldwin, *Notes of a Native Son* (1955; rpt. New York: Bantam, 1968), 148.

18. Meier and Rudwick, *From Plantation to Ghetto,* 356.

19. Robert L. Heilbroner, *The Future As History* (New York: Grove, 1960), 201–2.

20. The Southern Poverty Law Center, *Intelligence Report.*

21. National Anti-Klan Network, *Newsletter* (Atlanta: NAKN, 1982), 1.

22. "Attack on 2 Blacks Barely Draws Notice," *Chicago Tribune* (12 July 1985), Sec. 2, 1, 5.

7. Ancestral Quests

1. Frye, *Anatomy of Criticism,* 187.

2. Joseph Campbell, *Hero With A Thousand Faces* (1949; rpt. Cleveland: World, 1970).

3. Dorothy H. Lee, "*Song of Solomon*: To Ride The Air," *Black American Literature Forum* 16 (1982), 64–70.

4. Toni Morrison, *Song of Solomon* (New York: Knopf, 1977), 337. All further references to this work appear in the text.

5. Lee, "*Song of Solomon*," 70.

6. David Bradley, *The Chaneysville Incident* (New York: Harper and Row, 1981), 1. All further references to this work appear in the text.

7. Tate, ed., *Black Women Writers at Work*, 128.

8. Mel Watkins, "Talk with Toni Morrison," *NYTBR* (11 Sept. 1977), 50.

9. Harris, *Exorcising Blackness*, 162–83.

10. Janheinz Jahn, *Mantu*, trans. Marjorie Grene (New York: Grove, 1961), 108–10.

11. *The Interpreter's Dictionary of the Bible: An Illustrated Encyclopedia Identifying and Explaining All Proper Names* (New York: Abingdon Press, 1982), 399.

12. Mel Watkins, "Talk with David Bradley," *NYTBR* (19 April 1981), 21.

13. Tate, ed., *Interviews with Black Writers*, 126.

14. Watkins, "Talk with Toni Morrison," 50.

A Selected Bibliography

Andrews, William L. "A Reconsideration of *Charles Waddell Chesnutt: Pioneer of the Color Line.*" *College Language Association Journal* 19 (1975), 136–51.

——. *The Literary Career of Charles W. Chesnutt.* Baton Rouge: Louisiana State Univ. Press, 1980.

Aptheker, Herbert. *Afro-American History: The Modern Era.* New York: Citadel, 1971.

——. *American Negro Slave Revolts.* 1943; rpt. New York: International Publishers, 1963.

"Attack on 2 Blacks Barely Draws Notice." *Chicago Tribune* (12 July 1985), Sec. 2, 1, 5.

Attaway, William. *Blood on the Forge.* 1941; rpt. Chatham, N.J.: Chatham Bookseller, 1969.

Axthelm, Peter. *The Modern Confessional Novel.* New Haven: Yale Univ. Press, 1967.

Baldwin, James. *Go Tell It on the Mountain.* New York: Dial, 1953.

——. *Notes of a Native Son.* 1955; rpt. New York: Bantam, 1968.

——. Review of *Roots* by Alex Haley. *NYTBR* (26 Sept. 1976), 1–2.

——, and Margaret Mead. *A Rap on Race.* Philadelphia: Lippincott, 1971.

Baym, Nina. *Woman's Fiction: A Guide to Novels by and about Women in America, 1820–1870.* Ithaca: Cornell Univ. Press, 1978.

Bigsby, C.W.E. *The Black Writer,* Vol. 2. (Deland, Fla.: Everett Edwards, 1969), 80.

Blake, Susan L. "Ritual and Rationalization: Black Folklore in the Works of Ralph Ellison." *PMLA* 94 (1979), 121–35.

Bohannan, Paul. *Africa and Africans.* 1964; rpt. Garden City, N.Y.: Natural History Press, 1971.

Bone, Robert A. *The Negro Novel in America.* New Haven: Yale Univ. Press, 1965.

Bontemps, Arna. *Black Thunder.* 1936; rpt. Boston: Beacon Press, 1968.

Bradley, David. *The Chaneysville Incident.* New York: Harper and Row, 1981.

Brown, William Wells. *Clotel; or, the President's Daughter.* 1853; rpt. Upper Saddle River, N.J.: Gregg Press, 1969.

——. *Narrative of William Wells Brown, a Fugitive Slave. Written by Himself.* Boston: Anti-Slavery Office [18??].

Burrows, David J., et al. *Private Dealings: Modern American Writers in Search of Integrity.* 1969; rpt. Rockville, Md : New Perspectives, 1974.

Butterfield, Herbert. *The Historical Novel: An Essay.* Cambridge, England: Cambridge Univ. Press, 1923.

Callahan, John F. "Chaos, Complexity and Possibility: The Historical Frequencies of Ralph Ellison," *Black American Literature Forum* 11 (1977), 130–38.

Campbell, Joseph. *Hero With A Thousand Faces.* 1949; rpt. Cleveland: World, 1970.

Cash, Earl A. "The Narrators in *Invisible Man* and *Notes from Underground:* Brothers in the Spirit." *College Language Association Journal* 16 (1973), 505–7.

Chase, Richard. *The American Novel and Its Tradition.* Garden City, N.Y.: Doubleday, 1957.

Chesnutt, Charles Waddell. *The Marrow of Tradition.* 1901; rpt. Miami: Mnemosyne, 1969.

Chesnutt, Helen. *Charles Waddell Chesnutt: Pioneer of the Color Line.* Chapel Hill: Univ. of North Carolina Press, 1952.

Christian, Barbara. *Black Feminist Criticism: Perspectives on Black Women Writers.* New York: Pergamon Press, 1985.

———. *Black Women Novelists: The Development of a Tradition, 1892–1976,* Westport, Conn.: Greenwood, 1980.

Davis, Angela Y. *Women, Race, and Class.* New York: Random House, 1981.

Davis, Arthur P. *From the Dark Tower: Afro-American Writers, 1900 to 1960.* Washington, D.C.: Howard Univ. Press, 1974.

De Arman, Charles. "Milkman as the Archetypal Hero." *Obsidian* 6 (1980), 56–59.

Dostoevsky, Feodor. *Three Short Novels of Dostoevsky,* trans. Constance Garnett. Garden City, N.Y.: Doubleday, 1960.

Du Bois, W.E.B. *The Quest of the Silver Fleece.* 1911; rpt. Miami: Mnemosyne, 1969.

———. *The Souls of Black Folk.* 1903; rpt. Greenwich, Conn.: Fawcett, 1961.

Eckman, Fern. *The Furious Passage of James Baldwin.* New York: M. Evans, 1966.

Eisinger, Chester E. *Fiction of the Forties.* Chicago: Univ. of Chicago Press, 1963.

Elder, Arlene A. *The "Hindered Hand": Cultural Implications of Early African-American Fiction.* Westport, Conn.: Greenwood, 1978.

———. "Swamp Versus Plantation: Symbolic Structure in W.E.B. Du Bois's *The Quest of the Silver Fleece.*" *Phylon* 34 (1973), 358–67.

Ellison, Ralph. *Invisible Man.* New York: Random House, 1952.

———. *Shadow and Act.* New York: Random House, 1964.

Farrison, William Edward. *William Wells Brown: Author and Reformer.* Chicago: Univ. of Chicago Press, 1969.

Fischer, Russell G. "*Invisible Man* as History." *College Language Association Journal* 17 (1974), 338–67.

Fleming, Robert E. "Sutton E. Griggs: Militant Black Novelist." *Phylon* 34 (1973), 73–77.

Franklin, John Hope. *From Slavery to Freedom: A History of Negro Americans.* 1947; rpt. New York: Vintage, 1969.

Frazier, E. Franklin. *Black Bourgeoisie.* 1957; rpt. Glencoe, Ill.: Free Press, 1969.

———. "The Du Bois Program in the Present Crisis." *Race* 1 (1935), 11–13.

Frye, Northrop. *Anatomy of Criticism: Four Essays.* 1957; rpt. New York: Atheneum, 1969.

Fullinwider, S.P. *The Mind and Mood of Black America: 20th Century Thought.* Homewood, Ill.: Dorsey Press, 1969.

Gayle, Addison, Jr. *The Way of the New World: The Black Novel in America.* Garden City, N.Y.: Doubleday, 1976.

———, ed. *The Black Aesthetic.* Garden City, N.Y.: Doubleday, 1971.

Genovese, Eugene. Review of *The Black Family in Slavery and Freedom, 1750–1925*, by Herbert G. Gutman. *TLS* (25 Feb. 1977), 198–99.

———. *Roll, Jordan, Roll: the World the Slaves Made.* New York: Pantheon, 1974.

Giles, James R. "Revolution and Myth: Kelley's *A Different Drummer* and Gaines's *The Autobiography of Miss Jane Pittman.*" *Minority Voices* 1 (1977), 39–48.

Gloster, Hugh M. *Negro Voices in American Fiction.* Chapel Hill: Univ. of North Carolina Press, 1948; rpt. New York, Russell and Russell, 1965.

Graves, Wallace. "The Question of Moral Energy in James Baldwin's *Go Tell It on the Mountain*," *College Language Association Journal* 7 (1964), 215–23.

Griggs, Sutton. *Imperium in Imperio.* 1899; rpt. New York: Arno, 1969.

Gutman, Herbert G. *The Black Family in Slavery and Freedom, 1750–1925.* New York: Pantheon, 1976.

Haley, Alex. *Roots.* Garden City, N.Y.: Doubleday, 1976.

Harper, Frances Ellen Watkins. *Iola Leroy; or Shadows Uplifted.* 1893; rpt. New York: AMS Press, 1971.

Harris, A. Leslie. "Myth as Structure in Toni Morrison's *Song of Solomon.*" *MELUS* 7 (1980), 69–76.

Harris, Trudier. *Exorcising Blackness: Historical and Literary Lynching and Burning Rituals.* Bloomington: Indiana Univ. Press, 1984.

Hassan, Ihab. *Contemporary American Literature: 1945–1972.* New York: Frederick Ungar, 1973.

Heermance, J. Noel. *Charles W. Chesnutt: America's First Great Black Novelist.* Hamden, Conn.: Archon, 1974.

———. *William Wells Brown and Clotelle: A Portrait of the Artist in the First Negro Novel.* Hamden, Conn.: Archon, 1969.

Heilbroner, Robert L. *The Future As History.* New York: Grove, 1960.

Henderson, Harry B. *Versions of the Past: The Historical Imagination in American Fiction.* New York: Oxford Univ. Press, 1974.

174   **Mythic Black Fiction**

Herskovits, Melville J. *The Myth of the Negro Past*. 1941; rpt. Boston: Beacon Press, 1958.

Hopkins, Pauline E. *Contending Forces: A Romance Illustrative of Negro Life North and South*. 1899; rpt. Miami: Mnemosyne, 1969.

Huggins, Nathan Irvin. *Harlem Renaissance*. London: Oxford Univ. Press, 1971.

Jahn, Janheinz. *Muntu*. Trans. Marjorie Grene. New York: Grove, 1961.

————. *Neo-African Literature: A History of Black Writing*. New York: Grove, 1969.

Jordon, Winthrop. *White Over Black: American Attitudes Toward the Negro: 1550–1812*. Chapel Hill: Univ. of North Carolina Press, 1968.

Kail, Harvey A. "The Confessional Tradition and Selected Confessional Literature: 1821–1914." Diss. Northern Illinois Univ., 1977.

Kelley, William Melvin. *A Different Drummer*. 1959; rpt. Garden City, N.Y.: Doubleday, 1969.

————. "The Ivy League Negro." *Esquire* (Aug. 1963), 54–56 ff.

Keramidas, George (Vice-President, Television Research, American Broadcasting Company). Telephone interview, 17 June 1982.

Klotman, Phyllis. "An Examination of Whiteness in *Blood on the Forge*." *College Language Association Journal* 15 (1972), 459–64.

Kostelanetz, Richard. "The Politics of Ellison's Booker: *Invisible Man* as Symbolic History." *Chicago Review* 19 (1967), 5–26.

————. "Ralph Ellison: Novelist as Brown-Skinned Aristocrat." *Shenandoah* 20 (1969), 56–77.

Larousse Encyclopedia of Mythology. New York: Prometheus, 1959.

Lee, A. Robert, ed. *Black Fiction: New Studies in the Afro-American Novel Since 1945*. New York: Barnes and Noble, 1980.

Lee, Dorothy H. "*Song of Solomon*: To Ride the Air," *Black American Literature Forum* 16 (1982), 64–70.

Leisy, Ernest. *The American Historical Novel*. Norman: Univ. of Oklahoma Press, 1950.

Lerner, Gerda, ed. *Black Women in White America: A Documentary History*. New York: Random House, 1972.

Lillard, Stewart. "Ellison's Ambitious Scope in *Invisible Man*." *English Journal* 58 (1969), 833–39.

Lowenberg, Bert J., and Ruth Bogin, eds. Black Women in Nineteenth-Century American Life: Their Words, Their Thoughts, Their Feelings. University Park: Pennsylvania State Univ. Press, 1976.

Lukács, György. *The Historical Novel*. Trans. Hannah and Stanley Mitchell. London: Merlin, 1962.

Matthews, Brander. *The Historical Novel and Other Essays*. New York: Scribner's, 1901.

Meier, August, and Elliott Rudwick. *From Plantation to Ghetto.* New York: Hill and Wang, 1976.

Mellard, James M. "Prolegomena to a Study of the Popular Mode in Narrative," *Journal of Popular Culture* 6 (1972), 8.

————, ed. *Four Modes: A Rhetoric of Modern Fiction.* New York: Macmillan, 1974.

Mitchell, Louis D. "Invisibility—Permanent or Resurrective." *College Language Association Journal* 17 (1974), 379–86.

Morrison, Toni. *Song of Solomon.* New York: Knopf, 1977.

Moore, Robert E., ed. "On Initiation Rites and Power: Ralph Ellison Speaks at West Point," *Contemporary Literature* 15 (1974), 165–86.

National Anti-Klan Network. *Newsletter.* Atlanta: NAKN, 1982.

O'Brien, John. *Interviews with Black Writers.* New York: Liveright, 1973.

Rampersad, Arnold. *The Art and Imagination of W.E.B. Du Bois.* Cambridge, Mass.: Harvard Univ. Press, 1976.

Reilly, John. "The Dilemma in Chesnutt's *The Marrow of Tradition*." *Phylon* 32 (1971), 31–38.

————. *Twentieth-Century Interpretations of Invisible Man.* Englewood Cliffs, N.J.: Prentice-Hall, 1970.

Scruggs, Charles W. "Ralph Ellison's Use of the *Aeneid* in *Invisible Man*." *College Language Association Journal,* 17 (1974), 368–78.

Southern Poverty Law Center. *Intelligence Report.* Montgomery, Ala.: SPLC, 1981.

Standley, Fred L. "James Baldwin: The Artist as Incorrigible Disturber of the Peace." *Southern Humanities Review* 4 (1970), 18–19.

Staples, Robert. *The Black Woman in America: Sex, Marriage, and the Family.* 1973; rpt. Chicago: Nelson Hall, 1978.

Stark, John. "*Invisible Man*: Ellison's Black Odyssey." *Black American Literature Forum* 7 (1973), 60–63.

Starke, Catherine Juanita. *Black Portraiture in American Fiction: Stock Characters, Archetypes, and Individuals.* New York: Basic Books, 1971.

Stepto, Robert B. *From Behind the Veil: A Study of Afro-American Narrative.* Urbana: Univ. of Illinois Press, 1979.

Tate, Claudia, ed. *Black Women Writers at Work.* New York: Continuum, 1983.

Turner, Darwin T. "Black Fiction: History and Myth." *Studies in American Fiction* 5 (1977), 109–26.

"'A Very Stern Discipline:' An Interview with Ralph Ellison." *Harpers* March 1967, 76–95.

Watkins, Mel. "A Talk with Alex Haley." *NYTBR* (26 Sept. 1976), 2, 10.

————. "Talk with David Bradley." *NYTBR* (19 April 1981), 7, 20–21.

————. "Talk with Toni Morrison." *NYTBR* (11 Sept. 1977), 48, 50.

Weixlmann, Joe. "The Uses and Meaning of History in Modern Black American Fiction." *Black American Literature Forum* 11 (1978), 123.

Weyl, Donald M. "The Vision of Man in the Novels of William Melvin Kelley." *Critique* 15 (1974), 15–33.

Wilner, Eleanor R. "The Invisible Black Thread: Identity and Nonentity in *Invisible Man*." *College Language Association Journal* 13 (1970), 242–57.

Wilson, Harriett E. *Our Nig; or, Sketches from the Life of a Free Black*. 1859; rpt. New York: Vintage, 1983.

Woodward, C. Vann. *The Strange Career of Jim Crow*. New York: Oxford, 1966.

Wright, Richard. "A Tale of Folk Courage," review of *Black Thunder*, by Arna Bontemps. *Partisan Review and Anvil* 3 (1936), 31.

Young, James O. *Black Writers of the Thirties*. Baton Rouge: Louisiana State Univ. Press, 1973.

Young, Pauline A. "Black Thunder." Review of *Black Thunder*, by Arna Bontemps. *Journal of Negro History* 22 (1937), 355–56.

Index